THE HOLOGRAPHIC PARADIGM
AND OTHER PARADOXES

THE HOLOGRAPHIC PARADIGM AND OTHER PARADOXES

Exploring the Leading Edge of Science

Edited by Ken Wilber

SHAMBHALA

BOULDER & LONDON   1982

SHAMBHALA PUBLICATIONS, INC.
1920 13th Street
Boulder, Colorado 80302

Library of Congress Cataloging in Publication Data
Main entry under title:
The Holographic paradigm and other paradoxes.
  Includes index.
  1. Science—Philosophy. 2. Physics—Philosophy.
3. Holography. 4. Brain. I. Wilber, Ken.
Q175.H773 1982   501   82-50277
ISBN 0-87773-235-3
ISBN 0-394-52823-9 (Random House)
ISBN 0-87773-238-8 (pbk.)
ISBN 0-394-71237-4 (Random House: pbk.)

Contents

INTRODUCTION

Ken Wilber

OVER THE PAST THREE YEARS or so, an extraordinary dialogue (and debate) occurred in the pages of *ReVision Journal*. Its topic: perhaps the first serious and sustained look at the interface of "real science" (e.g., physics and physiology) and "real religion" (e.g., mysticism and transcendence), a topic that more than one scholar has termed "epochal." This book is the product and content of that dialogue.

The general, historical dialogue between science and religion itself goes back a long way—at least to Plato, Aristotle, and Plotinus (although "science" didn't mean quite the same thing then as it does now). Previously, however, the discussions usually centered on the *differences* between science and religion, their conflicts, their competing and apparently irreconcilable truth-claims (with an occasional strained discussion on a possible armistice and some sort of peaceful, if edgy, coexistence).

But here, rather suddenly, in the 1970s, were some very respected, very sober, very skilled researchers—physicists, biologists, physiologists, neurosurgeons—and these scientists were not talking *with* religion, they were simply *talking religion*, and more extraordinarily, they were doing so in an attempt to explain the hard data of science itself. The very *facts* of science, they were saying, the actual data (from physics to physiology) seemed to make sense only if we assume some sort of implicit or unifying or transcendental ground underlying the explicit data.

Why this is so is exactly the topic of this book. For the moment, however, let us simply note that, for various sophisticated reasons, these researchers and theoreticians from the "hard sciences" were saying that, without the assumption of this transcendental, spaceless, and timeless ground, the data themselves, the very results of

1

their laboratory experiments, admitted of no cogent explanation. Moreover—and here was the shock—this transcendental ground, whose very existence seemed necessitated by experimental-scientific data, seemed to be identical, at least in description, to the timeless and spaceless ground of being (or "Godhead") so universally described by the world's great mystics and sages, Hindu, Buddhist, Christian, Taoist. And it was *that* idea, unprecedented and far-reaching, that sparked and defined the *ReVision* dialogue.

Different investigative currents came together in this dialogue. There was, first, the pioneering research of Stanford neurosurgeon Karl Pribram, whose book *Languages of the Brain* is already acknowledged as a modern classic. As will be explained in the following pages, Pribram's studies in brain memory and functioning led him to the conclusion that the brain operates, in many ways, like a hologram. A hologram is a special type of optical storage system that can best be explained by an example: if you take a holographic photo of, say, a horse, and cut out one section of it, e.g., the horse's head, and then enlarge that section to the original size, you will get, not a big head, but a picture of the *whole* horse. In other words, each individual part of the picture contains the whole picture in condensed form. The part is in the whole and the whole is in each part—a type of unity-in-diversity and diversity-in-unity. The key point is simply that the *part* has access to the *whole*.

Thus, if the brain did function like a hologram, then it might have access to a larger whole, a field domain or "holistic frequency realm" tht transcended spatial and temporal boundaries. And this domain, reasoned Pribram, might very likely be the same domain of transcendental unity-in-diversity described (and experienced) by the world's great mystics and sages.

It was approximately at this time that Pribram became aware of the works of English physicist David Bohm. As we will see, Bohm's work in subatomic physics and the "quantum potential" had led him to the conclusion that physical entities which seemed to be separate and discrete in space and time were actually linked or unified in an implicit or underlying fashion. In Bohm's terminology, under the *explicate realm* of separate things and events is an *implicate realm* of undivided wholeness, and this implicate whole is simultaneously available to each explicate part. In other words, the physical universe itself seemed to be a gigantic hologram, with each part being in the whole and the whole being in each part.

It was at this point that the "holographic paradigm" was born: the brain is a hologram perceiving and participating in a holographic universe. In the explicate or manifest realm of space and time, things and events are indeed separate and discrete. But beneath the surface, as it were, in the implicate or frequency realm, all things and events are spacelessly, timelessly, intrinsically, one and undivided. And, Bohm and Pribram reasoned, the quintessential religious experience, the experience of mystical oneness and "supreme identity," might very well be a *genuine* and *legitimate* experience of this implicate and universal ground.

In some ways, this paradigm seemed to mark the culmination of a discernible historical trend: ever since the "quantum revolution" of fifty years ago, various physicists have been finding intriguing parallels between their results and certain mystical-transcendental religions. Heisenberg, Bohr, Schroedinger, Eddington, Jeans, even Einstein himself all held a mystical-spiritual view of the world. With the great influx of Eastern religions to the West (beginning principally with D.T. Suzuki's *Essays in Zen Buddhism*), these parallels were drawn with increasing clarity and forcefulness. On a popular level, Alan Watts began to use modern physics and systems theory to explain Buddhism and Taoism. A more scholarly approach was *The Medium, the Mystic, and the Physicist*, by Lawrence LeShan. But perhaps no book more captured the interest of scholars and laypeople alike as Fritjof Capra's enormously successful, *The Tao of Physics*.

All of these researchers—Pribram, Bohm, Capra—were part of the *ReVision* dialogue. Other voices joined in: Stanley Krippner on parapsychology, Kenneth Pelletier on neurophysiology, Sam Keen on the "cosmic connection," John Welwood on psychology, Willis Harman on the new science, John Battista on information theory and psychiatry, and many others. Special mention, however, should be made of the contributions of Marilyn Ferguson and Renée Weber. Marilyn Ferguson—whose most recent book, *The Aquarian Conspiracy*, is an important contribution to this whole topic—was instrumental (via *Brain/Mind Bulletin*) in initiating the general dialogue itself. And Renée Weber, besides contributing numerous articles and ideas herself, very skillfully conducted interviews with Bohm and with Capra that aided immeasurably in clarifying the central issues.

The order of the following chapters is not based on my judgements of merit or relative importance. The order is simply the same order that the articles, interviews, and responses chronologically appeared in the various issues of *ReVision*. In this way, the original order and flow of ideas remains intact, and the growth and maturation of the dialogue itself becomes apparent. Moreover, the dialogue is still continuing in the pages of *ReVision*; the various authors have continued to refine, sophisticate, and update their thoughts; thus the last chapter of this book is by no means the final word on the topic, but simply the most recent.

What follows is not, of course, the only types of dialogues possible between science and religion—far from it. But judging from the evidence, the theories and ideas represented in the following pages have generated as much or more excitement and enthusiasm as any. Nor is there any doubt that the ideas of such theorists as Pribram, Bohm, and Capra represent some of the most serious and sophisticated attempts to directly interface "hard science" with spiritual or transcendental realities. One may agree or disagree with the new paradigm—and both pro and con arguments are well-represented in this volume. And "the" paradigm itself actually has all sorts of different interpretations—some researchers have found it necessary to introduce hierarchical and evolutionary dimensions to the paradigm; other researchers have found, not a strict identity between science and mysticism, but merely some important analogs; still others have questioned whether a new *mental* map or paradigm, no matter how apparently unified, can actually lead to a *transcendence* of the mind itself (which is the real aim of genuine mysticism). All of those topics were debated in *ReVision*, and all of them are reported in the following pages.

But my point: agree or disagree with the new paradigm(s), one conclusion unmistakably emerges: at most, the new science demands spirit; at least, it makes ample room for spirit. Either way, modern science is no longer *denying* spirit. And that, *that* is epochal. As Hans Küng remarked, the standard answer to "Do you believe in Spirit?" used to be, "Of course not, I'm a scientist," but it might very soon become, "Of course I believe in Spirit. I'm a scientist."

This volume—like *ReVision* itself—is one of the first steps toward preparing the ground for that second, and more enlightened, response.

1

A NEW PERSPECTIVE ON REALITY

The Special Updated Issue of The Brain/Mind Bulletin

NEUROSCIENTIST KARL PRIBRAM of Stanford and physicist David Bohm of the University of London have proposed theories that, in tandem, appear to account for all transcendental experience, paranormal events and even "normal" perceptual oddities. The implications for every aspect of human life, as well as for science, are so profound that we have dedicated an issue to the subject.

This breakthrough fulfills predictions that the long-awaited theory would (1) draw on theoretical mathematics; (2) establish the "supernatural" as part of nature.

The theory, in a nutshell: *Our brains mathematically construct "concrete" reality by interpreting frequencies from another dimension, a realm of meaningful, patterned primary reality that transcends time and space. The brain is a hologram, interpreting a holographic universe.*

Phenomena of altered states of consciousness (which reflect altered brain states) may be due to a literal attunement to the invisible matrix that generates "concrete" reality. This may enable interaction with reality at a primary level, thereby accounting for precognition, psychokinesis, healing, time distortion, rapid learning . . . and experience of "oneness with the universe," the conviction that ordinary reality is an illusion, descriptions of a void that is paradoxically full, as in the Taoist saying, "The real is empty and the empty is real."

For several years those interested in human consciousness have been speaking wistfully of the "emerging paradigm," an integral theory that would catch all the wonderful wildlife of science and spirit. Here, at last, is a theory that marries biology to physics

5

in an open system: the paradoxical borderless paradigm that our schizophrenic science has been crying for.

In the 1963 book *You and Your Brain*, Judith Groch observed that paranormal events could be ignored just because they were inconvenient to the framework of our knowledge. Einstein, unable to reconcile inconsistencies within Newton's physics, "unlocked a theoretical door through which scientists then poured in pursuit of the knowledge that lay on the other side." Groch suggested that the brain awaited its Einstein.

It is appropriate that this radical, satisfying paradigm has emerged from Pribram, a brain researcher-neurosurgeon who was a friend of the Western Zen teacher Alan Watts . . . and Bohm, a theoretical physicist, close friend of Krishnamurti and former associate of Einstein.

WHAT IS HOLOGRAPHY

Holography is a method of lensless photography in which the wave field of light scattered by an object is recorded on a plate as an interference pattern. When the photographic record—the hologram— is placed in a coherent light beam like a laser, the original wave pattern is regenerated. A three-dimensional image appears.

Because there is no focusing lens, the plate appears as a meaningless pattern of swirls. *Any piece of the hologram will reconstruct the entire image.*

THE HOLOGRAM AS A MODEL FOR A NEW DESCRIPTION OF REALITY

Physicist David Bohm says that the hologram is a starting point for a new description of reality: the *enfolded* order. Classical reality has focused on secondary manifestations—the *unfolded* aspect of things, not their source. These appearances are abstracted from an intangible, invisible flux that is not comprised of parts; it is an inseparable interconnectedness.

Bohm says that primary physical laws cannot be discovered by a science that attempts to break the world into its parts.

There are intriguing implications in a paradigm that says the brain employs a holographic process to abstract from a holographic domain. Parapsychologists have searched in vain for the energy that might transmit telepathy, psychokinesis, healing, etc. If these events emerge from frequencies transcending time and space, they don't have to be transmitted. They are potentially simultaneous and everywhere.

Changes in magnetic, electromagnetic or gravitational fields and changes in the brain's electrical patterns would be only surface manifestations of seemingly unmeasurable underlying factors. J.B. Rhine, who pioneered modern parapsychology, was skeptical that an energy would be found. Psychologist Lawrence LeShan, author of *Alternate Reality*, believes that energy is a less useful concept in psychic healing than a certain merger of identity, perhaps a resonance.

PRIMARY REALITY MAY BE A FREQUENCY REALM

Is reality the product of an invisible matrix?

"I believe we're in the middle of a paradigm shift that encompasses all of science," Karl Pribram said at a recent Houston conference, *New Dimensions in Health Care*. He went on to spell out a powerful multifaceted theory that could account for sensory reality as a "special case" constructed by the brain's mathematics but drawn from a domain beyond time and space, where only frequencies exist.

The theory could account for all the phenomena that seem to contravene existing scientific "law" by demonstrating that such restrictions are themselves products of our perceptual constructs. Theoretical physics has already demonstrated that events cannot be described in mechanical terms at subatomic levels.

Pribram, a renowned brain researcher, has accumulated evidence for a decade that the brain's "deep structure" is essentially holographic—analogous to the lensless photographic process for which Dennis Gabor received a Nobel Prize.

Pribram's theory has gained increasing support and has not been seriously challenged. An impressive body of research in many laboratories has demonstrated that the brain structures see, hear, taste, smell and touch by sophisticated mathematical analysis of temporal and/or spatial frequencies. An eerie property of both hologram and brain is the distribution of information throughout the system, each fragment encoded to produce the information of the whole.

Although the holographic model generated fruitful answers, it raised a question that came to haunt Pribram. Who was looking at the hologram? Who was the "little man inside the little man," what Arthur Koestler called "the ghost in the machine"?

After agonizing over this problem for some time, Pribram said, he decided that if the question had stymied everybody since Aristotle, perhaps it was the wrong question. "So I asked, 'What if the real world isn't made up of objects at all. What if *it's* a hologram?' "

Pribram's conversation with his son, a physicist, led him to the recent theories of David Bohm. To his great excitement he found that Bohm speculated that the nature of the universe might be more like a hologram, a realm of frequencies and potentialities underlying an illusion of concreteness. Bohm pointed out that ever since Galileo, science has objectified nature by looking at it through lenses.

Pribram was struck with the thought that the brain's mathematics might be "a cruder form of a lens. Maybe reality isn't what we see with our eyes. If we didn't have that lens, we might know a world organized in the frequency domain. No space, no time—just events. Can that reality be 'read out of' that domain?" Transcendental experience suggested that there is access to the frequency domain, the primary reality.

"What if there is a matrix that doesn't objectify unless we do something to it?" The brain's own representations—its abstraction—may be identical with one state of the universe.

Pribram pointed out the extraordinary insights of mystics and early philosophers that preceded scientific verification by centuries. One example is the metaphysical description of the pineal gland as the "third eye." Recently it was found that the pineal may be something of a super master gland, since its secretion of melatonin regulates the activities of the pituitary, long considered the brain's master gland.

The eighteenth-century philosopher Leibniz described a system of "monads" that coincided strikingly with the new paradigm, Pribram observed. His discovery of integral calculus enabled Gabor to invent the hologram two hundred years later.

"How did these ideas arise for millenia before we had the mathematics to understand them?" Pribram asked. "Maybe in the holographic state—in the frequency domain—4,000 years ago is tomorrow.

"Eastern philosophy has come into Western thought in the past. Every once in a while we have these insights that bring us back to the infinite," he told his audience. "Whether it will stick this time or we'll have to go around once more will depend on you. The spirit of the infinite could become part of our culture and not 'a little far out.' "

PRIBRAM'S PARADOXES:
HOW DOES THE BRAIN KNOW?

Karl Pribram's research and theory encompass the whole spectrum of human consciousness: learning and learning disorders, imagination, meaning, perception, intention, paradoxes of brain function. Following are current key concepts:

• The brain's intricate mathematical devices may depend on interactions at the junctions between cells (synapses) via a network of fine fibers on the branching axons. Nerve impulses in this fine-fiber network manifest in **slow waves** with the potential to carry out the mathematics. (Other researchers have speculated that the **alpha brainwave rhythm** may be a timing device necessary for this computation.)

• Information in the brain may be distributed as a **hologram**. The brain apparently has a parallel-processing capability that suggests a model-like optics, wherein connections are formed by paths traversed by light, in addition to its more limited digital or linear computer-type connections. A distribution pattern similar to that of a hologram also would explain how a specific memory does not have a location but is scattered throughout the brain.

• A kind of **stereo effect** of sensory input—auditory, kinesthetic, etc.—causes point perception to leap out into space, as when two stereo speakers are so balanced that sound seems to project from a point midway between them. Such phenomena involve alternation of frequency and phase relationships.

• Pribram speculated that **transcendental experience** might also involve projection of some sort. He said his observations of transcendental experience suggest a possible role for circuits centering on the amygdala that control the joining of feedback and feedforward mechanisms in the brain. These circuits have been the site of pathological disturbances, he noted, as well as *deja vu* and the "consciousness without a content" of mystical states.

• He believes that the **neuropeptides** (*see B/MB, June 20, 1978*), the recently discovered large molecules, will prove to regulate the brain transmitters and represent a breakthrough in understanding brain function.

• Pribram finds mystical experience no stranger than other phenomena, such as the selective derepression of DNA to form first one organ, then another. The most productive scientists, he said, "are as ready and as capable to defend spirit as data. This is science as it was originally conceived: the pursuit of understanding. The days of the cold-hearted, hard-headed technocrat appear to be numbered."

• He suggested that there is no such thing as metaphor—or, in a sense, that all metaphor is true. "Everything is isomorphic." (In Eastern philosophy, "As above, so below.") We may now be experiencing the effects of a social hologram, a pattern of interconnectedness of individuals. **Synchronicity,** meaningful coincidence, makes sense in a meaningful, holographic universe. Pribram proposed that even random distribution is based on holographic principles and is therefore determined. "The uncertainty of occurrence of events is only superficial . . ." There are **underlying symmetries,** not just haphazard occurrences. He cited recent observations of "spin" in physics and Einstein's insistence that "God doesn't play dice with the universe."

THE THEORY'S IMPLICATIONS TOUCH ALL ASPECTS OF HUMAN LIFE

The new theory has awesome implications in terms of the individual's potential to affect his life—his "reality"—and impressive power to unify disparate discoveries in consciousness research.

Learning: Educators have known for decades that anxiety undermines the ability to learn. Judging from brainwave activity, anxiety is like static—a noisier, arrhythmic state. Teaching methods can attempt to foster harmonious, relaxed states in students by centering or meditative techniques, biofeedback, Suggestology-type blends of music and breath exercises. A deeper understanding of the brain as a complex frequency analyzer might engender greater respect for individual differences in learning style.

Health: Individual responsibility for health is underscored once it becomes fully apparent that there is access to the primary realm of reality that creates illness or wellness. This does not mean that environmental factors are unimportant: nutrients, light, ionization and sound affect health at the level of frequencies.

Healing approaches that combine imagery with altered states of consciousness—autogenic training, meditation, hypnosis, psychosynthesis—make a lot of sense if the image interacts with a simultaneous-everywhere state of all possibility. This could reassure skeptical patients—and save the cost of placebos!

Psychotherapy and religion: Figurative descriptions of a sense of flow—as in love, joy, confidence and the creative process—may actually reflect states of consciousness in resonance with the holistic "wave" aspect of reality. Anxiety, anger and "stuckness" would represent fragmented states.

Personal transformation: Are profound, transforming personal experiences coincident with attunement to underlying universal symmetries? Consciousness research already has tied activity in the brain's limbic system to such experiences. The term "transcendence" may prove a literal description—some sort of phase relationship between two brain processes usually considered mutually exclusive: the analytical and the holistic (like particles and waves), the intellectual and the intuitive.

Attention: Does truly focused awareness correlate with a state of universal harmony? Attention is little understood. Some biofeedback patients cure their migraines by raising their hand temperature, some by lowering it. Researchers are coming to believe that the quality of attention may be more important than the actual learning of physiological self-control.

Philosophy and evolution: Pierre Teilhard de Chardin's idea of a noosphere—an invisible planetary web of evolving consciousness—is interesting in light of the new theory. So is the age-old esoteric notion that other dimensions of reality exist at frequencies normally not perceptible to us. And consider the alchemists, who believed that they could transmute earth's elements if they could reach a point of utmost harmony in themselves.

The arts: Apparent universals in aesthetic quality could reflect underlying symmetry, frequencies, phase relationships to which our brains respond. Classical music is used increasingly to alter consciousness. One physicist has speculated that Beethoven's great chords activate the chakras.

IS CHANGE DUE TO RESONANCE, NOT TECHNIQUE?

A New York psychoanalyst has proposed that the hologram is a valuable model for the phenomenon of insight or sudden change in psychotherapy.

Edgar A. Levenson pointed out that such changes take place across the spectrum of psychoanalytic methods and must therefore be due to something other than a specific approach. Technique, he said, is nothing more than a series of ceremonial preparations for change.

"Sudden or insidious, dramatic or by default, change does not come at the behest of any technique or procedure. If his life depended upon it, no therapist could produce a therapeutic result on command. . . . Like the mystical or the aesthetic, the psychoanalytic experience is capricious and unreliable."

But there is a strong feeling when therapy is going well that an elusive pattern is emerging, a powerful central theme evident on all levels at once. The therapist is not saying anything *new* to the patient "but resonates with something the patient already knows and brings it into clearer focus. The change results as a consequence of the expansion of configurational patterns over time."

The therapist's interpretation in itself would not make for change "any more than one point in space makes a line. It is not so much that a therapist is correct in his formulations but that he is in harmony or resonance with what is occurring in a patient.

"It is as though a huge, three-dimensional, spatially coded representation of the patient's experience develops in the therapy, running through every aspect of his life, his history and his participation with the therapist. At some point there is a kind of 'overload' and everything falls into place."

The pattern, or theme, had emerged dramatically for the patient.

In an article in *Contemporary Psychoanalysis* (12: 1-20), Levenson cited Karl Pribram's holographic model of brain function and physicist David Bohm's concept of a holographic, "enfolded" level of reality.

The therapist does not succeed because he explains, Levenson said. He expands awareness of *patterning*. This activity of expansion and resonance hits closest to the real neuropsychological substrate of revelation.

"The holographic model suggests a radically new paradigm that might give us a fresh way of perceiving and connecting clinical phenomena that have always been known to be important but were relegated to the 'art' of psychotherapy. The error has been our model for communication: the transportation of a message across interpersonal space."

THE QUANTUM BRAIN-ACTION APPROACH COMPLEMENTS THE HOLOGRAPHIC MODEL

A torrent of comments, books, papers and leads continues to pour in, responding to the July 4 issue of *Brain/Mind Bulletin* devoted to the emerging holographic model of reality based on the theories of brain scientist Karl Pribram and physicist David Bohm.

Parapsychologists Stanley Krippner, Charles Tart and Douglas Dean commented that the holographic model is consistent with their experimental data, particularly as it postulates access to a domain transcending time and space; but Jule Eisenbud finds the theory too mechanistic.

Physicist Evan Harris Walker has framed a complementary quantum-mechanical theory of psychic phenomena. Recently he dealt specifically with subatomic events in the brain: "Quantum Mechanical Tunneling in Synaptic and Ephaptic Transmission" (*International Journal of Quantum Chemistry* 11: 102-127).

Terence and Dennis McKenna formulated a related theory in their book, *The Invisible Landscape* (Seabury, 1975), in an excellent section titled "Toward a Holographic Theory of Mind." They expanded holographic brain theory to the possibility that DNA and even subatomic particles operate on holographic principles.

Holographer Eugene Dolgoff told *B/MB* that his unsuccessful attempts to detect energy transfer in psi in the late 1960s led him to conclude that no transfer was necessary. "Nothing needed to go from here to there, because in that realm there isn't any 'there.' "

Melvin Werbach, psychiatrist and biofeedback clinician, believes that the hologram may not be our ultimate model, "but it can serve a most important purpose by providing those of us who are comfortable in thinking in holistic terms the possibility of a scientific base." William McGarey, director of the A.R.E. Clinic in Phoenix, and George Baker of Graduate Theological Union in Berkeley suggested metaphysical implications of a resonance model.

CHRONOLOGY OF AN IDEA

1714—Gottfried Wilhelm von Leibniz, discoverer of integral and differential calculus, said that a metaphysical reality underlies and generates the material universe. Space-time, mass and motion of physics and transfer of energies are intellectual constructs.

1902—William James proposed that the brain normally filters out a larger reality.

1905—Albert Einstein published his theories.

1907—Henri Bergson said that the ultimate reality is a vital impulse comprehensible only by intuition. The brain screens out the larger reality.

1929—Alfred Whitehead, mathematician and philosopher, described nature as a great expanding nexus of occurrences not terminating in sense perception. Dualism such as mind/matter are false; reality is inclusive and interlocking . . . and Karl Lashley published his great body of research demonstrating that specific memory is not to be found in any particular site in the brain but is distributed throughout.

1947—Dennis Gabor employed Leibniz's calculus to describe a potential three-dimensional photography: holography.

1965—Emmett Leith and Juris Upatnicks announced their successful construction of holograms with the newly invented laser beam.

1969—Karl Pribram, who had worked with Lashley as a neurosurgeon, proposed that the hologram was a powerful model for brain processes.

1971—Physicist David Bohm, who had worked with Einstein, proposed that the organization of the universe may be holographic.

1975—Pribram synthesized his theories and Bohm's in a German publication on Gestalt psychology.

1977—Pribram speculated on the unifying metaphysical implications of the synthesis.

References

For Karl Pribram's research and holographic brain-processing theory, *Languages of the Brain* (1971); for his synthesis of the holographic brain model with David Bohm's view of the physical universe, *Consciousness and the Brain*, edited by G. Globus, et al. (Plenum, 1976), and *Perceiving, Acting, and Knowing*, edited by R.E. Shaw and J. Bransford (Erlbaum/John Wiley, 1977).

David Bohm's theories appear in *Quantum Theory and Beyond*, edited by Ted Bastin (Cambridge U., 1971); *Foundations of Physics* 1 (4), 3 (2), and 5 (1); and in *Mind in Nature* (University Press of America, Washington, D.C.).

2

KARL PRIBRAM'S CHANGING REALITY

Marilyn Ferguson

IF YOU WANT TO KNOW where the next revolution in brain research will take place, find out what currently interests Karl Pribram. In the course of his career, the 58-year-old Stanford neuroscientist has been close at hand, if not a primary incendiary, at nearly all the major upheavals of prevailing thought about how the brain works.

Currently he is proposing a startling, all-encompassing model that is generating considerable excitement among those intrigued by the mysteries of human consciousness. His "holographic model" marries brain research to theoretical physics; it accounts for normal perception and simultaneously takes the paranormal and transcendental experiences out of the supernatural by explaining them as part of nature.

Like certain dicoveries of quantum physics, the radical reorientation of this theory suddenly makes sense of paradoxical sayings of mystics throughout the ages. Not that Pribram was the least bit interested in giving credence to mystical insights. The diminutive brain surgeon, researcher and professor was only trying to make sense of the data generated from his laboratory at Stanford where brain processes in higher mammals—primates, especially—have been rigorously studied.

This latest development in the thinking of Karl Pribram makes his own transition complete from (in his own term) a "staunch behaviorist" in the 1940s to a pioneer in cognitive psychology in the 1950s to an occasional ally of humanistic psychologists in the 1960s and early '70s to a radical defender of spiritual experience in the late '70s.

Biologist T.H. Huxley once wrote, "Sit down before fact like a little child, and be prepared to give up every preconceived notion, follow humbly wherever and to whatever abysses Nature leads, or you shall learn nothing." Pribram's innocent fascination with facts he has come across has led him to such abysses.

He was born in Vienna and came to the United States as an eight-year-old child. He attended the University of Chicago, where he obtained both his BA and his MD degrees in an astounding five years.

After residencies and internship in Illinois, he began to practice as a neurosurgeon in Florida. And that is where he first began doing research—at Yerkes Laboratories in Orange Park, under famous brain scientist Karl Lashley. (Also working at Yerkes were D.O. Hebb and Austin Riesen, who would later achieve eminence in sensory-deprivation research, and Roger Sperry, later a pioneer in split-brain research.)

For thirty years Lashley had searched for the "engram"—the site and substance of memory. He had trained experimental animals, then selectively damaged portions of their brains, assuming that at some point he would scoop out the locus of what they had learned. Removing parts of the brain worsened their performance somewhat, but it seemed that short of lethal brain damage, it was impossible to eradicate what they had been taught.

At one point, a nonplussed Lashley said wryly that his research demonstrated that learning was just not possible. Pribram participated in the writing up of Lashley's monumental research, and he was steeped in the mystery of the engram. How could memory be stored not in any one part of the brain but be distributed throughout it?

Pribram then went to Yale, where, during his 10-year stay, he contributed profoundly to brain science by developing surgical techniques that finally gave access to the mysterious primitive limbic brain. His investigation of such limbic structures as the hippocampus and the amygdala demonstrated that traditional theories of "higher centers" of the brain controlling lower ones was in need of radical modification. The older brain centers proved to have a richer complexity and more control than anyone had imagined.

Then Pribram demonstrated the processes whereby the limbic and frontal brains interact. And in 1960, he helped set off what he describes as "cries of pain" from fellow behaviorists. *Plans and the Structure of Behavior*, a book by George A. Miller, Eugene Galanter and Pribram, was later credited by the literature in the field with launching the "cognitive revolution"—the shift of scientific interest from behavior to thought. Both Miller and Pribram had been in the camp of the behaviorists until that time. The behaviorists depended on a simple stimulus-response model derived, in part, from early brain research on the reflex arc—simple cellular response—by Charles Sherrington. Pribram believed that Sherrington had never meant an entire psychology to be built on the model of the reflex. Subjective experience must be studied if brain research is to get anywhere. He and his coauthors called their approach "subjective behaviorism."

For a time Pribram also directed research at the Institute of Living, commuting to Yale. He also directed the Yerkes Laboratories briefly after Lashley's retirement.

When he accepted a position at the Center for Advanced Studies in the Behavioral Sciences at Stanford in 1958, he took with him a first draft of his book *Languages of the Brain*, which was to take roughly 15 years from its beginnings to its publication in 1971 and is a classic of clear theoretical writing about the brain.

Interestingly enough, Pribram's office was next to that of Thomas S. Kuhn, who was then at work on what became one of the most influential books of our time, *The Structure of Scientific Revolutions*, in which he described the process by which the scientific world view is periodically overturned in what he called a "paradigm shift."

Pribram and his coworkers were among the first to use computer modeling to understand aspects of thought and behavior. One of his most dramatic contributions was the discovery that the brain's motor centers are involved not only in movement but in thought processes preceding movement—*plans of action*. It became clear that there is a critical neurological connection between the motor centers of the brain and learning, a link that had been suspected by educational therapists.

A glance at the titles of the chapters in *Languages of the Brain* gives an insight into his intense interest in relating brain processes to actual human experience and behavior: "Images," "Feelings," "Achievement," "Signs," "Symbols," "Talk and Thought," "The Regulation of Human Affairs." Brain science, he has said, must deal with the awareness of awareness. It could no longer afford to shut out that part of the world we call subjective.

Pribram was still deeply troubled by the mystery that had drawn him into brain research: how do we remember?

In the mid-'60s, he read a *Scientific American* article describing the first construction of a hologram, a kind of three-dimensional "picture" produced by lensless photography. Dennis Gabor had discovered the mathematical principle of holography in 1947, a discovery that would later earn him a Nobel prize, but a demonstration of holography had had to await the invention of the laser.

The hologram is one of the truly remarkable inventions of modern physics, and eerie indeed when seen for the first time. Its ghostlike image can be viewed from various angles, and it appears to be suspended in space.

Its principle is well described by biologist Lyall Watson:

> If you drop a pebble into a pond, it will produce a series of regular waves that travel outward in concentric circles. Drop two identical pebbles into the pond at different points and you will get two sets of similar waves that move towards each other. Where the waves meet, they will interfere. If the crest of one hits the crest of the other, they will work together and produce a reinforced wave of twice the normal height. If the crest of one coincides with the trough of another, they will cancel each other out and produce an isolated patch of calm water. In fact, all possible combinations of the two occur, and the final result is a complex arrangement of ripples known as an interference pattern.
>
> Light waves behave in exactly the same way. The purest kind of light available to us is that produced by a laser, which sends out a beam in which all the waves are of one frequency, like those made by an ideal pebble in a perfect pond. When two laser beams touch, they produce an interference pattern of light and dark ripples that can be recorded on a photographic plate. And if one of the beams, instead of coming directly from the laser, is reflected first off an object such as a human face, the resulting pattern will be very complex indeed, but it can still be recorded. The record will be a hologram of the face.

Light falls onto the photographic plate from two sources: from the object itself; and from a reference beam, light deflected by a mirror from the object onto the plate. The apparently meaningless swirls on the plate do not resemble the original object, but the image can be reconstituted by a coherent light source like a laser beam. The result is a 3-D likeness projected into space, at a distance from the plate.

If the hologram is broken, any piece of it will reconstruct the entire image.

News that a hologram could really be built, based on Gabor's mathematics, stirred a lot of scientific interest. A handful of engineers observed that the idea might be applied to biology, and Bela Ulas of Bell Laboratories speculated on the possibility. It had also crossed Gabor's mind.

Pribram saw the hologram as an exciting model for how the brain might store memory. Perhaps it too deals in interactions, interpreting frequencies and storing the image, like the hologram, not localized but dispersed throughout the brain. In 1966, he published his first paper proposing a connection. Over the next several years Pribram and other researchers uncovered what appeared to be the brain's neural strategies for knowing, for sensing, using mathematical computations. It appears that in order to see, hear, smell, taste, the brain performs complex calculations on the frequencies of data it receives. *These mathematical processes have little common-sense relationship to the real world as we preceive it.*

Pribram believes that the intricate mathematics may occur as a nerve impulse travels along and between cells through a network of fine fibers on the cells. The fibers move in slow waves as the impulse crosses the cell and those waves may perform the calculating function. In taking a hologram, light waves are encoded and the resulting hologram that's projected then decodes, or deblurs, the image. The brain may similarly decode its stored memory traces. Another feature of a hologram is its efficiency. Billions of bits of information can be stored in a tiny space. The pattern on the holographic plate has no space-time dimension. The image is stored everywhere on the plate.

It was typical of Pribram that he would seize upon a new finding from outside his field in an attempt to understand memory. He has sometimes been criticized by more conventional neuroscientists— typically, a narrow, highly specialized lot—for his bold speculation.

Pribram recalls the remark of a pioneer memory researcher, Ewald Hering, that at some point in his life, every scientist must make a decision. "He begins to be interested in his work and what his findings mean," Pribram said. "Then he has to choose. If he starts to ask questions and tries to find answers, to understand what it all means, he will look foolish to his colleagues. On the other hand, he can give up the attempt to understand what it all means; he won't look foolish, and he'll learn more and more about less and less.

"You have to decide to have the courage to look foolish."

At a recent small conference at Stanford, Pribram was invited to debate an opponent of the holographic theory. He was effectively assaulted on technical points that suggest that the brain's holography is almost certainly a variant of optic holography rather than an exact analogy. "I held my own well enough, but they got me on details here and there," he recalls.

Afterward a young man came up and asked him how he could be so convinced. How could he go on and on, standing up to well-reasoned arguments?

"It's simple," Pribram replied. "This has been happening to me ever since I got into science—and I've always been right!"

If you are somewhere on the leading edge, he has said, you can't explain everything. "If you knew all about it, it wouldn't be the leading edge."

The famous physicist, Niels Bohr, once said that when the great innovation appears, it will seem muddled and strange. It will be only half-understood by its discoverer and a mystery to everyone else. For any idea that does not appear bizarre at first, there is no hope.

Pribram has said that we are now in a period where only technical excellence is rewarded; researchers are not expected to extrapolate, to think. "Europeans are much more theoretically oriented. Americans test hypotheses at best, forgetting that these emerge from a thesis. Even in our very successful science, we usually come up with nothing but a description of the terrain.

"That's sufficient to many people," says Pribram. "They say, 'Well, we've answered the question.' They seem to feel that they don't dare try to understand, especially if they have to get into fields they aren't complete technical experts in. They're afraid something will go wrong with their science."

Pribram himself shows no such timidity; he has undertaken to understand physics better and has enrolled in graduate classes in advanced mathematical methods. If the facts lead him to the abyss, he will go well informed.

In 1970 or 1971, a distressing and ultimate question began troubling him. If the brain indeed knows by putting together holograms—by mathematically transforming frequencies from "out there"—*who* in the brain is interpreting the holograms?

This is an old nagging question. Philosophers since the Greeks have speculated about the "ghost in the machine," the "little man inside the little man" and so on. Where is the I—the entity that uses the brain?

Who does the actual knowing? Or, as Saint Francis of Assisi once put it, *"What we are looking for is what is looking."*

Lecturing one night at a symposium in Minnesota, Pribram mused that the answer might lie in the realm of gestalt psychology, a theory that maintains that what we perceive "out there" is the same as—*isomorphic* with—brain processes.

Suddenly he blurted out, "Maybe the *world* is a hologram!"

He stopped, a little taken aback by the implications of what he

had said. Were the members of the audience holograms—representations of frequencies, interpreted by his brain and by one another's brains? If the nature of reality is *itself* holographic, and the
brain operates holographically, then the world is indeed, as the
Eastern religions have said, *maya*: a magic show. Its concreteness is
an illusion.

Soon afterward he spent a week with his son, a physicist, discussing his ideas and searching for possible answers in physics. His son
mentioned that an eminent physicist, David Bohm, had been thinking along similar lines. A few days later, Pribram read copies of
Bohm's key papers urging a new order in physics. Pribram was
electrified. *Bohm was describing a holographic universe.*

What appears to be a stable, tangible, visible, audible world, said
Bohm, is an illusion. It is dynamic and kaleidoscopic—not really
"there." What we normally see is the explicit, or unfolded, order of
things, rather like watching a movie. But there is an underlying
order that is mother and father to this second-generation reality. He
called the other order implicate, or enfolded. The enfolded order
harbors our reality, much as the DNA in the nucleus of the cell
harbors potential life and directs the nature of its unfolding.

Bohm describes an insoluble ink droplet in glycerine. If the fluid is
stirred slowly by a mechanical device so that there is no diffusion,
the droplet is eventually drawn into a fine thread that is distributed
throughout the whole system in such a way that it is no longer even
visible to the eye. If the mechanical device is then reversed, the
thread will slowly gather together until it suddenly coalesces again
into a visible droplet.

Before this coalescence takes place, the droplet can be said to be
"folded into" the viscous fluid, while afterward it is unfolded again.

Next imagine that several droplets have been stirred into the fluid
a different number of times and in different positions. If the ink
drops are stirred continuously and fast enough, it will appear that a
single permanently existing ink drop is continuously moving across
the fluid. There is no such object. Other samples: a row of electric
lights in a commercial sign that flashes off and on to give the
impression of a sweeping arrow, or an animated cartoon, giving the
illusion of continuous movement.

Just so, all apparent substance and movement are illusory. They
emerge from another, more primary order of the universe. Bohm
calls this phenomenon the *holomovement*.

Ever since Galileo, he says, we have been looking at nature through lenses; our very act of objectifying, as in an electron microscope, alters that which we hope to see. We want to find its edges, to make it sit still for a moment, when its true nature is in another order of reality, another dimension, where there are no *things*. It is as if we are bringing the "observed" into focus, as you would bring a picture into resolution, but the *blur* is a more accurate representation. The blur itself is the basic reality.

It occurred to Pribram that the brain's mathematics may also comprise a lens. These mathematical transforms make objects out of blurs or frequencies, making them into sounds and colors and kinesthetic sensations and smells and tastes.

"Maybe reality isn't what we see with our eyes," Pribram says. "If we didn't have that lens—the mathematics performed by our brain—maybe we would know a world organized in the frequency domain. No space, no time—just events. Can reality be read out of that domain?"

He suggested that transcendental experiences—mystical states—may allow us occasional direct access to that realm. Certainly, subjective reports from such states often sound like descriptions of quantum reality, a coincidence that has led several physicists to speculate similarly. Bypassing our normal, constricting perceptual mode—what Aldous Huxley called the reducing value—we may be attuned to the source or matrix of reality.

And the brain's neural interference patterns, its mathematical processes, may be identical to the primary state of the universe. That is to say, our mental processes are, in effect, made of the same stuff as the organizing principle. Physicists and astronomers had remarked at times that the real nature of the universe is immaterial but orderly. Einstein professed mystical awe in the face of this harmony. Astronomer James Jeans said that the universe is more like a great thought than a great machine, and astronomer Arthur Eddington said, "The stuff of the universe is mindstuff." More recently, cyberneticist David Foster described "an intelligent universe" whose apparent concreteness is generated by—in effect—cosmic data from an unknowable, organized source.

In a nutshell, the holographic supertheory says that *our brains mathematically construct "hard" reality by interpreting frequencies from a dimension transcending time and space. The brain is a hologram, interpreting a holographic universe.*

Pribram engagingly admits at times, "I hope you realize that I don't *understand* any of this." The admission generally provokes a sigh of relief in even the most scientific audiences, where everyone but the physicists—who know better—had been trying to apply linear, logical thought processes to a nonlinear dimension. You can't use cause-and-effect reasoning to understand events not bound by time and space.

Psychic phenomena are only by-products of the simultaneous-everywhere matrix. Individual brains are bits of the greater hologram. They have access under certain circumstances to all the information in the total cybernetic system. Synchronicity—those coincidental occurrences that seem to have some higher purpose or connectedness—also fits in with the holographic model. Such meaningful coincidences derive from the purposeful, patterned, organizing nature of the matrix. Psychokinesis, mind affecting matter, may be a natural result of interaction at the primary level. The holographic model resolves one long-standing riddle of psi: the inability of instrumentation to track the apparent energy transfer in telepathy, healing, clairvoyance. If these events occur in a dimension transcending time and space, there is no need for energy to travel from here to there. As one researcher put it, "There isn't any *there*."

For years those interested in phenomena of the human mind had predicted that a breakthrough theory would emerge; that it would draw on mathematics to establish the supernatural as part of nature.

The holographic model is such an integral theory catching all the wildlife of science and spirit. It may well be the paradoxical, borderless paradigm that our science had been crying for.

Its explanatory power enriches and enlarges many disciplines, making sense of old phenomena and raising urgent new questions. Implicit in the theory is the assumption that harmonious, coherent states of consciousness are more nearly attuned to the primary level of reality, a dimension of order and harmony. Such attunement would be hampered by anger, anxiety and fear, and eased by love and empathy. There are implications for learning, environments, families, the arts, religion and philosophy, healing and self-healing. What fragments us? What makes us whole?

Those descriptions of a sense of flow, of cooperating with the universe—in the creative process, in extraordinary athletic performances, and sometimes in everyday life—do they signify our union with the source?

Increasing numbers of individuals are experimenting with altered states of consciousness. Are they creating a more coherent, resonant society, feeding order into the great social hologram, like seed crystals? Perhaps this is the mysterious process of the evolution of consciousness.

The holographic model also helps explain the strange power of the *image*—why events are affected by what we imagine, what we visualize. An image held in a transcendental state may be made real.

Keith Floyd, a psychologist at Virginia Intermont College, said of the holographic possibility, "Contrary to what everyone knows is so, it may not be the brain that produces consciousness—but rather, consciousness that creates the appearance of the brain—matter, space, time and everything else we are pleased to interpret as the physical universe."

When a paradigm is shifting, Pribram pointed out, science is often forced to reexamine earlier concepts that had been rejected. Leibniz, the seventeenth-century philosopher and mathematician whose discovery of the integral calculus made holography possible, had postulated a universe of *monads*—units that incorporate the information of the whole. Leibniz maintained that the exquisitely orderly behavior of light indicated an underlying radical, patterned order of reality.

There are numerous cases of early thinkers explaining what should have been inexplicable in their time. Ancient mystics, for example, correctly described the function of the pineal gland centuries before science could confirm it. "How did ideas like this arise centuries before we had the tools to understand them?" Pribram asks. "Maybe in the holographic state—the frequency domain—4,000 years ago is tomorrow."

Similarly, Henri Bergson had said in 1907 that the ultimate reality is an underlying web of connection and that the brain screens out the larger reality. In 1929, Alfred North Whitehead, mathematician and philosopher, described nature as a great expanding nexus of occurrences beyond sense perception. We only imagine that matter and mind are different, when, in fact, they are interlocking.

Bergson maintained that artists, like mystics, have access to the *élan vital*, the underlying creative impulse. T.S. Eliot's poems are full of holographic images: "The still point of the turning world" that is neither flesh nor fleshless, neither arrest nor movement, "And do not call it fixity, where past and future are gathered. Except for the point, the still point/ There would be no dance, and there is only the dance."

The German mystic Meister Eckhart had said that "God becomes and disbecomes." David Hume, an eighteenth-century philosopher, anticipated David Bohm's theory of holomovement, saying that a human being is nothing but a bundle of perceptions "which succeed each other with inconceivable rapidity and are in perpetual flux and movement." Rumi, the Sufi mystic, said, "Men's minds perceive second causes, but only prophets perceive the action of the First Cause."

And, perhaps the most extraordinary ancient description of a holographic reality is in a Buddhist sutra:

> In the heaven of Indra there is said to be a network of pearls so arranged that if you look at one you see all the others reflected in it. In the same way, each object in the world is not merely itself but involves every other object, and in fact *is* every other object.

Since the gradual unfolding of Pribram's synthesis of the holographic brain with David Bohm's holographic universe, his idea has stimulated the interest of philosophers and humanistic psychologies. The Association for Humanistic Psychology sponsored two invitational one-day symposia last December in San Francisco so that Pribram could fully explain the concepts to an interdisciplinary group. Among those attending were George Leonard, Jean Houston, Charles Tart, Rollo May, Bob Samples, John Perry, Stanley Krippner, Arthur Deikman, Enoch Callaway, Huston Smith and Sam Keen. The theory was also the subject of a recent Canadian Broadcasting Corporation documentary that spurred one of the largest audience responses of any program in the history of the network.

"We're here in celebration of the paradigm shift," Pribram said with some amusement. When he noted that the theory sees everything in terms of vibrations, the audience laughed, and he said, "I guess I don't need to tell you that."

The brain he was raised on was a computer, Pribram told a San Diego audience in 1976, but "the brain we know now allows for the experiences reported from spiritual disciplines." Recently, at the large invitational conference in San Francisco sponsored by the Unification Church, Pribram discussed his approach to the physics of consciousness in a session with five Nobel laureates.

How brain processes can be altered to allow direct experience of the frequency domain is still a conjecture. It may involve a known perceptual phenomenon—the "projection" that permits us to experience the full, three dimensional stereophonic sound as if the sound emanates from a point midway between two speakers instead of coming from two distinct sources. Research has shown that the kinesthetic senses can be similarly affected; tactile stimulation on both hands at a particular frequency eventually causes the person to feel as if he or she has a third hand, midway between the other two. Pribram has suggested possible involvement for brain circuits centering on the amygdala that have been the site of pathological disturbances, déjà vu, and seem involved in the "consciousness without a content" of mystical experience. Some alternation of frequency and the phase relationships in these structures may be the Open Sesame for transcendental states.

Mystical experience, Pribram says, is no more strange than many other phenomena in nature, such as the selective derepression of DNA to form first one organ, then another. "If we get ESP or paranormal phenomena—or nuclear phenomena in physics—it simply means that we are reading out of some other dimension at that time. In our ordinary way, we can't understand that."

Pribram acknowledges that the model is not easily assimilated; it too radically overturns our previous belief systems, our common-sense understanding of things and time and space. A new generation will grow up accustomed to holographic thinking; and to ease their way, Pribram suggests that children should learn about paradox in grade school, since the new scientific findings are always fraught with contradiction.

Pribram predicted in 1977 that the soft sciences of today will be the core of hard science in 10 to 15 years, just as cognitive psychology, once considered soft, took precendence over behaviorism. He also predicted the emergence of a clear holism, a paradigm shift encompassing all of science.

Productive scientists must be as ready to defend spirit as data. "This is science as it was originally conceived: the pursuit of understanding," says Pribram. "The days of the cold-hearted, hardheaded technocrat appear to be numbered."

3
WHAT THE FUSS IS ALL ABOUT
Karl H. Pribram

THE PHYSICAL

DAVID BOHM IN HIS BOOK *The Special Theory of Relativity* has an appendix on Perception. In this appendix he covers problems dealing with the psychology of appearances, especially James Gibson's findings in an extended series of experiments. These experiments utilize two dimensional displays on cathode ray tubes which are perceived as three dimensional figures. Gibson argues from his findings that three dimensional perception is "direct," i.e., immediate and that all other forms of knowledge and the world are derived from this immediate reality.

In a paper in which I take issue with Gibson on the "directness" of appearances, I describe the constructional brain processes which are involved even when perceptions appear to be immediate. An example from everyday life is the immediacy of our awareness of a projected three-dimensional acoustic image in stereophonic high fidelity reproduction of music. We know the sources of the sound to be the speakers but we also know that by adjusting the phase relationships between acoustic waves generated by the speakers we can move the sound away from the two sources, to in between the speakers or in front of them.

Our ears and acoustic nervous systems (re)construct the sound to be perceived in a location we know to be incapable of producing that sound. Which then is the reality of the situation, the perceived appearance or what we know to be the physical arrangement that gives rise to the appearance? Gibson has emphasized the reality of appearances and the primacy of that reality. Most other scientists, however, when they are asked what they mean by the "real" world would answer that they mean the world of physics. If pushed, they

27

would even describe that world as being made up of material objects and the interactions among these objects. In the example given, they would give primacy to the reality of the sound (re)producing stereophonic high fidelity apparatus, not the perceptual awareness derived from the operations of that apparatus.

Pursuing this "objective" reality of the physical universe, I began to inquire into the investigations of modern physicists. Immediately, I ran into the writings of David Bohm, Bohr, Einstein, Heisenberg, Wigner, Weizacker and others. Bohm had worked with Einstein who was occupied in a search for a unified field theory because he did not like the probabilistic statistical view that at bottom the physical universe is composed of essentially haphazard movements of minute objects, particles such as electrons and photons. Einstein expressed this concern in his statement that he did not believe God played dice with the universe. Bohm conceptualized the dilemma by suggesting that beyond haphazard appearance lay a domain of constraints, a set of "hidden" variables which, when uncovered, would provide a consistent nonstatistical basis for the apparently haphazard comings and goings of individual particles.

Bohr had enunciated the principle of complementarity to deal with some of these problems. He suggested that particles and fields were complementary views of the same sets of occurrences and his followers have come to believe in a basic reality opposite to that held by Einstein and Bohm. The so-called "Copenhagen Solution" (Bohr was a Dane) insists that the wave function—the field characteristics of microphysics—describe an envelope over the statistical perturbations of particles. It is this view of the primary reality which Einstein and Bohm continued to counter.

Heisenberg, Wigner and Weizsacker make still another and perhaps even more profound point. Heisenberg notes that the complementary view of the basic physical structure of the universe—particles vs. waves—are derived when different observations are made, different techniques are used, and different experiments are performed. Each experiment yields consistent results but the results of some are incompatible with those of others. Complementary views are based on disparate sets of data. Heisenberg argues in his famous principle that there is therefore no way of knowing which of the views is the more basic.

Wigner has conceptualized this line of reasoning in the statement that modern microphysics studies the relationships between observations not between observables. An observable is an observation that remains consistent, constant over a range of different views. Gibson, the psychologist, speaks of such constancies as invariances or "information," and Weiszacker squarely faces the conclusion, as does Bohm, that modern microphysics must deal with information defined *psychologically*, i.e., through behavioral observations.

Thus modern physicists and modern perceptual psychologists have converged onto a set of issues that neither can solve alone. If the psychologist is interested in the nature of the conditions which produce the world of appearances, he must attend to the inquiries of the physicist. If the physicist is to understand the observations which he is attempting to systematize, he must learn something of the nature of the psychological process of making observations.

THE MENTAL

As a brain scientist, I have come into the midst of this convergence. Brain is an essence of the material world; still it is an essence of which observations are constructed. An easy conceptualization would suggest that perceptions are emergent properties of the interaction of brain (and body) with the physical universe. Much as gravitational and electromagnetic forces are composed of the interactions among material objects and particles, so perceptions and other mental phenomena are composed of the interactions between brain (senses and body) and its surrounding "real" world.

At one level such an easy explanation is, of course, tenable. But deeper penetrations into the ideas reviewed above suggest another equally plausible explanation. Relationships among observations *are* mental phenomena since observations and perceptions are mental. Perhaps the very fundamental properties of the universe are therefore mental and not material. Nuclear physicists remind themselves of this possibility when they attribute charm, colors and flavors to their "relationships among observations,"[4] the quarks, bosons and other most elementary particles that constitute the nucleus of atoms. And from time to time philosophers such as Leibnitz and Whitehead have proposed panpsychic ontologies to account for similar views obtained by following through to a logical conclusion the reasoning of their mathematical insights into the basic order of the universe.

The following statements place these two basic views into succinct apposition:

1) Brain, by organizing the input from the physical world, as obtained through the senses, constructs mental properties.

2) Mental properties are the pervasive organizing principles of the universe, which includes the brain.

Paradoxically, almost all behavioral and neuroscientists would today subscribe to some form of statement one, while, as noted above, statement two reflects the belief of many of the most influential theoretical physicists. Mathematicians have faced the dilemma more directly: how is it that the operations of their brains so often describe faithfully the basic order of the universe they perceive?

Whenever thoughtful inquiry produces an impasse, it is reasonable to ask whether the questions being asked are being properly phrased. In the present instance, could it be that the properties derived from the relations between organism (brain-senses-body) and environment (physical universe) that are called mental and those that are derived from relations among observations of the physical universe, though also called mental, are disparate? If so, the problem would be essentially a semantic one—the same name used for different properties. In view of the fact that the proponents of the two views are extraordinary sophisticated thinkers, this simplistic resolution of the problem is most likely to be wrong. Those who believe mind and consciousness to be extended in the universe really do mean to refer to the same set of properties that are referred to by those who see perception, attention, consciousness, etc. as, primarily, manifestations of brain functioning. The same naming indicates that the same meaning is intended.

But another possibility can be entertained which does not do violence to intended meaning. Could it be that one aspect of organism-environment relations and one aspect of relationships-among-observations shows a commonality which has been generalized to the entire range of mental properties? Such overgeneralization (or lack of differentiation) is a well-known attribute of thought processes, and much of scientific and philosophic inquiry is devoted to "unpacking" sets of concepts which, though related differ from each other in some nontrivial fashion. I believe that in the present instance there is evidence that "unpacking" of the concept "mind" is warranted.

THE NEURAL

The evidence comes from understanding the nature of the brain mechanism involved in constructing perceptions—the mechanisms necessary to prehend the world of appearances. The story begins, not with perception however, but with memory. Specific memories are incredibly resistant to brain damage. Removing a hunk of brain tissue or injuring one or another portion of the brain does not excise a particular memory or set of memories. The process of remembering may be disturbed in some general way, or even some aspect of the general process may be disrupted. But never is a single memory trace of some particular experience lost while all else that is memorable is retained. This fact has become well established both through clinical observation in man and through experiments on animals. Thus in some way or other memory must become distributed—the experienced input from the senses becomes spread over a sufficient expanse of brain to make the memory of that experience resistant to brain damage.

Until recently, brain and behavioral scientists could not conceive of any mechanism that was consonant with the facts of brain anatomy and physiology and at the same time spread sensory input sufficiently to account for the distributed memory store. Now a plausible mechanism has been discovered.

In the late 1940s Dennis Gabor suggested that the resolution of electron microscopy could be enhanced if instead of storing images directly, the photographic film would be exposed to the patterns of light diffracted (filtered through or reflected from) by the tissue to be examined. Gabor's suggestion was formulated mathematically. Only many years later in the early 1960s was his suggestion realized in hardware. These hardware realizations made it obvious that images of the objects that had initially diffracted the light could readily be reconstructed. Thus object $\longrightarrow$ wave storage $\longrightarrow$ image construction could be seen to be a simple linear process. Furthermore, Gabor's equations showed that the identical mathematical transfer function transformed object into wave storage and wave storage into image! The storage of wave patterns is thus reciprocally related to the imaging of objects!! The wave functions are transforms of objects and their images.

Gabor named the wave pattern store a *hologram* because one of its most interesting characteristics is that information from the object beomes distributed over the surface of the photographic film. Each point of light diffracted from the object becomes blurred and is spread over the entire surface of the film (the equations that describe this are called spread functions), as is each neighboring point of light. The spread is not haphazard, however, as the blur would lead one to believe. Rather, ripples of wave move out from the point of light much as ripples of waves are formed when a pebble strikes the smooth surface of a pond of water. Throw a handful of pebbles or sand into the pond, and the ripples produced by each pebble or grain will crisscross with those produced by the other pebbles or grains, setting up patterns of interfering wave fronts. The smooth mirror-like surface has become blurred, but the blur had hidden within it an unsuspectedly orderly pattern. If the pond could suddenly be frozen at this moment, its surface would be a hologram. The photographic hologram is such a frozen record of interference patterns.

It seemed immediately plausible that the distributed memory store of the brain might resemble this holographic record. I developed a precisely formulated theory based on known neuroanatomy and known neurophsiology that could account for the brain's distributed memory store in holographic terms. In the dozen or so years since, many laboratories including my own have provided evidence in support of parts of this theory. Other data have sharpened the theory and made it an even more precise fitting to the known facts.

Essentially, the theory reads that the brain at one stage of processing performs its analyses in the frequency domain. This is accomplished at the junctions *between* neurons not within neurons. Thus graded local waxings and wanings of neural potentials (waves) rather than nerve impulses are responsible. Nerve impulses are generated within neurons and are used to propagate the signals that constitute information over long distances via long nerve fibers. Graded local potential changes, waves, are constituted at the ends of these nerve fibers where they adjoin shorter branches that form a feltwork of interconnections among neurons. Some neurons, now called local circuit neurons, have no long fibers and display no nerve impulses. They function in the graded wave mode primarily and are especially responsible for horizontal connectivities in sheets of neural tissue, connectivities in which holographic-like interference patterns can become constructed.

Aside from these anatomical and physiological specifications, a solid body of evidence has accumulated that the auditory, somatosensory, motor, and visual systems of the brain do in fact process, at one or several stages, input from the senses in the frequency domain.* This distributed input must then, in some form, perhaps as changes in the conformation of proteins at membrane surfaces,

*Much of the weekend conference sponsored by The Association for Humanistic Psychology was devoted to presenting this evidence in detail.

become encoded into distributed memory traces. The protein molecules would serve the neural photographic hologram.

The explanation of the fact that specific memory traces are resistant to brain damage (remembering demands only that a small part of the distributed store remain intact in the same way that images can be reconstructed from small parts of a photographic hologram) has been only one of the contributions of holographic theory. Characteristics of the experience of imaging have been explained in an equally powerful manner. The projection of images away from their sources of origin has been demonstrated to result from processing phase relations (just as in the stereophonic audio systems described above). Simulations of image processing by computer have found no technique other than the holographic to provide the rich texture of scenes such as those that compose our experiences. And the complicated computations that go into three dimensional x-ray imaging by computerized tomography have relied heavily on the fact that such computations (mostly correlations) are performed readily in the frequency (holographic) domain.

THE PHILOSOPHICAL

But perhaps the most profound insight gained from holography is the reciprocal relationship between the frequency domain and the image/object domain. Recall that the fundamental question that is under consideration is whether mind results as an emergent property from the interaction of an organism with its environment, or whether mind reflects the basic organization of the universe (including the organism's brain). Images are mental constructions. They result from processes involving the brain (object), the senses (objects) in their interactions with the environment (considered objectively, i.e., as objects, particles such as photons, electrons, atoms, molecules and the objects of the reality of appearances). Images (one aspect of mind) are thus emergents in any objective, object-i-fying philosophical formulation.

But the process of image construction involves a reciprocal stage, a transformation into the frequency (holographic) domain. This domain is characteristic not only of brain processing, as we have seen, but of physical reality as well. Bohm refers to it as the implicate order in which points become enfolded and distributed throughout the brain.

In the implicate, holographic domain, the distinction between points becomes blurred; information becomes distributed as in the example of the surface of a pond. What is organism (with its component organs) is no longer sharply distinguished from what lies outside the boundaries of the skin. In the holographic domain, each organism represents in some manner the universe, and each portion of the universe represents in some manner the organisms within it. Earlier in this paper, this was expressed in the statements that the perceptions of an organism could not be understood without an understanding of the nature of the physical universe and that the nature of the physical universe could not be understood without an understanding of the observing perceptual process.

It is, thus, the fact that the holographic domain is reciprocally related to the image/object domain that implies that mental operations (such as mathematics) reflect the basic order of the universe. Of special additional interest is one characteristic of the holographic order. This domain deals with the density of occurrences only; time and space are collapsed in the frequency domain. Therefore the ordinary boundaries of space and time, locations in space and in time become suspended and must be "read out" when transformations into the object/image domain are effected. In the absence of space-time coordinates, the usual causality upon which most scientific explanation depends must also be suspended. Complementarities, synchronicities, symmetries, and dualities must be called upon as explanatory principles.

The answer to the initial question as the whether mind, consciousness and psychological properties in general are emergents or expressions of some basic ordering principle, rests on which of two reciprocally related domains is considered primary, the image/object or the implicate holographic. Scientists are, as yet, only barely acquainted with the implicate order which has, however, apparently been explored experientially by mystics, psychics and others delving into paranormal phenomena. Perhaps if the rules for "tuning in" on the holographic, implicate domain could be made more explicit, we could come to some agreement as to what constitutes the primary basic order of the universe. At the moment this order appears so indistinguishable from the mental operations by which we operate on that universe that we must conclude either that our science is a huge mirage, a construct of the emergence of our convoluted brains, or that, indeed, as proclaimed by all great religious convictions, a unity characterizes this emergent and the basic order of the universe.

4

FIELD CONSCIOUSNESS AND FIELD ETHICS

Renée Weber

BOHM'S THEORY REVEALS a remarkable cosmology. Perhaps no less remarkable than its content is its source, a physicist. In our epoch of professional compartmentalization, the question arises: why does an eminent theoretical physicist with a scientific reputation at stake devote himself to exploring consciousness? An emphatic grasp of Bohm's vision of the universe sheds light on this question.

His contact with Indian philosophy, notably the Indian sage Krishnamurti, has convinced Bohm that thought, the form of consciousness most familiar to us and in which we habitually function, corrupts reality. The ancient hope of metaphysics and physics, that thought might reveal reality, is necessarily doomed. Thought is a *reactive*, not an active ability, attuning man only partially to nature; distorting most of it. Thought is a fossilized kind of consciousness, operating within "the known" and thus by definition is uncreative. Reality or the ultimate (Bohm does not equate these two, but their clarification is beyond the scope of this paper), Bohm's investigations have convinced him, is always fresh. It is a living process. Since thought is bounded by time, it cannot grasp what lies beyond a spatio-temporal finite framework.

Bohm only reluctantly admits the theories of other thinkers into his discussions, insisting on working out a given problem afresh without leaning on the past. Still, he allows that there are parallels between his views and those of certain philosophers of the past. A case in point is Plato, whose Allegory of the Cave (*Republic* VII) coheres surprisingly with Bohm's cosmology. When pressed, Bohm agrees to the correlation of Plato's cave with the explicate order, and that of Plato's metaphor of light with Bohm's implicate order. Both

Plato's light (sun) and Bohm's implicate order can be apprehended only through insight, both lie beyond language, and both are inaccessible except to those willing to undergo strenuous and single-minded change. The domains Bohm characterizes as "infinitely beyond" even the implicate order—namely truth, intelligence, insight, compassion—compare to Plato's ultimates: truth, beauty, the good, the one.

Other historical traditions come to mind. In the West, Plotinus, Leibniz, and Spinoza; in the East, Buddha, Shankara, and *jnana* yoga. *Jnana* yoga, whose affinity with Krishnamurti and Bohm is striking, is the yoga of discernment and discrimination. It eschews metaphysics and exoteric religion, ritual and symbol-systems in favor of a pure awareness without frameworks or filters. It is known in the tradition as "the path that goes straight up the side of the mountain," and is reputed to be the most direct and difficult path there is. Only the very few are said to be willing to meet its demands or are capable of this feat. According to those who have left us the record of their experience, its high point is silence. Thus Meister Eckhart (to turn to an unexpected source) asserts that "there is nothing in all the universe so much like God as silence," and connects this finding to methodology: "Why do you prate of God? Don't you know that whatever you say is untrue?"

Beyond these few remarks, we must leave tradition behind. Though it may be of historical and psychological interest to link ourselves to other explorers of this fecund stillness, to get stuck in the past is a hindrance and betrayal of the freshly minted living moment, in which Bohm's total focus lies. However interesting may be the philosophers or systems one injects into a discussion with him, Bohm firmly reduces these to a minimum and brings the subject back to the present, to this *moment*. It is his commitment to this living moment-to-moment manifestation of reality that links his work in physics with his interest in consciousness.

Atom-smashing can occur only in the present and must occur ever afresh. The analogy of the atom with thought, and with an alleged thinker who authors thought, is crucial. The thinker is like the atom, cohering in time through its binding energy. When the binding energy of the pysical atom is released in an accelerator, the resultant energy, staggeringly huge, becomes freed. Analogously huge amounts of binding energy are needed to create and sustain the "thinker" and to maintain his illusion that he is a stable entity. That energy, being tied up, is unavailable for other purposes, pressed into the service of what Bohm terms "self-deception" (a phenomenon described in detail by Buddha as ignorance, *avidya*, literally "not really seeing."). Thought, or what Bohm terms the 3-dimensional mind, mistakenly believing itself autonomous and irreducible, requires and hence squanders vast amounts of cosmic energy on this illusion. Energy thus pre-empted cannot flow into other grooves. The consequence is an unsound cosmic ecology, polluting the holomovement in at least two destructive directions. First, the holomovement misunderstands itself, chosing fiction over fact, and therefore enslaves itself. Second, the holomovement lacerates itself, substituting the isolated self for the consciousness of mankind in an abstraction founded on fallacy, enslaving others through its anger, greed, competitiveness and ambition. The result of both these missteps is a world of personal and interpersonal suffering.

The first misstep, the illusion of an ego, I, personal self or thinker, is intimately related to time and death. Let us be clear. The thinker, not consciousness, is death-bound. Death, according to these views, is precisely the psychological atom-smashing described above and need not be synonymous with the dissolution of the physical body (as has been noted by many recorders of the esoteric tradition). Psychological death occurs when consciousness keeps step with the ever-moving and self-renewing present, allowing no part of itself to become caught or fixated as residual energy. It is residual energy that furnishes the framework for what will become the thinker, who consists of undigested experience, memory, habit-patterns, identification, desire, aversion, projection and image-making. This is not a purely personal process but the energy of aeons of such processes sclerosed through time, persisting on both personal and collective levels. Ego-death dismantles this superstructure, moving it into its rightful place in the background of our lives, instead of dominating and disordering the foreground as is presently the case. Bohm argues that such a move entails greater not reduced biological adaptation and health, and it need not threaten us. On the contrary, "death" thus conceived is really its negation, ushering us into the timeless present beyond death's reach.

Our second point above concerns ethics. Through the centuries, the thinker has prattled on about absolutes unquestionably noble— God, cosmic consciousness, universal intelligence or love—but the domain where he daily dwells has remained destructive and chaotic. This need not surprise us. The 3-dimensional quality of thought necessarily blocks the thinker's own experiencing of reality about which he has chattered for centuries. Logical and substantive incommensurability, not ill-will nor insufficient effort account for this. The nonmanifest, as Bohm painstakingly argues, is n-dimensional and atemporal, and cannot be handled in any way whatever by 3-dimensional thought. Consciousness functioning as thought (as opposed to insight) cannot know truth or compassion at first hand, and herein lies the root of its failure to embody these energies in its daily life.

Only when the individual has dissolved the 3-dimensional self consisting of gross matter, can the ground of our being flow through us unobstructedly. To a theoretical physicist, the parallel of this state of affairs with quantum mechanics is evident. Bohm extends its applicability to psychology, urging on us the dissolution of the thinker as the highest priority the seeker for truth can undertake. With this view he teeters on the very edge of what is culturally acceptable, in the interface between physics and religion. It is a strange terrain, since our current culture, lacking any conceivable concept to explain it, rejects such a link as muddled if not absurd. However strange and novel it may be, this integration is justified by Bohm's model of the universe as a holomovement. The dismantling of the thinker yields energy that is qualitatively charged, not neutral or value-free. It is energy unbound and flowing, characterized by wholeness, n-dimensionality, and the force of compassion. Physics and ethics also become one in this process, for the energy of the whole is somehow bound up with what we term holiness. In short, the energy itself is love.

The atom-smashing applicable to consciousness Bohm and Krishnamurti term "awareness." Such a process provides consciousness with direct access to that energy, leading it to experiential certitude, based on evidence, that the ultimate nature of the universe is an energy of love. Mystics have proclaimed this with one voice. What is arresting is that a contemporary physicist finds such a theory and its method of interest. It is of course true that in many respects the aims of the mystic coincide with those of the physicist, i.e., contact with what is ultimate. But there is one critical difference. Smashing the atom is a dualistic enterprise; the physicist (subject) works on an object considered to lie outside himself. Changing the object does not fundamentally change him. By contrast, destructuring the thinker necessarily involves the operator or experimenter himself, for he is the test-object in question, at once the transformer and what is undergoing transformation. Hence the resistance, arduousness and great rarity of such an event.

Though rare, it does occur, and as suggested above, Bohm relates its achievement to ethics. Psychological atom-smashing unpollutes what countless illusory egoic clusters (analogous to spasms that reduce the flow within the whole) have polluted with their misplaced sense of separateness and their ego-borne priorities, resulting in universal sorrow. The psychological atom-smasher thus coincides with the saint, who no longer adds to the collective sorrow of mankind and instead becomes a channel for the boundless energy of compassion. Consciousness becomes a conduit aligned with the energy of the universe, radiating it to the creature and human world without distorting it or diverting it for its own self-centered pursuits.

Oddly, in spite of Bohm's conviction that this is the true and desirable state of affairs with which our knowledge simply has not yet caught up, he is reluctant to discuss it other than in brief allusions to it. His emphasis is on the methodology of the self-deconditioning process, not on the promised land which might lie at the end of it. His rationale for this is simple. In its conditioned state, the mind can in any case do no more than translate what is unconditioned into conditioned patterns and, thus, lose the essence of what it sought. Faithful to the credo of science, Bohm holds out for experiential, not verbal proof. The consequence of this position is strange if not bizarre. Nothing in the realm of knowledge, not even the elusive paradox of quantum mechanics, can quite rival it. On some level it seems at odds with our psychological make-up, for even those in full intellectual accord with this view encounter difficulty coming to grips with it on the existential level of their lives, as anyone who has experimented with Krishnamurti's teachings will attest. What is this paradox? Just this: that the more we talk about or even think "the truth," the further away we push it from ourselves (the analogy with Heisenberg's Indeterminacy Priciple is obvious). It is the *I*, the thinker, the creator of the thought about the holy or God who, in that act itself, introduces the impurities (time, self, language, dualism) and thus beclouds what would otherwise be *unsullied* (Krishnamurti himself used that word in this context in a talk we had together in Ojai in 1976).

This claim is hardly novel, but its articulation has rarely been put forward with such single-minded eloquence as that found in the tone and language of Krishnamurti or with the clarity of Bohm. We need in fact not roam far afield. Kant comes to mind. Already in the late eighteenth century he insisted on our impossibility—grounded in logic or the laws of thought and thus constituting an obstacle that cannot be overcome—to experience what is ultimate. Kant called that domain the thing-in-itself, i.e., what Krishnamurti and Bohm call intelligence or compassion (Buddha, the *dharma*, and Plato "the good"). Kant killed metaphysics by carefully demonstrating in the *Critique of Pure Reason* that whatever is thinkable and namable must necessarily conform to the inherent structure of the mind: space, time, quality, quantity, casuality, etc. The Kantian categories are what Bohm refers to as the realm of 3-dimensionality, with the distinction that the latter is wider, containing emotion, will, intent and other psychological as well as cognitive qualities. All these concern the world of sensible experience (the manifest or explicate order, in Bohm's language), and they account for our ability to function in the phenomenal domain. In that dimension, we have no choice but to filter *that which is* through the universal perceiving apparatus just described. Our capacity for translation is useful when properly employed (i.e., biologically or in certain practical affairs of daily life). But we do so at a heavy price, as Kant realized. The noumenon or thing-in-itself, not capable of being caught in our net, remains inscrutable to us. Knowledge for both Kant and Bohm is the process of tuning in on the manifestation (phenomenon) of the nonmanifest in order to make it accessible to creatures structured as we are. This filter and consequent distortion is inbuilt and universal. By definition, the thing-in-itself can never appear to us as it would be without our "tuning in" on it with our finite receiving apparatus.

Here the ways part. Krishnamurti, Bohm, and the whole mystical tradition agree with Kant's analysis regarding phenomenal experience. They move beyond Kant, however, to proclaim the possibility of a state of consciousness lying outside these barriers. For Kant, whose views on the subject have been accepted as definitive by Western philosphy, *no other capacity in us is available* on which to draw in order to approach the noumenon. Bohm and those mentioned maintain that such a capacity exists in the universe, not in us strictly speaking. The challenge for the individual locus of consciousness is to provide the condition that allows the universal force to flow through it without hindrance. The result is not knowledge, in the Kantian sense, but direct nondualistic awareness, a state for which Kant made no provision and for which he had no vocabulary. Its precondition is emptiness, as Bohm repeatedly insists, which entails a suspension of the Kantian categories and of 3-dimensional space-time. Such emptiness brings about the cessation of consciousness *as the knower* and transforms us into an instrument receptively allowing the noumenal intelligence to operate through us, irradiating our daily lives and those of others. The specific mechanism at work is difficult to understand. Perhaps we become akin to electrical "transformers" capable of stepping down the staggering cosmic energy in ways that permit us to *focus* it on the microcosmic level where we live and act. However this may be, the rare individual who functions as such a channel seems to those who come in contact with him to belong to a new species of man. (Krishnamurti, for anyone who has met him, clearly is such a case in point.) Such a human being radiates clarity, intelligence, order and love by his mere presence. He seems capable of transmuting our chaotic interpersonal world into an ethical realm by his very *atmosphere*, which unmistakably is charged with energies for which we have neither names nor concepts. At best we can vaguely capture the presence and power of that atmosphere in metaphorical and approximate terms.

Kant, by contrast, leaves us no doubt as to his unfamiliarity with such states of being, which a handful of humanity has recorded with remarkable consistency and intersubjective agreement. Bohm, like Kant, performs an invaluable service in delineating clearly where the limits of knowledge must lie. To paraphrase Kant: humankind is in a bind symbolized, as we might state it today, by a species universally endowed with contact lenses. Without these lenses, we cannot see at all, i.e., we can have no knowledge whatever. But as the lenses come pre-equipped with their own built-in tinted filters, with their aid we can "see" only what the filters permit. Thus we see either nothing or else distortedly. In neither case do we contact what is ultimate.

Perceiving (not visually, of course) things as they really are requires inactivating these lenses, in Bohm's terms, by-passing the ego or self that manipulates the world through them, and becoming the empty channel for the wholeness that is our source. Nothing in that emptiness can be characterized, as already explained, because characterization is the translation of noumenon into phenomenon, of nonmanifest into manifest. Therefore all languages will fail to capture the essence of the whole, even the purest of languages, mathematics, as Plato conceded in the *Republic*. Only silence is commensurate with its nature and appropriate to its universe of "discourse" (*samadhi*, the rapturous culmination of yogic meditation described by Patanjali, literally means "total silence" or "complete stillness").

These remarks should shed light on Bohm's uncompromising stance. The hope of apprehending the noumenon through phenomenal eyes is founded on a logical absurdity, what Bohm calls confusion and self-deception. The age-old philosophical effort to tune in on the purity of being and perceive it as it would be in itself without being perceived by a knower is therefore a vain hope. To approach the infinite cosmic intelligence, love, or insight of which Bohm speaks entails that the knower has stepped aside altogether in favor of pure nondualistic awareness. In the light of this necessity, Bohm's priorities become understandable and seem inevitable. Atom-smashing confined to gross matter—the province of the particle physicist—is but a first step in our reaching out to reality, and it is the path presently pursued by the community of physicists. But Bohm runs far ahead of the pack. The shape-shifting (cf. *Tibetan Book of the Dead*) of subatomic particles (gross matter) will not yield up the secrets of the universe. All it can offer us is knowledge, restricted to the 3-dimensional realm, as we have seen.

Bohm holds out for atom-smashing of a subtler kind: to slow down and ultimately to still the shape-shifter's dance itself, i.e., the death of the 3-dimensional thinker and his rebirth within the n-dimensional domain of consciousness. Such an event would usher in the dynamic state Bohm refers to, in which creation and dissolution and creation would flow through us simultaneously, like quanta of energy born and borne away in the split micro-second, ever welling up afresh without being arrested, clutched at, or sullied. The consequence—were such a task successful—is a new paradigm of the universe, of consciousness and of human reality. No longer is it a question of a knower observing the known across the gulf of knowing which separates them. That model of consciousness has failed us through the centuries in which we have stubbornly clung to it.

It must be swept aside, as Bohm so clearly argues. Its replacement is the austere paradigm of a unified field of being, a self-conscious universe realizing itself to be integrally whole and interconnected. Knower and known thus are falsehoods: crude constructs based on abstraction. They are unwarranted by the way things really are, namely the monism which Bohm claims is most fully compatible with the message of modern physics, based on its penetrations into nature thus far. Although the data is accepted by physicists, their interpretation of it remains restricted to realms that exclude themselves as conscious beings.

It is this reluctance and restriction that Bohm is challenging. He is willing to explore *all* the consequences of quantum mechanical theory and is risking his reputation on his commitment to the holomovement. His vision is a unified field theory undreamed of by science, in which the searcher and what is sought are apprehended as one, the holomovement becoming translucent to itself. That unified field is neither neutral nor value-free as current scientific canon requires, but an intelligent and compassionate energy, manifesting in an as yet unborn realm where physics, ethics and religion merge. For human life, widespread awareness of such a realm will be revolutionary, leading us from information to transformation and from knowledge to wisdom.

5

THE ENFOLDING-UNFOLDING UNIVERSE: A CONVERSATION WITH DAVID BOHM

conducted by Renée Weber

WEBER: I think the first question that we ought to explore is what is the holographic model of the brain or of consciousness and how does it differ from currently held concepts or what we've always believed the truth of the matter to be?

BOHM: Well, the holographic model of consciousness is based on the notion that information from which the consciousness works is not stored in particular places but rather is stored all over the brain or over large areas of the brain, and each time the information is used, a selection is made by gathering it together from all over as happens with the hologram outside the brain.

WEBER: How is it gathered?

BOHM: You really should do an interview with Pribram for that, but you can imagine that the brain is a network of connections of cells and, let's say, information. Last year I heard a theory which said that memory may be stored in rings of circuits going round and round between certain cells, and it leaves a kind of plastic deformation of the brain so that when energy is supplied to those rings again, a pattern is evoked which is similar to the one that produced those rings. It's not so different from the principle of tape recording.

WEBER: It takes the path of least resistance?

BOHM: Well, not exactly that, but when you see something which stirs up that ring it will record, but then when you see something similar, it may stir up an energy which comes from that record.

WEBER: Retrieves it?

BOHM: Retrieves it. Those rings may not only be local but there may also be many such rings all over the brain, a tremendous number of them, interconnected, so if, for example, you are looking at a particular item of information such as a rock, the simplest view, like the lens, would be to say that the rock is stored in one cell of the brain. And then the second rock is in another cell, the tree is in another cell and so on. Another view would be that the rock is analyzed into many many features such as lines, curves, edges, colors and all the different information might produce some sort of plastic deformation all over the brain. Therefore to retrieve the information about this rock, somehow there must be a collection of information from all over the brain. In other words, if we put it that way even the word "rock" may be stored all over the brain and all the various attributes which the rock has are stored, not necessarily in one place but all over, and those attributes could be recombined in different ways for different kinds of objects. Therefore, you could say to form any concept whatsoever or any picture or memory or whatever, you need to take information which is not in a one-to-one correspondence with some sort of card index, or something like that, but rather is in its holographic storage. In fact computer people are working on holographic storage of information as a far more effective way than the present digital storage.

WEBER: Is that related to the notion that any part of any cell can reproduce the whole?

BOHM: Well, not necessarily only one cell but any part of one cell has information about the whole. The more cells you bring together the more detailed the information. See, it is characteristic of the hologram that if you illuminate a part of the hologram you will get the information about the whole picture but it will be less detailed and from less angles, so the more of the hologram you take, the more detailed and the more ample the information is always going to be. But the subject or object of the information is always this one whole. The different parts of the hologram are not in correspondence with different parts of the object. But rather each one is somehow impressing something of the whole.

WEBER: In other words it would conflict with or even lay to rest what philosophers used to call the correspondence theory of truth: the image, the photographic plate, the object.

BOHM: Well, it doesn't really cohere with that. And in fact Pribram had an interesting way of looking at it; that is he was thinking about this holographic model and then he read my papers and thought about that, and he asked himself the question: "What is the hologram the hologram of?" And according to the view we're proposing, the world itself is constructed or is structured on the same general principles as the hologram. I don't know how much of the implicate order I should explain?

WEBER: As much as you like; we'd be very interested in it.

BOHM: I'm saying the hologram is an example of the enfolded or implicate order.

WEBER: Can you give us a model of the implicate order?

BOHM: We had sort of a device in London consisting of two concentric glass cylinders with a very viscous fluid such as glycerine between them, that could be turned very slowly so that there was no diffusion of the viscous fluid. If you put a droplet of insoluble ink into that viscous fluid and turned it slowly, it would be drawn out into a thread that was invisible and when you would turn it back, it would be suddenly visible again. Now, you can say the thread was enfolded like the egg is folded into the cake. You cannot unfold the egg out of the cake but you can unfold the thread in this case because there is this viscous mixing, and not diffusive mixing; you can unfold the ink droplet out of the glycerine by turning it back slowly so that there is no diffusion. Now you could imagine that you could enfold another ink droplet and it would also look much the same, but there is a distinction between the two enfolded ink droplets because one is going to unfold into this and the other into that. This distinction is in the *enfolded* order; it is not the ordinary *unfolded* order which we see, which is our ordinary description of reality. Ordinarily we think of each point of space and time as distinct and separate and that all relationships are between contiguous points in space and time, right? In the enfolded order we'll see, first of all, that when we've taken the droplet and enfolded it, it's in the whole thing and every part of the whole thing contributes to that droplet. Let's now imagine a situation where we put in another droplet. The two droplets are in different positions but when they are enfolded they sort of mix up with each other; is that clear?

WEBER: They mix with each other or they distribute through the whole?

BOHM: They distribute through the whole but they are interspersed with each other; they interpenetrate each other, but when you unfold, they separate and form two droplets. So, now if you have a situation which the ordinary language doesn't describe, this is an interpenetration in the whole and we must make a distinction between that whole which is going to produce a droplet here or one which will produce one there or one which will produce two droplets and so on. See, the ordinary order of description in physics is the Cartesian order in which we take a Cartesian grid and we say all points are entirely outside of each other and have only contiguous relation. You can then make a smooth curve for example, but if we enfolded that smooth curve we would get a whole with everything interpenetrating, and yet it would unfold into a smooth curve. Another smooth curve could be folded up. The result would look the same, very nearly, and yet the two would be different. So, there would be a set of distinctions that we make which are different from those that we make in the ordinary Cartesian order; namely, that there are all these enfolded orders which are different and yet don't look different from the gross view, from the ordinary view.

WEBER: So the Cartesian model is one of atomistic entities?

BOHM: Ultimately. Either atomistic or continuous flow. Continuous field is still the Cartesian model but all the connections are contiguous; namely, the field connects only with field elements very near to it in space and time; it has no direct connection with distant elements. Now, we'll see in a moment that this is not so in the enfolded order. I'm going to give you another image, another model: we enfold a droplet by turning the machine a certain number of times, "n" times. We now put in another droplet in a slightly different place and then enfold that n-times, but meanwhile the first one is enfolded 2-n times, right? Now we have a subtle distinction between a droplet which has been enfolded n-times and, one which has been enfolded 2-n times. They look the same but if we turn one of them n-times, we get this droplet; turn it another n-times we get that one. Now let's do it again with a slightly different position, so that it goes n times and the second 2-n times, and the original 3-n times. We keep it up until we've put in a lot of droplets. Now we turn the machine backward and one drop emerges and manifests to our vision and the next one does and the next one, so if this is done rapidly, faster than the time of resolution of the human eye, we will see a particle apparently continuously crossing the field.

But this description of the particle is absolutely different from the

Cartesian description. In the Cartesian description the particle exists and its essence is to be at one place, then another, then another. Here we say it is the whole which is manifesting, as the particle is always the whole but its parts are only in manifestation, namely it manifests to our eye because our eye only sees the droplet when the intensity, the density of ink droplets is beyond a certain point. So only those which have collected and been gathered to a very dense state are visible at that moment. And when they go back in, another set come out, so you see a particle crossing. But you see, the particle crossing is only an abstraction which is manifest to our vision and the reality is the enfolded order which is always whole and which is essentially independent of time. It's unrelated to time because two elements which are closely related to each other are those which are going to unfold one after another, but originally they are all interspersed. And so the basic relation has nothing to do with space and time.

WEBER: To make them manifest to us, it is as if we have to elicit them in the kind of condition that a human being, structured as we are, can get hold of.

BOHM: That's right. They manifest in a form which can be open to our perception. Ordinarily the whole enfolded order cannot be all made manifest to us, but some aspect of it is manifest. Then when we bring this enfolded order into that manifest aspect we get an experience of perception. But that doesn't mean that the whole of the order is just what is manifest. That would be the Cartesian view: that the whole of the order is at least potentially manifest though we may not know how to make it manifest on our own. We might need microscopes and telescopes and various instruments.

WEBER: It's *res extensa*. Isn't that what holds it up; it's the postulate for Descartes that (except for the "I" and God) only what is materially visible and extended is ultimately real.

BOHM: Right. At least that it should be potentially visible to our finer instruments if not directly visible.

WEBER: Through surrogates.

BOHM: Yes. But, now we're saying that in the implicate order it is different. I'm going to say these ink droplets are only a model, but the hologram is infinitely finer; there are no ink droplets, really. And now we could say that what is going to be visible is only a very small part of the enfolded order, and therefore we introduce the distinction between what is manifest and what is not manifest. It may fold up and become nonmanifest or unfold into the manifest order and then refold again. And we say the fundamental movement is folding and unfolding. Whereas the fundamental movement of Descartes is crossing space in time, a localized entity moving from one place to another.

WEBER: Through space he would say.

BOHM: Through space, right. Or else a field transmitting a force from one place through space to another. See, the field model is just as Cartesian as the particle model; in fact Descartes favored the field model. He had a hydrodynamic vortex model of the world, not a particle model.

WEBER: Would this apply to current fields? Einstein's field?

BOHM: That's right; Einstein's field is still Cartesian.

WEBER: Why is that?

BOHM: Because he insists on local connection, on contiguous connection.

WEBER: Isn't there also so-called action at a distance?

BOHM: No, that is entirely outside of Einstein's view.

WEBER: It is? That would be Newton?

BOHM: Newton didn't like it. He said he had to have it, but he was trying to get rid of it. Newton and Einstein and Descartes all agreed on this point, though they may have differed on various other points.

WEBER: Now, exactly how does the implicate order differ from those three models?

BOHM: In the implicate order we not only always deal with the whole (which the field theory also does), but we also say that the connections of the whole have nothing to do with locality in space and time but have to do with an entirely different quality, namely enfoldment.

WEBER: In other words, what is significant here is that it's not crossing or traversing certain places?

BOHM: In these earlier models, either a particle crosses certain places or a force or an energy field crosses that place and therefore from the point of view of the implicate order, we don't have a fundamental distinction between Einstein and Newton, you see. We say they are different to be sure, but they both differ equally from the implicate order.

WEBER: Isn't time in some sense then, the key issue here?

BOHM: Well, we are going to go into time later. We have to put time into the implicate order but we haven't got there yet.

So we have this notion, this notion which is the implication parameter, the degree of implication. See the ink droplet that has turned "n" times differs from the one that has turned 2n times. That difference is of no significance in the Cartesian view. But here it's the *fundamental* thing because we say: those things are connected which have very nearly the same degree of implication, however far they may be spread across space and time.

WEBER: Could you go into that a little more?

BOHM: Well, we'll go back to our ink drop model, and we are going to say that the fundamental relationship in this ink drop model is the degree of implication. Let's say it takes "n" turns to unfold a droplet to our perception, and "n" plus 1 turns for the next droplet. Now there's another droplet that takes say, a million more turns and we say that droplet is very far, very disconnected from the first, so the two droplets that are connected are those which are close to each other in enfoldment. That's the view. Therefore, in the whole, we say all connections are in the whole, having nothing to do with locality but having to do with this quality of enfoldment which is always of the whole.

WEBER: But doesn't that subtly sneak back sequence?

BOHM: No, we'll see that this is not basic. For the moment, we are putting sequence in time but the actual existence of this sequence is not in time; you can see immediately the implicate order is there all at once, having nothing to do with time. Sequence is not necessarily time. See, the most primitive order is sequence but we're not introducing a sequence at points in space or points in time.

WEBER: No, but can I just be anthropomorphic for a moment in my question? From what you've said, one gets the picture: it's as if you say, they are all there and they're throughout the order but the droplets waiting furthest back in line so to speak, not yet ready to be unfolded but still enfolded, sounds as if they're further back in time and space.

BOHM: Well, they're not further back, they are all present together.

WEBER: But they are not ready to come out.

BOHM: Yes but that's another difference, you see. They're not further back but we must introduce differences or distinctions and orders and relationships to have anything to talk about, and the key issue is what are they going to be? Are they going to be contiguous connections in space and time or something else. Now I say they're something else. If you have no order at all, we have nothing to talk about, nothing to look at or anything. This is a very primitive example of implicate order but later we'll get much more complex examples where there will be many parallel orders, not necessarily just one sequential order, or many criss-crossing orders or interpenetrating orders and so on. So, first of all the notion of simple sequence is only the beginning. Now for the view I'm proposing, let's go back to the hologram which works in a similar way.

We want to say that the hologram is merely an image or a fixed image of the state of the electromagnetic field, or whatever you want to call it in that space where you put the photograph, the photographic plate, and that's a state of movement. I call that the holomovement. That's an example of it. Also electron beams could do the same thing or sound waves could make holograms, any form of movement could constitute a hologram, movements known or unknown and we will consider an undefined totality of movement, called the holomovement and say: the holomovement is the ground of what is manifest.

WEBER: The holomovement is the ground. . . .

BOHM: The total ground. . . .

WEBER: Of what is manifest.

BOHM: Yes. And what is manifest is, as it were, abstracted and floating in the holomovement. The holomovement's basic movement is folding and unfolding. Now, I'm saying that all existence is basically holomovement which manifests in relatively stable form. I remind you that the word "manifest" is based on "mani" which means to hold with the hand, or something that can be stably held with the hand, something solid, tangible and so on. Also visibly stable.

WEBER: The flux arrested for the time being.

BOHM: Well, at least coming to balance for the time being, coming into relative closure, like the vortex which closes on itself, though it's always moving.

WEBER: I think yesterday you said these would be denser forms of matter rather than subtler and less stable ones.

BOHM: Yes, they are more stable forms of matter, let's put it that way. See, even the cloud holds a stable form so the cloud can be regarded as a manifestation of the movement of the wind. Now, in a similar way matter can be regarded as forming clouds within the holomovement and they manifest the holomovement to our ordinary sense and thought.

WEBER: You said, "All entities are forms of the holomovement." That would obviously include man with all his capacities.

BOHM: Yes, all the cells, all the atoms. And, I should add, to complete the picture, this begins to give a good account of what (quantum) mechanics means: this unfoldment is a direct idea as to what is meant by the mathematics of (quantum mechanics). What's called the unitary transformation or the basic mathematical description of movement in quantum mechanics is exactly what we are talking about. In mathematical form, it is just simply the mathematical description of the holomovement. But at present in quantrum mechanics there is no physical notion of what movement means so we merely use the mathematics to produce results, to calculate results, saying that they have no meaning whatsoever other than that.

WEBER: Would the community of physicists accept this interpretation?

BOHM: What, the holograph?

WEBER: Your characterization of the present state of physics?

BOHM: Oh, I think they have to, yes. They do use the idea of fields and particles and so on but when you press them they must agree that they have no image whatsoever what these things are, and they have no content other than the results of what they can calculate with their equations.

WEBER: So it's pragmatic.

BOHM: Well, at least it's in pragmatic language though it isn't consistently pragmatic because all sorts of nonpragmatic ideas are allowed to be introduced in the mathematics. It's confused rather, I would say; it's a mixture of some pragmatic aspects and some highly speculative nonpragmatic aspects but in a very unbalanced way. It's saying speculation is only allowed in the equations, but in the physical ideas they are rather fixed and essentially the physical ideas are only images of the equations, that is, they have no content other than as the convenient vehicles for stating imaginatively what the equations compute, so that you can grasp it in some imaginative though confused form.

WEBER: But isn't that like saying that they are not anchored in anything real, that they have no actual ground?

BOHM: Their only anchor is in the experimental results. They're saying that these numbers that they get out of the calculations agree with numbers that come out of the experiments.

WEBER: And how would you perceive this differently?

BOHM: Well, we are trying to give a description of reality whether wrong or right, we are proposing a view of reality, a description of reality which will faithfully be about or fit this reality, and we can now regard this mathematics as a way of calculating what's happening within this reality.

WEBER: It's a very different claim from this current utilitarian one.

BOHM: Yes. In the old Newtonian view you supposed that matter was really made of particles or whatever and you said that the equations enabled you to calculate what these things are going to do. But you didn't in those days say that there's nothing but equations and measuring instruments and that the equations enable you to do nothing but calculate the numbers that are going to come out on your measuring instruments. Today, by contrast, you put in various images to enable you to sum up the effects of the equations quickly, but you assert that these images cannot be regarded as in any sense the descriptions of reality.

WEBER: Which is perhaps why the philosophical impasse about quantum physics seems to be that man cannot *know* reality at all. I gather you don't accept that.

BOHM: That's somewhat of an absurd notion, because reality is whatever man can know, by definition. Reality is based on the word *res*, meaning "thing," and the thing is what is known. You see, the word *res* is based on the word *rere*, meaning to think, and the thing is what you can think about, essentially. So reality is just what man can know. Now, essentially what they [contemporary physicists] are saying (although it doesn't make sense) is that man's reality is confined to the results of some operations of scientific instruments but they wouldn't seriously argue for that either. It's confused. See, on Sundays when they are being philosophical, they say that man's reality is confined to the result of scientific instruments; and on weekdays they say it's really made of hard solid little particles, which they know cannot be so because they have all properties of waves and many properties that particles could never have. So, therefore, I think that the general result is confusion and you judiciously jump from one image to the other to enable you to quickly get mathematical results that you can compare with the experiments, and that's really the main point of the operation anyway; everything else is either useful for that purpose or window dressing, as they used to say, or frosting on the cake or whatever, but they would argue that it isn't really the main point.

WEBER: Now, the implicate order clearly changes that, but in what way?

BOHM: Because it says reality is the implicate order and the equations are describing that.

WEBER: Whereas in the other view, i.e., that of most contemporary physicists, the equations are as it were almost both the means and the end?

BOHM: Yes, the equations are the truth.

WEBER: The truth about what, is the question?

BOHM: In the first instance the results of scientific instruments, but then people can't say that that is all there is. Then they say it's the truth about these hard little particles which the equations deny could exist and we just go off into confusion, and then we finally say let's give up all those questions because we just can't answer them and there is no point to them. The only thing that has a point is to get results to work. It sort of slips around from one thing to another and you can't pin it down on any one point because its characteristic confusion is to jump from one idea to another. Whenever the pressure gets too great on one idea, you jump into another and therefore, you keep on jumping through ideas that don't cohere. And I think you could say the situation in physics today is thoroughly confused.

WEBER: You said yesterday that quantum mechanics when mapped partly onto the implicate order can handle the other aspect of the particle as somewhat in the implicate order even though not in the manifest. Could you go into that?

BOHM: Yes. If you take this picture of the ink droplets converging to form a particle and going out, the particles are actually all over space. If you were to put obstacles in the way of the particle it would converge differently, like a wave. It would begin to show a wave-like property and so on. So you see, all the properties of the particle are in the whole order. They are not a particle, what we call a single particle. Thus we begin to see a reality, a kind of reality which would make comprehensible the whole behavior of this thing. Then we could say it is a thing, *res*, and a thing that we know through thought, *rere*. The relation between thought and the thing is this: action being formed from thought will consistently meet that thing, and therefore it is the role of the experiment to test that.

WEBER: Could you further clarify the manifest/unmanifest relationship?

BOHM: Well, perhaps we should finish this business of the holomovement. If you follow through the mathematics of the present Quantum Theory, it treats the particle as what is called the quantized state of the field, that is, as a field spread over space but in some mysterious way with a quantum of energy. Now each wave in the field has a certain quantum of energy proportional to its frequency. And if you take the electromagnetic field, for example, in empty space, every wave has what is called a zero point energy below which it cannot go, even when there is no energy available. If you were to add up all the waves in any region of empty space you would find that they have an infinite amount of energy because an infinite number of waves are possible. Now, however, you may have reason to suppose that the energy may not be infinite, that maybe you cannot keep on adding waves that are shorter and shorter, each contributing to the energy. There may be some shortest possible wave, and then the total number of waves would be finite and the energy would also be finite. Now, you have to ask what would be the shortest length and there seems to be reason to suspect that the gravitational theory may provide us with some shortest length, for according to general relativity, the gravitational field also determines what is meant by "length" and metric. If you said the gravitational field was made up of waves which were quantized in this way, you would find that there was a certain length below which the gravitational field would become undefinable because of this zero point movement and you wouldn't be able to define length. Therefore, you could say the property of measurement, length, fades out at very short distance and you'd find the place at which it fades out would be about 10^{-33} cm. That is a very short distance because the shortest distances that physicist have ever probed so far might be 10^{-16} cm. or so, and that's a long way to go. If you then compute the amount of energy that would be in space, with that shortest possible wave length, then it turns out that the energy in one cubic centimeter would be immensely beyond the total energy of all the known matter in the universe.

WEBER: In one cubic centimeter of space?

BOHM: Yes. And therefore, how is one to understand that?

WEBER: How *do* you understand it?

BOHM: You understand that by saying: the present theory says that the vacuum contains all this energy which is then ignored because it cannot be measured by an instrument. The philosophy being that only what could be measured by an instrument could be considered to be real, because the only point about the reality of physics is the result of instruments, except that it is also said that there are particles there that cannot be seen in instruments at all. What you can say is that the present state of theoretical physics implies that empty space has all this energy and matter is a slight increase of the energy, and therefore matter is like a small ripple on this tremendous ocean of energy, having some relative stability, and being manifest. Now, therefore, my suggestion is that this implicate order implies a reality immensely beyond what we call matter. Matter itself is merely a ripple in this background.

WEBER: In this ocean of energy, you are saying.

BOHM: In this ocean of energy. And the ocean of energy is not primarily in space and time at all. We haven't discussed time yet, but let's discuss space. It's primarily in the implicate order.

WEBER: Which is to say unmanifest, not manifest.

BOHM: Right. And it may manifest in this little bit of matter.

WEBER: The ripple.

BOHM: The ripple, you see.

WEBER: But the source or the generative matrix, you're saying, is in the implicate order and that's this ocean of energy, untapped or unmanifest.

BOHM: That's right. And in fact beyond that ocean may be still a bigger ocean because, after all, our knowledge just simply fades out at that point. It's not to say that there is nothing beyond that.

WEBER: Something not characterizable or namable?

BOHM: Eventually, perhaps, you might discover some further source of energy but you may surmise that that would in turn be floating in a still larger source and so on. It is implied that the ultimate source is immeasurable and cannot be captured within our knowledge. So that's the general suggestion. That really is rather what is implied by contemporary physics and this implication has been avoided by saying that we mostly look at the equations and just work out what our instruments will do and how instruments will give results according to these equations.

WEBER: This view is of course very beautiful, breathtaking in fact, but would a physicist who pressed you on this, would he find some kind of basis *in physics* for allowing such a vision to be postulated?

BOHM: Well, I should think it's what physics directly implies. See, you have to ask the question, how do physicists manage to avoid facing this basis? And the answer is that they avoid it through this philosophy by which they say that anything that doesn't show in the instruments is of no concern to physics. So they decide to subtract off this infinity and say it's not there.

WEBER: But in the calculations and in the data, you say it is either implied or there?

BOHM: It's implied or there but then when you find the implications of this data through what our instruments would show, then it's not there because it's subtracted out; see, the instruments do not directly respond to this background. Because they are floating in it. It's like a fish not being aware of the ocean.

WEBER: I understand. But the theory, you're saying the extension of the theoretical part of physics warrants this kind of inference?

BOHM: Not only that but it's almost unavoidable to infer it. It's just been very ingenious that people could avoid considering it. I mean that they feel a tremendous pressure never to consider such ideas whereas in fact such ideas would be the obvious thing to consider had it not been for this philosophy which says that we should never consider these things.

WEBER: In other words a tacit assumption that we shall only *acknowledge* what is measurable by our instruments?

BOHM: Yes, that is our reality. What is measurable by our instruments is considered to be our reality and the things that our theory talks about, and therefore the theory itself should not actually talk about things which are not measurable by our instruments. I think this has been implicit, a kind of positivism. And at the same time it has been consistent, because people also want to say that our theory is considered a good hard solid reality such as the particle and they like to imagine that our instruments are measuring particles because they see tracks. But tracks are no proof of particles any more than the track of an animal is a proof of an animal. Somebody could have put the tracks there or anything.

WEBER: Wouldn't they in that metaphor accuse you of violating Occam's Razor and the principle of parsimony?

BOHM: Yes, but that's another idea, another thing, that's why I call it "philosophy." You see, I say Occam's Razor is a philosophical idea. I mean, it doesn't follow from the instruments that you must interpret them through Occam's Razor; it merely means that people, having been historically conditioned in a certain way, believe that Occam's Razor takes priority over anything else.

WEBER: But even measured by that criterion, is the implicate order not in fact simpler and more elegant?

BOHM: It is simpler. Basically, you see, it's not Occam's Razor so much as the belief that you must only discuss your instruments. From the point of view of an idea, it's much simpler. In fact you must engage in logical gymnastics in order to accommodate the present view. The typical reaction of a student who studies quantum mechanics is that at first he doesn't understand it and by a year or two later he says there is nothing to understand because it's nothing but a system of computation. At the same time they've got to say, no, it isn't just that, we're discussing reality. After all, physicists would have no motive for doing the work they do if they didn't believe that these particles are really the building blocks of the universe. So, you see, you have to engage in and become very skillful at mental gymnastics in order to sustain this myth. It's actually not so easy. It takes several years and a lot of skill to train people to be able to do it [i.e., to avoid the above philosophical implications].

Now, I say from the point of view of an idea, the implicate order is much simpler, but if you say that anything which is not register-able by our instruments is to be cut out by Occam's Razor then, of course, you will do so. I don't even know if Occam meant his razor in that sense. I mean, he didn't have any instruments. He might have meant just simplicity in the construction of ideas for all I know, which would have been an entirely different view.

WEBER: But let's take that criterion of simplicity. A quote from John Wheeler comes to mind. He said, "We will only understand how strange the universe is when we realize how simple it is." What is your reaction to that?

BOHM: He would have to mean simplicity in the idea. You know, simplicity means, as we say, onefoldness, it comes from some simple germ but it might unfold to encompass the complexity of the universe.

WEBER: The idea of an unmanifest source or realm? (I don't know if realm is too substantive).

BOHM: Well, unmanifest reality. It's simple enough. I mean people have had this for ages, you know; the ether was one form of that. It seemed very natural at a certain period for people to postulate that this ether was not ordinarily manifest and to claim that the things we see were manifestations of that. Now at some stage it got very complicated, it became very difficult for people to accommodate the facts of physics, and then came the positivist philosophy which said if it's not directly manifested we should ignore it. After that it became sort of a custom or fad to say that we must never consider such ideas. Whereas the fad before it was that such ideas were very natural; in fact people preferred those ideas. So, I don't think all of that has any great signigicance [i.e., the concensus of the scientific community at any given moment in history].

WEBER: Now, you said yesterday that in fact your theory would explain quantum mechanics better, and therefore by the criterion of explanatory power there is something to say for it even from the point of view of physics.

BOHM: Yes. I will give a better explanation and, on the one hand physicists might appreciate that. On the other hand they may be so influenced by this operationalist, positivist, empiricist philosophy that they say explanation is not the point of physics but prediction and control are. And they say if it doesn't enable you to predict and control anything then it's just frosting on the cake. That's the sort of language they would have used thirty years ago anyway.

WEBER: Speaking of prediction and control, what would you say about the notion of a physicist, a colleague of mine at Rutgers, who claims that Bohm is really subtly holding out for Cartesian type of prediction and control in not accepting the statistical methods of quantum mechanics, that Bohm is subtly reintroducing complete control and therefore mechanism?

BOHM: I don't know why he says that. He couldn't have read what I wrote very carefully. The first point is that I don't say there are no statistics. In this implicate order there is plenty of room for statistics. You may just as well use statistical distributions as determinate laws and in fact I proposed statistical distributions. It's not statistics I object to at all, but it's really the statement that the statistics of quantum mechanics is nothing but an algorithm for cranking out how our instruments are going to operate, not a statistic for what is there in reality. The second point is, I think he has it all wrong. It's the ordinary physicist who says: unless I can control and predict, I'm not interested.

WEBER: His question is: are you rejecting that method because it doesn't provide *enough* control?

BOHM: No, it has nothing to do with control. I'm rejecting it because it's confused. I'm saying that in fact the ordinary physicist is only interested in prediction and control. Statistics is also a means of prediction and control, to predict and control large numbers on the average. If the formulae of quantum mechanics did not enable a physicist to predict what the average results of his instruments were going to be, he would say: there's no point to it. He'd drop it. The ordinary physicist cares about nothing but what is predictable and controllable by any means whatsoever, whether by deterministic methods, statistical methods or, as I said yesterday, doing yoga or standing on his head, if that would help.

WEBER: Which is like saying that he is not primarily concerned with the truth of the matter?

BOHM: Well, with the reality. He's primarily concerned with what he can predict and control and it's rather surprising for your colleague to say that other physicists are not and that I am the one who's concerned with it.

WEBER: He added (and this issue would bring out the difference between your view and some others): what is wrong with conceiving of the universe as a machine? Why won't Bohm accept that?

BOHM: I think it's confused. I'm not objecting to conceiving the universe as a machine or in any other way, I'm saying that the particular conception that they are proposing is thoroughly confused.

WEBER: How?

BOHM: In present-day quantum mechanics, in the ways we've already touched on and going a little further, we can say that quantum physicists, on the one hand, claim that there is reality, that particles are really real, and they have an intense conviction about this reality, which is behind their motive for doing their work. On the other hand they say that these particles have no reality whatsoever, that the only reality is our instruments, and that there is no way to describe this reality. They may have some faith that somehow there is a reality there but it's confused to say that.

WEBER: Is it fair to state that essentially your creative work in these new directions is motivated by the original search of physics, the search for reality, not for just predictibility?

BOHM: And the search for clarity as well. You see, I'm saying that we not only want to consider what is reality but we want clearly to understand it and physicists say clarity is of no importance, only results count. Any way of getting results which are predictible and controllable will do.

WEBER: You've spoken of clarity often today and in the past: therefore, isn't it necessary at this point to consider consciousness and the knower, the one who is or isn't clear?

BOHM: Yes, we could come to that. The point is that consciousness is confused. Confusion is nonclarity. And if you say, a person is not clear, you mean he's confused, although it is more polite to say he's not clear. And confusion means "melting together." Things that are different are seen as one and things that are one are seen as broken up into many. So confusion clearly causes chaos.

WEBER: With respect to the implicate order and the manifest/ unmanifest domains, shall we say, what are the implications of those ideas of consciousness, for the way we think, and I would even like to ask, for the way we act?

BOHM: I think it would come back to what we were discussing about Pribram, the hologram model of the brain. You can see now that we are saying that the brain may function on something like this implicate order and manifesting in consciousness by memory.

But there is an order beyond which is not manifest. This involves both space and time. Time itself is an order of manifestation, you see. We are going to say that it is possible to have an implicate order with regard to time as well as to space, to say that in any given period of time the whole of time may be enfolded. It's implied in the implicate order when you carry it through, that the holomovement is the reality and in the holomovement, what is going on in the full depth of that one moment of time contains information about all of it.

WEBER: The whole thing. The moment is atemporal, you're saying.

BOHM: Yes, that's right, the moment is atemporal, the connection of moments is not in time but in the implicate order.

WEBER: Which you said is timeless.

BOHM: Yes. So let me propose that also for consciousness; let me propose that consciousness is basically in the implicate order as all matter is, and therefore, it's not that consciousness is one thing and matter is another, but rather consciousness is a material process and consciousness is itself in the implicate order, as is all matter, and that consciousness manifests in some explicate order as does matter in general.

WEBER: The differentiation between what we call matter and consciousness would be, I think you said yesterday, the state of density or subtlety.

BOHM: The state of subtlety, yes, that consciousness is possibly a more subtle form of matter and movement, a more subtle aspect of the holomovement.

WEBER: Yes. And matter is very dense or heavy or congealed.

BOHM: Whatever. Less subtle, yes.

WEBER: When you say consciousness do you refer to thoughts, emotions, desires, will, the whole mental or psychic life?

BOHM: Yes, all that.

WEBER: And you're saying that the source of what we perceive both of the so-called external world and of ourselves, our so-called inner processes, lies in this nonmanifest.

BOHM: Yes, and the nonmanifest itself lies in something immensely beyond that.

WEBER: Can that something beyond, immensely beyond that be (well I know it can't be known), can it be approached?

BOHM: Well, no, anything that could be approached could only be approached through the manifest. Let's try to say that it may act, the whole may act in each aspect, but the aspect cannot approach the whole, right?

WEBER: The ocean is wider and contains the droplet.

BOHM: The droplet has no way of approaching the ocean.

WEBER: But it can, the ocean (. . . what's the word? . . .) *acts* on the droplet, is present in it.

BOHM: It's present in the droplet and acts on and in the droplet, yes.

WEBER: With varying degrees of intensity or energy?

BOHM: Well, yes, but I think there's a certain danger here because [of what we are doing now]. We must now come back to thought. And I say thought is a material process and insofar as it is based on memory, it is manifest. You see, thought is the manifestation of some deeper mind. Now the relation between thought and the deeper mind might be like the relation between matter and this very much greater energy of emptiness. So thought is really a very tiny little thing. But thought forms a world of its own in which it is everything, right?

WEBER: Yes. It encapsulates itself and reifies itself.

BOHM: It reifies itself and imagines there's nothing else but what it can think about itself and what it thinks about. Therefore thought will now take the words, "the nonmanifest" and form the *idea* of the nonmanifest; and therefore, thought thinks the manifest plus the nonmanifest together make up the whole, and that this whole thought is now a step beyond thought, you see. But, in fact, it isn't. This nonmanifest that thought imagines is still the manifest, by definition, because to imagine is also a form of thought. It's a form of thought; it's the manifestation of thought. So, therefore, it's very easy to get into self-deception and possibly a lot of people thinking about it in this general way may have got caught in this throughout the ages. The point is that there is danger in doing this, namely that thought will imagine that it has captured the whole. Obviously, the nonmanifest that we talk about is a relative nonmanifest. It is still a thing, although a subtle thing.

WEBER: It's still material and governed by certain conditions.

BOHM: Yes. Conditions and laws and so on. And it may help us to understand the subtlety to which matter can reach, but at the same time, you see, however subtle matter becomes, it is not true ground of all being. Remember the word "truth" in Latin, *verus*, means "that which is," and the word "true" in English, means "straight": honest and faithful and straight. We could say that consciousness can be honest and faithful and straight but it is not . . . it is not *that which is*.

WEBER: All right. It comes out of that which is.

BOHM: Right, somehow it does. But we have to be careful because we've implicitly postulated that thought has already gotten down to that which is . . . , in that way you immediately find yourself *imagining* the deeper thing which is, and thought coming out of that. Now that is a self-deception.

WEBER: Yes, I see that, but on the other hand, if in trying in any way to deal with it (that's a poor word), one frames it as cautiously as possible, can't one say—which I think you've been implying—that one can entertain the possibility *that* it is but not *what* it is?

BOHM: Well, yes, we can consider that maybe that is what is, but, at the same time we have to be very careful to say that thought cannot grasp it, so at some stage thought has to put this question aside as to what is, you see. Thought cannot grasp that which is. And any attempt to grasp that which is engages us in serious self-deception which confuses everything. So that thought has to learn or somehow come to a state of discipline, or whatever you want to call it, spontaneous discipline, its own discipline.

WEBER: Order?

BOHM: Yes, order, in which it does not attempt to grasp the questions which are beyond it, such as the question of that which is. It can grasp any relative question which is conditioned, or in some way, conditional. So even the nonmanifest consciousness of the nonmanifest matter, which is highly subtle, is still within the possible area of thought.

WEBER: This is slightly aside from self-deception, but I just want to leave the phenomenological aspect for a moment to get back to the cosmology. You've said the nonmanifest generates and really governs what is manifest.

BOHM: Well, the manifest is really within the nonmanifest. It's like the cloud within the air.

WEBER: Okay. Is it a subset of it?

BOHM: In some form, well it's hard to express it, but the cloud is a form within it, it's really not very substantial, but it is a form within the whole. It is really our thought, which abstracts from our perception, and thought that abstracts that cloud; and in some sense, memory abstracts from the whole nonmanifest a certain sub-something, which is manifest.

WEBER: But also our perception, no? Because only what is accessible to us can be handled as manifest.

BOHM: Yes, but we're discussing consciousness. We say consciousness is whatever it is, with its content. It's a matter of being carefully logical; we may discuss a broader universe which is material and eventually fading off into something that is beyond.

WEBER: Spirit?

BOHM: What we call spirit. Let's discuss that a little bit. Matter, I would say, is that which we contact through our senses, our instruments, and through our thought. And any extension of that we still call matter. A field is still matter. Now what is spirit? Spirit has traditionally been opposed to matter. Spirit comes from the word *spiritus*, breath and wind. It basically means that which is nonmanifest, but which moves the manifest. I think the usual view of spirit is something beyond matter, for example, that which has created matter. In fact, that's the view in Genesis.

WEBER: God?

BOHM: Some people call it that. And you may try to get a view of spirit as the notion of God as immanent. But both immanent and transcendent God would have to be beyond thought. Now, we deceive ourselves if thought thinks spirit or God is immanent, and then it has captured it; or if God is transcendent and now it has already transcended itself, right? There's the self-deception. We have to be very careful here, very clear, you see, otherwise we'll start confusion going. Let us say first that thought itself has established a distinction between matter and spirit. And it's clear what the distinction is: whatever does not have obvious solid form and which moves something else, is called spirit, as the wind does; later we then discover that the wind is actually matter, right? But then we might say there was a spirit beyond the wind, and therefore we have this infinite regress.

So, finally we could now say a consistent view is to maintain that something like the nonmanifest matter is playing a role similar to what we thought of as spirit. It's moving manifest matter, but they are both matter, matter subtle and matter gross. Now, whatever we would mean by what is beyond matter we cannot grasp in thought. I mean, thought can pose the question, but it cannot go any further.

WEBER: But, can we reasonably assert that there must *be* something beyond that?

BOHM: No, we can't. We can say it would be reasonable to say there is, but we can't say by thought whether there is or isn't.

WEBER: Can we do it by any other means?

BOHM: Well, that's the question. But you see, at the moment we are discussing thought. Thought attempting to do this must deceive itself and produce confusion. Then the question would be what would be involved in not using thought? That would involve the cessation of thought; therefore that would get us outside the scope of what we're discussing. But we would say that it is only when thought actually is *not* there that it would be possible to perceive what is beyond thought. When thought is there, attempting to capture what's beyond cannot work.

WEBER: It is the filter that would filter it out.

BOHM: Yes, then it would therefore not be *it* anymore. Thought would filter according to its measure, and its measure is rather small, and it would filter this immense reality or totality into some little corner, some little thing which thought can hold.

WEBER: So thought is really the sentinel guarding it, making it impossible for something to come through.

BOHM: Thought has its place; but thought trying to go beyond its place blocks what is beyond.

WEBER: Yes. But something came up yesterday that was relevant to this, the idea of not thought. What you called insight, what Krishnamurti and you have called insight, can pierce through that state of affairs, and change the matter itself.

BOHM: Yes, the matter in the brain itself. You see we could suppose that there is an insight that may arise in this unknown totality, and this insight acts directly on brain matter either at the subtle nonmanifest level or possibly at the manifest, or it may more likely act in the subtle nonmanifest, which then changes the manifest. Thus the brain matter itself can change and be made orderly through insight. And thought itself changes in that case, not by thinking, not by reasoning, but rather a direct change takes place in thought.

WEBER: By being. It becomes something else.

BOHM: It is something else. It has been transformed in its being.

WEBER: Can I take that one question further? Are you saying that subtler manifestations of what you called matter, or matter-energy have the power to transform less subtle ones?

BOHM: That's right. Just as the wind moves the clouds, (well the clouds may have some effect on the wind, too, it works both ways) . . . but the primary source is the subtler.

WEBER: Is that because they have more energy?

BOHM: Also, because they are more inclusive. We're saying the subtle is what is basic and the manifest is its result. You see we're turning it upside down. The usual view is to say what is manifest is what is real, and what is subtle rather unimportant, it's just weak. You know, it's something unimportant.

WEBER: This is exactly the reverse. The nonmanifest is the subtler, and the subtler has power to transform the gross but not vice versa. The gross blocks the subtler?

BOHM: That's right. Yes, the gross cannot handle the subtler.

WEBER: So, insight would be almost an instrument for letting these energies come through.

BOHM: It's more than an instrument. I think that these energies are an instrument of insight. The insight is beyond these energies. The suggestion is that insight is an intelligence beyond any of the energies that could be defined in thought.

WEBER: An active intelligence?

BOHM: Yes, active intelligence. It is active in the sense that it does not pay attention to thought. It directly transforms matter; it sort of bypasses thought as of little consequence.

WEBER: Tells it to be quiet, or let's say it knocks it out of commission for the time being.

BOHM: Well, not only that, it changes it around and removes all the blocks in it and all the confusions and so on. It's like taking a magnet and rearranging the particles in the tape, you know. Only it would be done intelligently so as to wipe out the noise and keep the message right.

WEBER: But that metaphor of the magnet, you're saying, if I understand it, that the magnet can only attract according to its own nature and constitution. It can catch, let's say, in that net, whatever it is capable of catching. Now to rearrange that magnet, to use the metaphor of the insight means I have changed myself so that I perceive different realities.

BOHM: Yes, it's the insight that does it, you see, the insight is not you, right? The insight being supreme intelligence is able to re-arrange the very structural matter of the brain which underlies thought so as to remove that message which is causing the confu-sion, leaving the necessary information and leaving the brain open to perceive reality in a different way. But at present it's blocked, the conditioning blocks us, because it creates a pressure to maintain what is familiar and old, and makes people frightened to consider anything new. So, reality is limited by the message which has already been deeply impressed on the brain cells from early child-hood. Now the insight actually removes that message, that part of the message which is causing this block.

WEBER: And makes us then commensurable with it?

BOHM: It opens thought up to be fresh and new again so that it can operate rationally. One could say that to remain within this block is completely irrational. It's the result of pressure. You adopt the idea that this block is truth because it relieves the pressure of uncertainty.

WEBER: I see. But, when you see the term "rationally" or "reason-ably," shall we be very clear? You don't mean what the Enlighten-ment meant or Descartes, you mean something far beyond that.

BOHM: Reason may have two sources. One is the memory, which is mechanical, rather like a computer.

WEBER: Combining the right things?

BOHM: Yes. We may reason from there, and that is subject to all the irrational pressures which are also in the memory: emotional pressures, fears, all those experiences and so on, and so that kind of reasoning is very limited. It can very quickly get caught in self-deception.

WEBER: And to you that signifies a barrier. That is not what you're speaking of.

BOHM: That's right. But then there may be a reason which flows from insight and a reason which is operating as an instrument of intelligence. That is an entirely different kind of reason.

WEBER: It implies what? Order, but not mechanical order?

BOHM: Not mechanical order and not limited by pressure, you see. Let's take a physicist. If he's been subjected to all these courses in quantum mechanics and pressures to think in this way: he'll be approved of if he does, disapproved of if he doesn't, he gets a job if he does, not if he doesn't, and so on and so on, the minute the idea occurs of thinking in another way, there will be an intense pressure which will blot it out. So, therefore, that isn't reason anymore, it's unreason.

WEBER: But, he'll think it's reason. He'll rationalize it.

BOHM: He'll think it's reason, yes, he'll say it's reason because he's blotted out all this pressure. It all happens very fast and automatically.

WEBER: And he's confirmed by the consensus of the physical community?

BOHM: Well, everybody's doing the same thing, you see. They all reinforce each other and they all say it's right, but it's all the same.

WEBER: Can we go back for a moment? This possible state that you speak of where intelligence or insight operates because it's unblocked because I've taken away the obstacles. . . .

BOHM: It is insight that has taken away the obstacles, not me, right?

WEBER: All right. What it would be in touch with, you imply is beyond the nonmanifest, is the source of the nonmanifest. Are you implying that that's the domain of, shall we call it "the sacred"?

BOHM: Well, it has been called the sacred. As we know "holy" is based on the word whole, it could be called whole, or wholeness. See, the word "sacred" has unfortunately come to mean something different from its original root, that is to say a sacrifice that you make. Now it's closely connected with the idea of organized religions making sacrifices and things like that, and it has a great many connotations which are unfortunate.

WEBER: But you feel the word whole, holy is . . .?

BOHM: Is a bit better, yes. The word sacred can be used, but then you must remember all these wrong connotations.

WEBER: All right, and dissociate it from those. If someone pinned you down and said, "Are you then saying that if the implicate order is found to fit that it will also entail confirmation of a universal intelligence?"

BOHM: No, it doesn't confirm it. The implicate order is still matter, and it would still be possible to regard it, if you stopped there, as still a sort of more subtle form of mechanism.

WEBER: No, I mean to go all the way up . . .

BOHM: Yes, but then you're merely saying that the implications of the implicate order, the ultimate implications, are this [i.e., all the foregoing], but again you're in danger of being in this trap of thought imagining that it has captured this *whole*.

WEBER: Well, no, we've agreed that aware thought realizes it *cannot* capture the whole, but we're talking now about insight, insight, what . . . coming to see that the source? . . .

BOHM: But you see, there is a danger here. I think that it's necessary to be very disciplined or austere or whatever you want to call it, because thought can very easily, if there is not actual insight present, postulate insight, then in the next moment you will say mistakenly that this is insight. Therefore, we have to be very, very clear as to what we can do with this, and we can go a certain distance with this, a certain way and . . .

WEBER: And not project?

BOHM: And not project. You see, the temptation to project has to be understood; we have to be careful about that, observe it carefully, otherwise this could become a trap.

All we can say is that this view is consistent with the notion that there's a truth, an actuality, a being beyond what can be grasped in thought, and that is intelligence, the sacred, the holy.

WEBER: Order?

BOHM: It's order, it's truth, numerous names have been given, and that is that which is, in which all the things that thought can deal with unfold and manifest, but as something relatively small.

WEBER: A small but natural consequence.

BOHM: Yes, coming out of that in some sense, but at the same time, you have to be careful, having said that, we have to be careful not to linger on that too long.

WEBER: Not to exploit it in the cheap way.

BOHM: Yes, not to do anything with it really, because there's nothing we can do with that, you see, and therefore we have to return and say what we do with the implicate order is still in the domain of thought. In other words, we can then bring order, the implicate order can bring greater order into that domain which we call the ordinary domain.

WEBER: That is so, and yet, implied in what you're saying and in your works as I'm aware of it is the acknowledgment that though we cannot say more than we've just said about that other realm, if we're willing to go through the very hard work that is required in dismantling thought or the obstacle, there is a possibility for human beings to become related (maybe that's a poor word) to that.

BOHM: I understand what you're saying, that the implicate order helps to remove some of the logical barriers to this work. You see, if we accept the idea of the explicate order of everything outside of everything else, everything manifest, then it becomes absurd to think of human beings all becoming one, and so on, you know the universe as one whole. But now we say that that earlier view itself [i.e., the explicate order as the ultimate or whole of reality] was a tremendous abstraction. It was really very coarse, gross, and that by following science itself we have been led to a view which is compatible with the wholeness of mankind, or its holiness, if you want to call it that. Mankind has now splintered and fragmented into countless bits, not only nations and religions and groups, but each individual in families, isolated from each other; and within, each individual is in many fragments; and this tremendous fragmentation gives rise to chaos, violence, destruction and very little hope of any real order coming about. And now that is supported by the general view of everything, you know, that the basic reality consists of little bits, all outside of each other.

WEBER: Atomistic?

BOHM: Atomistic. In other words, that gets its confirmation and its reinforcement, so when people have this fragmentation, when they look at science they see a confirmation of the necessity of this fragmentation, right? And that strengthens it. If we look at science in this other [explicate] way, we say we are fragmented, but when we look at the material world we see that we are really totally out of line with the material world. There's no justification for our fragmentation in the material world whatsoever.

WEBER: You mean because that isn't the true state of affairs.

BOHM: No, no, the true state of affairs in the material world is wholeness, you see. If we are fragmented, we must blame it on ourselves.

WEBER: Our false view?

BOHM: Our false view, right, or the pressure which makes us adhere to this view, in spite of evidence to the contrary.

WEBER: Could you—this I think we haven't touched on—could you try to say something directly about that link; in other words, the wholeness of mankind as a consequence of this new understanding.

BOHM: Well, it won't be a consequence, but we want to say it's compatible with it. This new understanding won't bring about the wholeness of mankind. I feel quite sure of that.

WEBER: Because it's just thought?

BOHM: It's just thought, but it's compatible with the whole, it is the way of thinking that is compatible with the wholeness of mankind, therefore it may help to create a better climate for the wholeness.

WEBER: And can you, as it applies now to man, describe that wholeness or, put it in your words?

BOHM: Yes, well let's come back to the nonmanifest implicate order of consciousness. In the nonmanifest order, all is one. You see, there is no separation in space and time. In ordinary matter, this is so and it's equally so or even more so for this subtle matter which is consciousness. Therefore, if we are separate it is because we are sticking largely to the manifest world as the basic reality, where the whole point of the manifest world is to *have* separate units. I mean relatively so anyway, separate but interacting and so on. Now, in nonmanifest reality it's all interpenetrating, interconnected in one. So we say deep down the consciousness of mankind is one. This, we say, is a virtual certainty because even matter is one in the vacuum; and if we don't see this it's because we are blinding ourselves to it.

WEBER: And, therefore, you are saying it's we who construct space and time, really, in the Kantian sense and beyond Kant even?

BOHM: Yes, space and time are constructed by us for our convenience although they are created in such a way that when we're doing it right, it really is convenient. The word convenient is based on "coming together," "convene," to come together. Now, our conventions are convenient, and that is not purely subjective, they actually fit the reality of matter. So conventions are not just an arbitrary choice made to please us, to gratify us, but rather they are conventions which are convenient, which fit matter as it is. And now, we are saying space and time is a convenient order for a certain range of purposes.

WEBER: In the manifest?

BOHM: In the manifest.

WEBER: But you're saying it has no place in the nonmanifest.

BOHM: It is not the fundamental order. It's only place is in the nonmanifest . . . it has a place, but only as a relationship. It has a certain place but it is not the fundamental place.

WEBER: It's this n-1 and n-2 that you spoke about earlier?

BOHM: Yes, that's right.

WEBER: But in actuality, in the nonmanifest, you say mankind's consciousness or mind is one. And you mean this quite literally, not metaphorically or poetically.

BOHM: No, it is one consciousness, and you can see as evidence of this that the basic problems of mankind are one. You see they're the same: namely fear, jealousy, hope, confusion, you know the problem of isolation and so on. If you go around you will see that deep down all the problems are the same.

WEBER: So it's a universal stratum of some sort.

BOHM: Yes, we may say that these problems originate in the consciousness of mankind and manifest in each individual. You see, each individual manifests the consciousness of mankind. That is whay I say.

WEBER: Because he is, in a way, that consciousness.

BOHM: He is that manifestation.

WEBER: Right. And as he perceives himself, in the manifest, he's isolated himself out, he's made himself an abstraction.

BOHM: Yes, if he says that manifestation is independently existent, it's like saying the cloud exists on its own apart from the air.

WEBER: Or the particle without the whole ocean, the whole background?

BOHM: Or the ink droplet without the whole background.

WEBER: So the individual, as he thinks of himself, is but the overt manifestation just as the chair is, of that underlying background?

BOHM: Yes, as the chair is, and the mountain, because they're a manifestation of a deeper energy, a deeper order, a deeper reality which is not manifest.

WEBER: And you're saying this is not mysticism, it's good physics.

BOHM: Well, I'm saying that it's more consistent with physics than any other view that I know.

WEBER: If one really were to take this seriously in one's daily life, how differently would one interact with another human being?

BOHM: Well, it would be a tremendous change, but you see, to do this we have to get clear of the recording in the brain of this other view which has been deeply recorded in the material structure of the brain. We could call that the corruption of mankind, that the brain and the consciousness and the deeper levels, not only in the manifest levels of the brain but also in the nonmanifest, that there has been left this pollution, which is this whole view which leads to all this violence, corruption, disorder, self-deception. See, you could say that almost all of mankind's thought is aimed at self-deception, which momentarily relieves pressures arising from this way of thinking, of being separate, and it produces pressures. When a person is under pressure, any thought that comes in to relieve that pressure will be accepted as true. But immediately that leads to some more pressure because it's wrong and then you take another thought to relieve that thought.

WEBER: It's robbing Peter to pay Paul.

BOHM: Yes, and that has been the major way. If you watch how international negotiations go on you see no truth whatsoever there. It's entirely the result of pressures: fear, gain, greed, compromise, trade-offs, pressures to achieve and what not. You accept as true any statement that will relieve that pressure. And then in the next moment that's overturned and people will take another one.

WEBER: And do you think this happens on the miniature level too?

BOHM: It happens in families obviously. People are compelled in the family to state things which the pressure of the family says are true. It happens in organizations, in institutions.

WEBER: But you're saying it doesn't have to happen.

BOHM: No, but that would require this material change in the content of the brain.

WEBER: And therefore, what you've been saying is that the first order of priority is to address that.

BOHM: Yes, because without that it's all confused.

WEBER: And, even talking about the realms beyond the nonmanifest is therefore going to reflect that confusion. So, one mustn't catapult oneself up to those realms, but tackle what to you is the block.

BOHM: Yes, that's right. We can bring order into the realms which thought can touch, because that's the beginning, and the insight is primarily what is needed to bring that order into the brain itself. And I think that this present [positivistic and pragmatic] view of science has contributed considerably to the disorder in the brain, because insofar as people take it seriously, they are going to give it a lot of weight. Therefore it's going to contribute confusion to all that's in the brain.

WEBER: Now if one would ask you how someone convinced of the disorder of his daily life would begin to make the resolution of that his priority, what would you say? Would you talk along Krishnamurtian principles?

BOHM: Well, you're really asking, in turning the question toward Krishnamurti: what is the essence of what he says, right? And, in what way does it differ from what other people have said?

The first point is that we observe the chaos in our daily life and in the large scale as well, in human relationships. We see that chaos is the pervasive factor and order is only relative and limited and occasional. And we see that the origin of that chaos is in our thought, in our fragmented, atomistic thought.

WEBER: Untruthful, from what you've said. Our untruthful way of thinking.

BOHM: Our untruthful thought. It would not produce chaos unless it were untruthful, right? If it were truthful it would produce order. Here you see the first difference [of Krishnamurti] from a great many philosophies of the ages because philosophers have looked at a lot of these questions, but it has been part of their belief that ultimately they could arrange thought in an orderly way and that would help bring mankind to order. Now we're saying that thought is the source of the disorder.

WEBER: Not the content, but thought itself, its very form.

BOHM: Its very nature itself. Its form, yes.

WEBER: It can't be fixed up because it is . . .

BOHM: It is disorder. Therefore, we are saying that we have got to be aware of this disorder, being careful not to imagine we are beyond it, and to observe it as it happens, as it goes on around us and in us, the point being that we have to bring about order in this limited field of thought because that is the source of the disorder which prevents this larger field from operating. Ultimately it takes insight to bring that about, as I said, and a state of high energy.

WEBER: Whereas, you're saying, that most of us live in a state of low energy?

BOHM: Yes. And that exhausts us.

WEBER: . . . All this exhausts us: wrong thinking, living, feeling.

BOHM: We have to come to a state of high energy, and one of the points that Krishnamurti makes is to begin on certain simple things, not waste energy on, let's say, drinking and smoking and quarreling and various things like that. People waste fantastic energy on that: you can see how quarreling in the family in various ways—how much energy it wastes.

WEBER: It drains us.

BOHM: It drains. It's very destructive. So, that itself is already a beginning: when you watch the pressures that make this quarrel you're already required then to look inwardly at what's driving you into this irrational and destructive behavior. And you can see the pressures that are driving you. Then, you go on from there (and we will only sum it up now) to an insight into not merely this pressure or that pressure or the other pressure but into the whole of pressure, its root. We say pressure probably originates—if I use my language—I would say pressure probably originates in this nonmanifest consciousness and then it manifests. And *as* it manifests it comes back in to pollute this nonmanifest consciousness further, and then it piles up. So we could say all pressure has basically one germ, all the confusion. And the insight into that germ will remove that germ and allow the whole thing to clear up. Now, when it clears up, you know, even as you start to clear it up, energy starts to rise and builds up, you see. Energy has also been called passion. In other words, clarity and passion together are needed.

WEBER: The mind and the heart it used to be called.

BOHM: Yes. It used to be called the mind and the heart. Intelligence and passion. Clarity and passion.

WEBER: Or intelligence and love?

BOHM: Yes. But love in the sense of some very intense energy—and not just. . . .

WEBER: Sentiment.

BOHM: Sentiment.

WEBER: No. Love without a content, is what you're saying. Without a mental image. All right, you say the roots of all these endless disparate problems that we stumble on in the manifest in our daily lives lie not in the manifest, but in the nonmanifest.

BOHM: They lie in the nonmanifest. And that whole corruption of the nonmanifest—that pollution which has accumulated over the ages—we could call the sorrow of mankind. It is not just in an individual. It is in the nonmanifest consciousness of mankind.

WEBER: Is it a collective?

BOHM: Well, it's more than collective. It can be thought of as collective. But, it's not a collection of consciousness.

WEBER: It's not additive. It's one, you said.

BOHM: It's one. Yes.

WEBER: So, in that sense collection isn't so good a term maybe. What would you call it?

BOHM: Well, just simply the nonmanifest, the universal consciousness of mankind. That sorrow is there, you see. And sorrow creates this immense pressure to relieve it which further corrupts and pollutes everything.

WEBER: And yet the oddity about it (and maybe that's what gave

rise to the conviction of the separate self as primary and not derivative), the oddity is that it is the individual nonetheless who has to,
as it were, clear up—clean up his own—what? His own corner of it?

BOHM: That's right. Yes. Therefore, you see, this thing is far more
subtle because we could say that in some sense the individual has
direct access to the cosmic totality. And therefore it is through the
individual that the general consciousness has to get cleared up, to
get started clearing up.

WEBER: But only in a sense his own corner of it?

BOHM: No, it's not his own corner of it, because he, the individual
goes beyond. The individual is an actuality which includes this
manifestation of the consciousness of mankind, but he is more.
Every individual is his own particular contact. Every individual is in
total contact with the implicate order, with all that is around us.
Therefore, in some sense he is part of the whole of mankind and in
another sense he can get beyond it.

WEBER: He's a focus for the universal.

BOHM: He is a focus for something beyond mankind.

WEBER: And yet the paradox that troubles me is this: you would
think if the nonmanifest collective is the source of the root of the
conflict—then if a saint, let's say, a saintly human being achieves
integrity—then the whole thing ought to be, as you said, unpollut-
ed. But that isn't so. Now why isn't it so?

BOHM: Well, I think it takes a higher degree of energy. You see,
it's something like the transformation of the atom. In the early days
they transformed a few atoms, we could call that the transformation
in germ—the transformation of the atom, you know, and then it
spread like a flame and became . . . a power and a chain reaction.
The individual who see this [principle about inner energy and intel-
ligence] may be like the one who has discovered the transformation
of the atom. In principle he has already transformed mankind, but it
has not yet come about, right?

WEBER: That's a difficult thing to understand. Could you say
something more about that?

BOHM: You see, it takes a still higher energy to reach the whole of
the consciousness of mankind. But he has reached the principle of
the consciousness of mankind, right?

WEBER: But in actuality, not just in theory.

BOHM: In actuality. But still he hasn't quite the energy to reach the whole, to put it all on fire, as it were. It's a bit damp.

WEBER: Why?

BOHM: It's soggy. Because of the pollution of the ages.

WEBER: You're saying he's outweighed.

BOHM: He's outweighed by this massive pollution that has gone on over the ages. But this pollution can be burned up. It has burned up for that individual. The point is, we need a still more intense energy than that individual can give. Now, where will that come from? What I propose is that it is possible now for a number of individuals who are in close relation and who have gone through this and can trust each other to establish a one-mind of that whole set of individuals. In other words, that that consciousness is one, acting as one. If you had as many as ten people, or a hundred people, who could really be that way, they would have a power immensely beyond one.

WEBER: Because it's not mathematically additive.

BOHM: No.

WEBER: It's some other heightening altogether.

BOHM: An intense heightening, yes. And I think that that would begin to ignite, really, this whole consciousness of mankind. It would have such an effect. Even one man like Hitler who had a great passion, had a tremendous effect, though for destruction. If there had been ten people with Hitler's passion, all working together, nobody could have resisted them.

WEBER: Is this somewhat like sympathetic resonance?

BOHM: Well, I wouldn't use that analogy. Let me add that Hitler was, of course, only adding to the pollution, because he and people in general were ignorant of what is involved here. It's far beyond anything which we know. I am merely saying that taking this view, consciousness, deep down, is one, the whole of mankind. But then any part of mankind may establish a one-ness within that part of consciousness. And if ten people can have their part of consciousness all one, that is an energy which begins to spread into the whole.

WEBER: And changes it; it's *bound* to change some of it.

BOHM: Yes. Some of it—or perhaps deeply.

WEBER: Deeply. So you're saying that prior to this current awareness of the centrality of consciousness, what we've been trying to do is hopeless because we've addressed small social problems all in the wrong domain, so to speak.

BOHM: Yes. Well, really not going to their source at all.

WEBER: Not to their source. And therefore, wouldn't it seem to follow that it's no longer a question of what the ancients called "finding my own salvation" but much more responsibility towards the rest of mankind?

BOHM: Individual salvation actually has very little meaning, because, as I have pointed out, the consciousness of mankind is one and not truly divisible. Each person has a kind of responsibility not, however, in the sense of answerability or guilt. But in the sense that there's nothing else to do, really, you see. That there is no other way out. That is absolutely what has to be done and nothing else can work.

WEBER: Because of the very way that you've analyzed the connections?

BOHM: You can see that this view may be all wrong but if what I said is right then there is nothing else possible but that.

WEBER: Well. It's a very challenging world picture.

SECOND SESSION

WEBER: We had talked somewhat about this build-up of energy. But I don't think we had quite enough time to spell it out clearly. Would that be possible?

BOHM: Spell out what?

WEBER: You talked about the build-up of energy such that you really change the one mind of mankind when a group is united and in harmony, and when it really understands that the roots of its problems lie in this nonmanifest. . . .

BOHM: Yes. We say that the germ is in the nonmanifest. And out of that, you see, the manifest problem is arising. I think that we discussed the example of the live oak tree growing in California, which never loses its foliage. The leaves are continually forming and some are dropping off at the same time, so that it looks as if it's a constant tree. But it's from the nonmanifest that the tree is continually forming and into the nonmanifest that it is dying. And therefore you don't understand the tree by considering it to be static or more or less a static object which is just manifest at this moment to our concepts.

WEBER: You mean, you would say that to understand the tree you have to understand that as much as or more a part of what you see is something you don't see, that gives rise to it.

BOHM: That's right. What is manifest, what you can see and touch and so on, is the outcome of what is not manifest. And obviously the nutrition of the tree and so on, which is necessary for the way it manifests, is based on how it's continually being maintained or not maintained.

WEBER: And as you said the live oak provided such a good example because of the fact that it dies and is self-renewing. . . .

BOHM: All the time! Whereas in the deciduous tree you have a time alternation. See, you appear to have the period of quiescence when the leaves are all dead and then they all come out and then they go back and die again. Now, the live oak is an example of something which in a gross observation always looks very nearly the same, and yet the dying and being regenerated are going on constantly side by side. And interpenetrating the leaves which are dying are the leaves which are being generated.

WEBER: So creation and dissolution and creation all coexist in that live oak.

BOHM: Yes. Yes.

WEBER: That brings up another question that might not have been altogether clear earlier. You know, you said that the source of objects and also of the root of conflict of thoughts lies in the nonmanifest and it gave the impression as if the nonmanifest is the matrix of what we would call the problems. Is it also the source of compassion and love? Or does that come from elsewhere?

BOHM: No. See, anything that can be put into thought is limited. The nonmanifest is much bigger than the manifest, but still it is related to the manifest and the two together complete each other; but I'd say that compassion, love, intelligence, and insight are beyond these.

WEBER: In what you earlier called spirit or something unnamable?
BOHM: Yes.

WEBER: This makes it look as if the so-called negative factors only dwell in that nonmanifest. Is there something positive in it?

BOHM: Yes. Because you see if you were to ask about a tree which is living, that comes out of the soil and the air, whose matrix is the water, the sunlight . . . there's a nonmanifest energy out of which it's coming. But, that isn't this ultimate truth that we were talking about. Right? This tree may either be diseased or healthy, and whether it is diseased or healthy we can only understand through the nonmanifest. If you're going to treat the tree, you have to consider this whole unseen movement of its nutrition, of its light, you know, all that's going on with respect to it.

WEBER: So in that sense its nourishment, its nutritive factors also come from this nonmanifest, not just the problems.

BOHM: Yes. That's right. We'll say that the physical matter has its root in the nonmanifest. And also thought has its root in some nonmanifest consciousness. But all of that is still limited.

WEBER: But is that the best characterization if one has to give it a characterization?

BOHM: What?

WEBER: Limited. Not destructive, necessarily?

BOHM: No. It's not; it's only when it goes into disorder that it's destructive, you see.

WEBER: Maybe that's my question: Is it orderly?

BOHM: Yes. We say that living life is orderly. It's manifestation and also nonmanifest process. And of course, life can go off order. We're asking the question whether the life of the mind is orderly. And in general it has become disorderly. The same as in the body, the cells may grow harmoniously or you may have cancer which is growing independently. Disorder arises when all the different elements chaotically grow independently of each other, don't work together. Now, in cancer that has started to happen. And you could say that our thought process somewhat resembles a cancerous growth.

WEBER: But when the thought process is orderly, and has its place—nothing usurps any other element—then the source of that order is in the nonmanifest thought.

BOHM: That's right. Yes. And ultimately, perhaps, beyond that. But still the nonmanifest consciousness is what will give rise to thought.

The difficulty now is that thought has become self-moving. It provides the stimulus for its own movement which is disorderly.

WEBER: To relate this to the holographic world, would you say that there are two possible interpretations from all the foregoing: would you say that the world or the universe is a holograph. . . .?

BOHM: Yes. Call it the holomovement. Because "graph" is too static. It's what has been written, right?

WEBER: Right. Is there a holomovement looking at itself? Or are there two—is there a holographic consciousness looking at a holomovement which is then dualistic?

BOHM: Well, I think consciousness is part of the whole. Now, we have the whole of nature and within it we exist and we are also; the whole is in each part and consciousness is of that nature too. On the other hand consciousness, as Krishnamurti was discussing yesterday, may be the instrument of an intelligence beyond all of this. That is, if it is self-moving then it will be disorderly. But when it is not self-moving then it may be orderly. Now, I think we should say consciousness is a material process if we say consciousness is thought, feeling, desire, and will, and various other factors of a similar nature. And then we would have to say consciousness is a material process, more subtle than the usual material processes that we look at with our senses, or with our scientific instruments.

WEBER: Yes. But now how would you complete the explanation of this in terms of the holomovement, of the universe?

BOHM: I said the holomovement is an undefinable term. In mathematics there's the notion of the undefinable which, however, can become the source of definable relations. Now, the holomovement is fundamentally an undefinable term which has various factors or features, such as light, electrons, sound, neutrons, neutrinos, you know, and also thought, feeling, desire, will, and so on. And we can't necessarily reduce one of these to another, though they are all interrelated. Right?

WEBER: Yes. But now to get back to this question of what makes consciousness possible in this? I mean, there are two models, isn't that so? The old one would have said—even to use your new terminology—it's the holographic mind/brain looking at the holomovement. And you're saying something else.

BOHM: Well, that would lead to an infinite regress. Because there would then have to be another and another holomovement. Say holomovement B looked at holomovement A, but holomovement C would have to look at holomovement B, and so on, right? See, you say holomovement B is looking at holomovement A then applies further back as holomovement C looking at holomovement B looking at holomovement A.

WEBER: Why?

BOHM: Well, if you say holomovement B looks at holomovement A you are already implicitly outside of holomovement B looking at it. So your consciousness is already holomovement C.

WEBER: Yes, to describe it, to assert that. To be capable of stating that.

BOHM: Yes. To assert that there is a holomovement B you must have holomovement C in your consciousness. Then you immediately reflect on that and say, "That's holomovement C," but it was already holomovement D which is doing that, right?

WEBER: Which was the old Cartesian or dualistic model.

BOHM: Right. It also leads to infinite regress, unless you end it by God or somewhere.

Now I think we come to a point where we're raising a question which was similar to what was raised in yesterday's discussion. How long can we go on trying to talk about what is beyond thought by making an intellectual construction? You see, because when we make such an intellectual construction we have a content and we always have implied that the one who is constructing it is also supposed to be beyond that content. So he evades the very thing we attempt to include him in and in that very attempt he gets out. And so it seems that there is some limit to how far you can go in that process, in that approach. Therefore it's best to say that in this approach in which we attempt to make a map, or a sketch of some kind of what reality is, that we are really dealing with something limited. Korzybski used to say: "Whatever we *say* it is, it isn't."

WEBER: The map is not the territory. . . .

BOHM: That's right. Yes. And therefore what we are doing is making maps, making sketches, making concepts. And see, that's why I said the other night that science, for example, theoretical science, is not primarily concerned with observing things but with observing ideas. People think that by saying ideas are a mere concomitant of the things they observe, that they are avoiding giving excessive importance to ideas, and so on, that they are avoiding idealism. But in fact, they are making ideas all-important by doing that, because they are saying that the ideas with which they examine things are either true or just figments. And if they are true then that's it. Therefore the idea with which you finally examine this material reality is never questionable. If you do question it you then just do it with another idea, right?

WEBER: Which has to be certified.

BOHM: That's right. Or it's implicitly certified so that the final idea with which you're doing all this is truth. So the attempt to say that you're dealing only with material reality forces you to put ideas in the realm beyond material reality and therefore of the value of truth. And that's self-deception. So I'm saying that the pragmatist is not really pragmatic because he does not look at his ideas pragmatically. He accepts his ideas nonpragmatically, with no pragmatic basis whatsoever, as truth. Or else he completely rejects them—again with no pragmatic basis.

WEBER: In other words he hasn't made that last step. He hasn't understood that the currency that he's using isn't necessarily pragmatic at all?

BOHM: No, but it is pragmatic, that's the point. It is pragmatic but he is not treating it pragmatically. He is treating it as something beyond question, beyond dispute, just simply to be accepted as truth. He is not looking at ideas as material processes. He is saying ideas are either figments of the imagination or they are truth and reality itself. Then he says those ideas which are figments he discards and those which are truth and reality, he says, that's it, that's the way the world is. On the one hand he is giving ideas no significance whatsoever and on the other hand he jumps to giving them supreme significance.

WEBER: His own methodology, for example.

BOHM: Yes. That's right. And he pretends that all this is coming from matter. But this whole way of looking at it does not come from observing matter. It is just simply the way which has come about due to the long process of conditioning, historically. Now, we were discussing the other night that we could say ideas are material processes which grow from a seed. See, the word "idea" is based on a Greek word which means "to see" basically, but it also includes the idea of "image"—the notion of "image" which is not to see, right? The image is an imitation of seeing.

WEBER: That came later, though, don't you think?

BOHM: Yes. That came later. That's right.

WEBER: Plato wanted *ideein* to be direct reception, direct seeing.

BOHM: But *eidòlon* is image, which comes from the same root. So there is the perception and there's the image of perception. Now, the image of perception is not perception. Right?

WEBER: Exactly.*

BOHM: But it may be confused with perception, it may be treated as perception. Now, if we take an idea, the perception grows from a seed in the nonmanifest order and unfolds as the seed grows in the manifest order. When we apply the idea, the idea is being realized. It is unfolding, growing, dying, and so on. What sort of result or plant does this idea produce? Does it produce one which is harmonious and orderly or roughly speaking, is it a useful plant or is it a weed? Our brain may be said to be now mostly a field of weeds. But we don't look at this at all. We don't say that this is material. We say whatever that is—that's our equipment, that's what we work with, that's where we start. And we put various injunctions in—we should think this way or that way. But we don't question that those injunctions are also ideas. And now, what I'm saying is look at ideas— every idea just has to be looked at for what it is: what is it and what does it do? So let us look at our ideas pragmatically. Therefore, the principal function of the theorist is to work with ideas pragmatically.

WEBER: Which is not even considered, at the moment.

BOHM: Yes. Well, instead of saying they are truth and what-not, that once you have the right idea which has been checked by an experiment, that's the truth, I'm saying that an idea is a pragmatic instrument. . . .

WEBER: For what?

BOHM: For grasping some broader reality. And without an idea you can't do it.

---

*This is the very point Plato makes in his Allegory of the Cave in the *Republic*. In a later conversation, I asked Prof. Bohm about the similarity between Plato's philosophy and his own nonmanifest/manifest distinction. He agreed with the similarity, and pointed especially to Plato's notion of shadows and images in the Cave, contrasted to the sun outside, which is Plato's light of reality. (RW)

WEBER: But you're saying the idea isn't just the vehicle or the instrument, like a scoop by means of which I scoop up an earthful of reality, it is itself. . . .

BOHM: Actual.

WEBER: Actual. And therefore forms as much the data as the so-called content.

BOHM: That's right. You must look at the idea as much as you look at the thing that it scoops up.

WEBER: Exactly. It's not privileged and exempt. . . .

BOHM: No.

WEBER: . . . And to be unquestioned.

BOHM: No. It must be treated just as pragmatically as the data itself.

WEBER: It *is* data, you're saying.

BOHM: It *is* data. Yes. The idea is a functioning instrument which brings in a certain part of reality in some way or even helps to determine reality. And man's reality is shaped entirely by ideas. Natural reality goes beyond any human idea but the extent to which we can bring it in to *our* world depends on our ideas. So we may completely miss natural reality because our ideas don't bring it in. So that is the point: that ideas have to be looked at pragmatically. Now, there's a limit to what any idea can scoop up, if you want to put it that way. And an attempt to say that we can form an idea that handles everything is just going to lead to chaos. Even this idea of the implicate order, and the nonmanifest and so on, has some limit. It will bring about a certain contact with reality up to some vaguely defined limit. But it will not grasp the whole.

WEBER: Yes, because of the very nature of thought. I think we went into that a little earlier in the conversation. We said that. But that having been acknowledged, isn't it also true that if I take you to be saying that the whole universe is a holomovement. . . .

BOHM: Well, that's merely an idea, you see. I'm saying that our idea—we'll call it the universe of discourse in terms of the holo-movement—is limited. What the universe *actually* is, is unsayable, right?

WEBER: Yes. All right. I think the reason this assumed importance, at least in our discussion, was that it's connected with the notion of nondualism, which already eliminates one such idea that mankind has carried with it to its detriment for centuries and it no longer would beg the question of observer and observed and therefore of time. (Which, incidentally, I thought we would say a few things about later. You talked about it briefly but we didn't go into it.) But to return to this topic, what you are emphasizing is that the holo-movement is itself a limited idea? Because the totality is unutterable?

BOHM: Yes. What we're saying is that these ideas (of the holo-movement) are much better able to deal with our reality, I think, than the other ideas we have, but we must notice that these ideas are also limited. See, we're going to have to have some kind of idea to deal with reality and the ideas we have now are sheer chaos. They may allow for some technical progress but in general they lead to chaos. I think this idea is a more harmonious one, one that accords better with what is and really brings things together into harmony.

WEBER: It would lead to less chaos, you're saying? Even though it has still the limitation of all ideas.

BOHM: If you considered that it was unlimited you would proba-bly end up with just as much chaos, but this idea contains within it the idea that it is limited, you see, whereas the old idea contains implicitly the idea that once you get the right idea, that's it. There-fore the old idea encourages you to chaos in every way.

WEBER: Let's be clear: it's limited when contrasted with that about which nothing can be said.

BOHM: Yes. Well, it's limited because it's an idea. You see, every idea is limited and it can grasp some limited aspect or factor of reality. Now we are looking at the nature of ideas, looking at them both pragmatically and theoretically, in the same way we would look at anything else. We are saying: ideas are not to be exempted from the whole scientific approach. Ideas are not sacred things which are either true or else they are just nothing at all. All ideas are limited and we must look at them all. Some ideas have this advan-tage, some have that one, some have very little value and so on, and there's no ultimate idea. But we can look at all these ideas, the way in which they are related and not related and so on. We are just looking at ideas, you see, just as we look at the world as a whole. Our mind contains a collection or an aggregate of ideas which is always changing.

WEBER: Or our mind *is* that.

BOHM: It *is* that, yes. And that we can look at, just as we look at the things which we see around us.

WEBER: Does time come into this question of ideas?

BOHM: Let's discuss time. Time is something which our present ideas don't cover very well. Now see, one of the basic troubles with the present notion of time is contained in Zeno's paradox. First of all, it does not handle movement. If you have a series of frames of the cine-camera, this is not the same as movement. A thing is here and it's not moving, right? And having it jump from here to here is not movement. Or more generally, you can look at the problem of time like this: to say that, considering the present moment we have the past, which is considered to be behind us, but actually the past is present in us in the form of memory, and the future is also projected from the present. It's really a response of memory. Now, if we say the past therefore does not exist actually as such, nor does the future, and if the present is the dividing line between these two, it also cannot exist. So therefore, something is wrong. We must say neither past, present, nor future exist as far as present thought looks at it, that it's really nothing but an abstraction. So, if we want to say from the holomovement, you can say all time is in each moment, and one of the basic features of time is this sequence by which there comes a later movement which contains the earlier movements in its past but not the other way around. So there's a natural sequence like this series of Chinese boxes within boxes. And the present moment might be called the box which contains all these previous moments as its content, that is, the thought content. We could also say that any knowledge held in the present is knowledge about the past. You see, the present does not seem to know itself.

WEBER: Because of this lag.

BOHM: It takes time to be recorded and become part of thought and knowledge. So the present does not know itself and we could say the present knows its past so there's a relationship: each moment has its past and its future. Now, if we try from the past at the present to predict the future what we will be trying to predict is the past of the future, right? In other words, the knowledge which will exist in some future moment. So we say knowing what we know at present, we predict that in the future we well be able to know such and such. So the present is, as it were, unspecifiable, indescribable.

One of the basic features of matter is recurrence or even with greater regularity, periodicity. And if there is a recurrent tendency in the development then we can say that though we do not know the present and the immediate future, it's sufficiently recurrent so that we can be fairly confident of it from the past. Now that is the kind of situation to which our scientific technology or knowledge addresses itself, saying that the structure of the holomovement is such that it is fairly recurrent and therefore, although surprises may occur, we can get some fairly reliable knowledge but nothing absolutely certain. That is, there is no possibility of an absolutely certain prediction or control, because there's always more; there's always contingency. There's no absolute necessity in our knowledge.

WEBER: That's Hume.

BOHM: Yes. Nevertheless, we say the very structure of the holomovement is recurrence; we don't say the human mind *only* contributes this regularity or recurrence, but the very structure of the holomovement is such that it contains this feature of recurrence. Otherwise our thought of recurrence would have no value whatsoever. You see, the idea of recurrence meets the fact that recurrence is common in matter: the recurrence of the seasons, the continual recurrence in the live oak, which says that though everything is changing the general pattern recurs again and again. So there is the idea of recurrence which somehow meets a fact of recurrence in matter, right in the holomovement. And this is our idea.

WEBER: But our idea was encouraged to hold that, because, as you say, it met it in the holomovement.

BOHM: It meets it up to a point but since the holomovement is infinite, it goes beyond any limits. Therefore the idea does not always meet it. There may be anything new in there.

WEBER: And this is what we have not grasped. We've shut that out.

BOHM: Yes. So we say that although we may reasonably expect quite a bit of recurrence, the mind is always open and does not insist on that as an absolute necessity. And therefore the mind is always open to saying it hasn't recurred, let's look again.

WEBER: Can we focus on a slightly different but related notion? In the holomovement, if I understand it, you said that the whole is contained in each part and that applies both to so-called space, right, "the world in a grain of sand," and also to so-called time, the atemporality of a given moment. We said it a little bit earlier about space. Could you now say something about it in terms of time?

BOHM: First of all, you can see that in memory you have the past contained in the present, right? That's an example of the holomovement. Now also, in the movement which is going on: if you think of the light in any particular part, it contains obviously the entire past of those waves which came from everywhere to reach that part. And it contains some implication about the future, although not a complete implication. You see though it implies the whole, it does not give complete detail of the whole. In other words, it is about the whole. The holomovement of each part is about the whole, it refers to the whole. But no part contains all the detail of the whole. So therefore it does not give us a complete view of the past nor of the future.

WEBER: But you say it implies it.

BOHM: Yes. It implies it and refers to it. Just as the partial hologram refers to the whole but it will be of less detail and of less use. So you will have to say that the information in the part does not actually cover the whole completely.

WEBER: But what does it mean to say it implies it? It gives intimation of it?

BOHM: Yes. Well, it gives a certain amount of information, in the same way that if you illuminate a part of a hologram you will get information about the whole, not about some part of the object. And yet not the full information. It will be somewhat vague.

WEBER: What does that mean for us as knowers or consciousness? How should we intelligently interact with the holomovement given these features?

BOHM: You see we *are* of the holomovement; we can't interact with it. Consciousness itself is a feature of the holomovement in this view. Remember, always, this is an idea about this whole subject, right? We say consciousness is a feature of the holomovement, and therefore the content of consciousness refers to the whole of the holomovement.

WEBER: It's not there looking at it. It is itself embedded in it.

BOHM: It's a little bit like Leibniz, if you want to say that: each monad refers to the whole but with different degrees of completion and perfection.

WEBER: Mirrors it, he says.

BOHM: Mirrors it. I would rather say "refers to." I could say mirrors it, but let us say refers to the whole in the sense not merely of mirroring it but of moving toward it and being able to grasp it.

WEBER: It's more active.

BOHM: It's more active. Yes.

WEBER: But when it grasps it: (this is just another way of saying what I crudely said earlier, dualistically I said it) when it grasps it, that's what we used to call knowledge or consciousness. It's an active part, right?

BOHM: Yes. Well, also the knowledge itself is the recording of all that, including the skills which have been left in the person who has done it. But see, the whole movement of knowledge is knowledge as holomovement. Or knowledge is part of the holomovement.

WEBER: There *is* only the holomovement in the speakable domain.

BOHM: That's right. Yes. In this universe of discourse the holomovement is all there is, which, however, doesn't mean that it *is* all there is.

WEBER: I understand. There is what we called earlier spirit or whatever we want to call it.

BOHM: You can call it truth or. . . .

WEBER: Something . . . beyond.

BOHM: Beyond, right.

WEBER: And then you said there could be—that could shade off infinitely into many other such domains. . . .

BOHM: Yes.

WEBER: . . . that about which we can say nothing.

BOHM: Yes.

WEBER: But may I then rephrase my question? I'll use the word "grasp." Since you said we're filled with disorder and this has translated itself into a disorderly and dangerous world, what is the most intelligent and orderly way then for this holomovement to grasp itself?

BOHM: Well, you see, so far we have been just simply making an idea, that is to say, we've let the holomovement have a certain idea of itself, a correct idea of itself. That is one approach, right?

WEBER: In history, throughout history?

BOHM: No. This is what we're doing now. See, we're saying this holomovement is forming a correct idea of itself, right?

WEBER: At this very moment.

BOHM: Yes. That's part of the grasp. It says: the holomovement agrees that the idea of the holomovement is part of the holomovement. And it doesn't say there's the holomovement and besides that another idea of the holomovement which somehow has to relate to the holomovement.

WEBER: This is so important. Could you perhaps say it once again?

BOHM: Well, that the idea of the holomovement is part of the holomovement. And that the idea of the holomovement contains also the idea that the idea itself is part of the holomovement.

WEBER: And therefore, what?

BOHM: And therefore this idea is considered to grasp other aspects of the holomovement and one could even go so far as to say that possibly the entire holomovement is to a certain extent of the nature of an idea, in the sense that the nonmanifest is the germ of the manifest or that the DNA is the germ of the living organism and so on. The idea of the holomovement will be a kind of germ in consciousness that can grasp something broader. This germ grows in the whole, in the soil of the whole of existence into something which can also produce more germs itself.

WEBER: But "grasp?"

BOHM: It means fit, to grasp. You see, the word "perceive" is "percipere." It means to take hold of thoroughly, the same as capture. The word "comprehend" means to take hold of it all, and many similar words arise. Discipline is the same word, it means to take in something mentally, really, to grasp it, to grasp it apart, "discipere."

WEBER: Is grasping as you use it to become one with it?

BOHM: Well, it's more . . . to contact it so that it enters, as Piaget would have put it, into a cycle of movement which is assimilated into the one whole.

WEBER: So it is to become one with it, in a way.

BOHM: It's like a kind of digestion, as it were. We even say we digest the idea mentally.

WEBER: It becomes part of the living organism.

BOHM: That's right. When you take food in it becomes part of the living organism. So when you take something else in, it becomes also part of the living consciousness.

WEBER: It circulates.

BOHM: It circulates and the living consciousness is also part of that. See, the living tree is part of the whole environment as the environment is part of the tree.

WEBER: That brings up, if you don't mind, what we talked about the other night, this exciting idea which you made so clear. The notion that most of us have the idea that our own inner space stops where we're bounded. Now you claim this is false. Could you say something about that?

BOHM: Yes. There are two views of space. One view is to say the skin is the boundary of ourselves, saying there's the space without and the space within. The space within is the separate self, obviously, and the space without is the space which separates the separate selves, right? And therefore to overcome the separation you must have a process of moving through that space, which takes time. Is that clear?

WEBER: That's how human beings have always thought of it, earlier.

BOHM: Yes. That's right. So now, if we took the view of the holomovement, with this vast reserve of energy and empty space, saying that matter itself is that small wave on empty space, then we could better say that the space as a whole (and we start from the general space) is the ground of existence, and we are in it. So the space doesn't separate us, it unites us. Therefore it's like saying that there are two separate points and a certain dotted line connects them, which shows how we think they are related, or to say there is a real line and that the points are abstractions from that.

WEBER: Demarking the boundaries of the line.

BOHM: Yes.

WEBER: So it's the other way around.

BOHM: The other way around. The line is the reality and the points are abstractions. In that sense we say that there are no separate people, you see, but that that is an abstraction which comes by taking certain features as abstracted and self-existent.

WEBER: And I think you carried it even one step farther the other day. You said that wherever we have formerly thought of as empty space and where we're not, that's the only place where, in fact, "we" are.

BOHM: Well, that would be the nonmanifest ground of our existence.

WEBER: Which you're saying is nonmaterial.

BOHM: Well, it's matter in its . . .

WEBER: In its subtle state?

BOHM: It's subtle matter but beyond that, of course, there's more, and therefore ultimately we have to say that the ultimate ground is beyond anything we call matter. But there is that much subtler state. We can do two things. One is to extend the notion of the subtlety of matter, which we are doing now. I think the universe of discourse can only be the universe of matter. That is the only reasonable content of the universe of discourse. The attempt to make spirit part of the universe of discourse is not going to work.

WEBER: Except to say there is something which the universe of discourse as matter doesn't exhaust.

BOHM: It doesn't exhaust the totality. That's all of it. But having said that, then we leave that aside.

WEBER: Would there be an analogous new way in the holomovement to look at what we call "time" with regard to other people, in the way that you've just described about the boundaries of space?

BOHM: Well, yes. I think we could take an interval of time and say the two moments are either real and the time between is an abstraction, or the holomovement is the reality and the moments are abstractions. You know, the moments which begin it and end it.

WEBER: So that the interval between the moment is the real.

BOHM: It could be considered to be that. But see, if we take the view that the space is what is real, then I think that we have to say that the measure of space is not what is real. The measure of space is what matter provides. So the space goes beyond the measure of space. It's the same with time. If we want to say that this interval is real, then the measure of time cannot be taken as fundamental. Therefore we are already outside of what we ordinarily would call time. But rather, if we have silence and emptiness, it does not have the measure either of space or of time. Now *in* that silence there may appear something which is a little ripple which has that measure. But if we thought that the little ripple was all that there is and that the space between was nothing, of no significance, then we would have the usual view of fragmentation.

WEBER: May I just go back one step? When you said awhile ago that just as taking the line to be primary and not the two points that limit it or define it with respect to space, so taking what we shall call events, as the points. . . .

BOHM: Yes. Events are the points.

WEBER: Like the line. Events are the points.

BOHM: Well, that's the usual way we talk of it.

WEBER: But the line then, it would seem to me, if you don't allow time to be measured by events. . . .

BOHM: Then it's flowing movement, right?

WEBER: Well then in a way it's silence. That would seem to be the implication. . . .

BOHM: It's just flow. If you look at nature and say, there's no event in nature, really, then it's just flowing. It's the mind that abstracts and puts an event in there.

WEBER: But, doesn't it follow then that that flow or that silence cannot be broken up by any distinguishing characteristics by any properties?

BOHM: Yes. Except that's what thought puts in, the distinguishing characteristics.

WEBER: I understand. But in this other way of looking at it. . . .

BOHM: It can be, but then we have to realize that they have their place the same as we're saying thought does; if you know the place of thought, then it won't interfere, right? The distinguishing characteristics have their place in a certain limited domain of the explicate order and of the manifest.

WEBER: Still, I think to some people it's going to seem very strange. First of all, it challenges everything we've known or have been taught. Secondly, it at least appears to be counter-intuitive, certainly to those who have been trained in modern science, and thirdly, I think it will appear frightening or threatening. So let's maybe spell it out. You're saying that the events are always distinguishable, they have characteristics, they are what we call happenings, and they're the ones we've seized upon as what transpires in the world, as the world's business, so to speak. Those, you're saying, are secondary, derivative, and less important than the absence of all that. And the absence of all that is—call it emptiness, silence, *sunyata*, whatever.

BOHM: On the level of this theory it would be the holomovement, you see, the flowing movement. But it goes beyond that. We could say that even at this level of thought there is a way of looking at it in which emptiness is the plenum, right? That's the way this level of thought treats it. And I'm saying that what we call the things that are real are actually tiny little ripples which have their place, but they have been usurping the whole, the place of the whole.

WEBER: Also emptiness isn't—we don't mean by it a substantive emptiness, like an "empty" box. We're talking about a plenum.

BOHM: It's emptiness which is a plenum. Yes.

WEBER: An emptiness which is a plenum: now what does plenum say to you? What does that mean?

BOHM: You see, this is a well-known idea even in physics, that if you take a crystal which is at absolute zero it does not scatter electrons. They go through it as if it were empty. And as soon as you raise the temperature and (produce) inhomogenities, they scatter. Now, if you used those electrons to observe the crystal (e.g., by focusing them with an electron lens to make an image), all you would see would be these little inhomogeneities and you would say they are what exists and the crystal is what does not exist. Right? I think this is a familiar idea, namely to say that what we see immediately is really a very superficial affair. However, the positivist used to say that what we see immediately is all there is or all that counts, and that our ideas must simply correlate what we see immediately.

WEBER: From that, of course, it would follow that history and all these multiplicity of objects and events are just ripples.

BOHM: Yes. They're merely ripples and their meaning depends on understanding what underlies the ripples.

WEBER: And you're saying what underlies the ripples is the true profundity. That's what's actual.

BOHM: Yes.

WEBER: And you've also said that man can fit himself to grasp that emptiness.

BOHM: Well, he doesn't grasp it, you see. You can't—any more than you could grasp empty space.

WEBER: Well, then what's the word we should use?

BOHM: I think that at this stage we have to say that this is an idea and therefore there's a limit to how far we'll go.

WEBER: In discourse.

BOHM: This only works in the universe of discourse which works in the real universe up to a point. See, to make this emptiness a reality in the consciousness of man, as Krishnamurti was saying, consciousness would empty itself of all these ripples. When the mind is full of all these ripples and little movements, they scatter the energy, as it were, and it looks as if they are all there is. The plenum which consciousness is is not seen, or is not able to operate. So the notion is that if the consciousness can empty itself of its content, which is all these ripples, then possibly we could say that this holomovement is then. . .

WEBER: Unobstructedly there?

BOHM: Unobstructedly there, yes. And I think that's about as far as you could go. If we say consciousness is the manifest content, it is the nonmanifest movement beneath, and it is something far beyond that, and the point is by ending these ripples in the manifest and the nonmanifest, ending these ripples in the manifest and the germs in the nonmanifest which create them, then we have an emptiness which makes consciousness somehow a vehicle or an instrument for the operation of this totality—of intelligence, compassion, truth. But if consciousness is full of all this content which then begins to keep itself going, self-generated, it becomes just chaos.

WEBER: And if consciousness empties itself of all these ripples, is this what yesterday I took Krishnamurti to be saying is religion?

BOHM: Yes. That's the first step. It's the notion of ending conflict, you see, religion as wholeness which means ending fragmentation and conflict.

WEBER: And he said "total listening." Now by that I suppose he meant total listening to that wholeness or void-plenum but not to the little surface things?

BOHM: Well, also to the surface, you see. To listen to it all.

WEBER: To all of it.

BOHM: Yes. What interferes with listening as you could see very clearly yesterday, is that thought jumps in very fast with a word and all its associations which then goes so fast that thought takes that to be [direct] perception.

WEBER: And thus it ends any further . . . probing in depth?

BOHM: That's right. It says that's what reality is. Therefore thought begins to ponder, to move in it, so it gets caught in itself. And it begins to make comments about itself which in turn seem real, and it keeps on going and building up all these ripples.

WEBER: It skates on the ripples and concentrates on that dimension and never gets beyond them.

BOHM: Yes. But in doing that it keeps this whole chaos moving, you see.

WEBER: I understand. To change the subject somewhat, you said one other thing that would be helpful to clear up. You know you talked earlier about the implicate order, the nonmanifest. When we discussed the matrix that makes possible and governs objects, you said it's as if there's a sequence, at least we can think of them as a sequence. But then you said that's only a simple rendition of it and that there is so much more, that they crisscross and are all part of one another. Could you go into this crisscross of factors in the implicate order?

BOHM: Well if you ask: how is three-dimensional space described? One-dimensional space could be taken to be simple sequence on a line, one of the dimensions of space. Now in order to have two dimensions we must have two sequences. Which interrelate, and in fact you could say that it's a sequence of sequences because each sequence forms a line and a line of lines makes a plane, and a line of planes makes a solid and so on. That is usually stopped at three dimensions. Now even in those three dimensions you can see you could orient those lines in many different ways and still cover the space, right? And therefore you have to say you have the possibility of a tremendous number of orders, not just those three that you happen to have chosen for the coordinate system. Is that clear?

WEBER: Orders meaning part dimension?

BOHM: Each line is an order. Now ordinary space could be called the product of three orders in three different directions. But you could choose those directions arbitrarily. This way or that way. You can rotate your frame or you can deform your frame, and any one of those frames is as good as any other. And therefore each order is potentially an infinity of orders. And at present you could say it could all be reduced to any three of those orders, or to any other three such orders. That's the notion of the vector. That every vector could be described by three components in any three directions. And therefore you could reduce any order to any three orders chosen as your standard. That's the meaning of the three dimensionality of space. Now when you go into quantum mechanics of a two-particle system you find not a three-dimensional space but a six-dimensional space. In other words, you have an order of orders: any three dimensional order is itself ordered in the three dimensions of the other particle. So it has to be treated as six-dimensional—an ordinary particle. An ordinary object with, say, 10^{24} power particles would have to be treated as 3×10^{24} dimensional, and so on. The universe would be treated as infinite dimensional. Is that clear? That is called configuration space or sometimes phase space if we extend it a bit.

In classical mechanics this configuration space is seen to be an abstraction, a descriptive abstraction. We say you really have to deal with particles located in certain places in three dimensions. But in quantum mechanics it is not an abstraction. This is the meaning of the Einstein, Rosen, and Podolsky experiment, that you cannot reduce this six-dimensional space to three-dimensional space. Some things happen in there which could only be understood by keeping it six-dimensional or more generally, 3n-dimensional. Right? How do we look at that? What happens is that we have what's called a wave function or else an algebraic operator in this 3n-dimensional space and properties of that determine or refer to the whole system and smaller operators refer to some parts of the system. So we cannot reduce the whole. In classical physics we can reduce the whole to parts. We say the whole has, say, 3n-dimensions, but we can always say that's an abstraction for a lot of different things which are all in the same three dimensions, and therefore we can reduce this whole to some function of a set of parts, to a mathematical function. Now in quantum mechanics we can't do that. We have to think that this 3n-dimensional space is just as elementary as the three-dimensional space, and that fundamentally the laws of quantum mechanics provide a relation between the 3n-dimensional space and the various three-dimensional spaces of each particle.

WEBER: Does the mathematics for this already exist?

BOHM: Oh yes. It's being used all the time. But people say it doesn't matter; it's only a way of calculating what's happening to solid little particles in three-dimensional space. And the paradox of Einstein, Rosen, Podolsky is that they're not comprehensible, but people sort of put it aside and say it's not really important because we're getting results. By using this mathematics we are correctly predicting how our instruments are going to behave. We say it's true, we don't understand how it comes about, but that is considered to be unimportant.

WEBER: Many people I suppose who read this don't know what the paradox of Einstein, Rosen and Podolsky is.*

BOHM: It doesn't matter.

WEBER: It doesn't matter. But you're saying it has specific implications or ramifications for the n-dimensionality of space.

BOHM: For the 3n-dimensionality of matter.

WEBER: Can you explain that somewhat?

BOHM: The manifest matter must be put into three dimensions if the deeper reality is 3n-dimensions. You can see by studying the mathematics that nonmanifest matter in 3n-dimensional and manifest matter is three-dimensional.

WEBER: The nonmanifest matter is 3n-dimensional?

BOHM: Yes. That's really what I'm saying, and whatever matter is manifest is three dimensional; the relation between those two is essentially what quantum mechanics tells you. The laws of quantum mechanics are essentially relating the 3n-dimensional to the three-dimensional. Our equipment reveals itself in 3n-dimensions and the calculation is carried out in 3n-dimensions and by means of certain rules that connect them. What you do in n-dimensions is related to what you can observe in three dimensions.

WEBER: What does that imply?

BOHM: Now at present what most physicists would say is that the three-dimensional reality is all there is and that quantum mechanics

---

*A. Einstein, N. Rosen and B. Podolsky, *Phys. Rev.*, 47, 777 (1935). " . . . an example suggested by Einstein, Rosen, and Podolsky . . . gives a case in which one can demonstrate explicitly the inconsistency of supposing that the precise details of the fluctuations described by the indeterminacy principle could be ascribed to disturbances of the observed subject by the observing apparatus." David Bohm, *Causality and Chance in Modern Physics* (University of Pennsylvania Press, Philadelphia, Pennsylvania, 1971).

is nothing but a set of rules, a different set of rules for discussing the three-dimensional reality.

WEBER: They turn it into something pragmatic?

BOHM: Yes. Now what I'm proposing is that the 3n-dimensional reality is what is and that we have a set of rules for showing how 3n-dimensional reality manifests in three-dimensional reality, the two together forming the whole larger whole.

WEBER: Is there an analogue here for three-dimensional consciousness which is thought and 3n-dimensional consciousness which is awareness? Could you say that?

BOHM: Yes, you could say that. I would propose that analogy. I mean, the nonmanifest consciousness is awareness, intelligence and something possibly beyond.

WEBER: Energy?

BOHM: Energy. Now thought could be compared to the three-dimensional except that it's a bit more subtle than that. But it's rather limited compared with this deeper—this whole thing. I mean, we actually have more dimensions in thought than three, but still, it's very limited.

WEBER: And you could say, maybe that it stands in that same relationship to the n-dimensional as the three-dimensional object to the 3n-dimensional matter, right? Not that it's exactly the same, it's more fluid. . . .

BOHM: Yes.

WEBER: Are you asserting that, so to speak?

BOHM: Yes.

WEBER: So you're saying that when consciousness breaks free from those restraints of three-dimensionality it encounters something altogether new and different.

BOHM: Well, it becomes—it *is* something new and different.

WEBER: It *is*. Yes. And that would be the connection, then, you would draw between the new physics and our understanding of consciousness.

BOHM: Yes. Insofar as we consider consciousness to be some material process we could say it could move into new domains of matter as in physics we have been moving in super-conductivity and super-fluidity, new highly ordered domains of matter, new highly ordered domains of consciousness. Now I think that some people are looking at this notion, but in general, of course, physicists are not terribly interested in it.

WEBER: For the reasons you talked about earlier?

BOHM: Yes.

WEBER: But then you're saying that just as physics—the new physics has revolutionized the way we look at what we think of as the world out there, so you're saying the new consciousness revolutionizes the way we look at what before we thought of as the observer.

BOHM: Yes. Well that's part of it. But see, I think that primarily what we are doing is getting rid of this tremendous discrepancy between consciousness and the material world which is its content, saying that they are both of the same general nature. But to get beyond them we have to come up to the end of thought. It's not enough to say we are going to consider a consciousness which is more than this limited three-dimensional kind. The trouble is that we are still using the three-dimensional consciousness to guide us in that.

WEBER: To talk about it?

BOHM: To talk about it. The point of meditation would be to stop doing that.

WEBER: This was the last question, if you don't mind, that I would like to bring up. What does meditation tell us in all these factors that we've been talking about: the holomovement, space and time, and 3n-dimensional reality. Could you say something about meditation?

BOHM: I think that meditation would even bring us out of all [the difficulties] we've been talking about. You see, the point is that we have been talking about something which is a kind of bridge. This whole construction of the implicate order is a kind of bridge. We can put it in our ordinary language but its implication leads somewhere beyond. At the same time, however, if you don't cross the bridge and leave it behind, you know, you're always on the bridge. No use being there!

WEBER: Yes, that's true, you're stuck there!

BOHM: So the purpose of a bridge is to cross. Or more accurately, we could perhaps think of a pier, leading us out into the ocean and enabling us to dive into the depths. So we could say that if we could consider it seriously, aside from its utility in understanding matter, the bridge or pier would help us to loosen our way of considering consciousness so that it doesn't hold so rigidly. But I think that the question of consciousness is, is beyond. The actuality of this 3n-dimensional consciousness could not be attained by studying physics with our three-dimensional consciousness. It might form a bridge or pier of some sort that moves us a certain way but, somewhere we've got to leave thought behind, and come to this emptiness of this manifest thought altogether and of the conditioning of the nonmanifest mind by the seeds of manifest thought. In other words meditation actually transforms the mind. It transforms consciousness.

WEBER: On the spot.

BOHM: On the spot. And we cannot use what we have produced in consciousness to replace that transformation.

WEBER: Then you're saying it's in the doing of it itself, without any gap or postponement or intent, that this process becomes active.

BOHM: Yes . . . yes.

WEBER: So just to relate it to this notion of emptiness. If we say that our daily busy activities for most people are the events, or the absence of emptiness or the overlay, then meditation does what?

BOHM: Well, it empties the mind of all that.

WEBER: Right. And so. . . .

BOHM: . . . makes possible something different. From that point of view, you could say that even to linger on the implicate order would then make it become part of the same general thing.

WEBER: You mean an obstacle, it's another thought.

BOHM: Yes. It's like the fellow who stays on the pier and never dives into the depths of the ocean.

6

COMMENTARIES ON THE HOLOGRAPHIC THEORY

Reflections on the Holographic Paradigm

KEN DYCHTWALD, PH.D.

NEW THEORIES ABOUT THE MIND or the body serve the double function of educating us to new ways of understanding ourselves and the contexts within which we live, as well as challenging us to explore and revision the very beliefs and structures within which we proceed to try and understand them. The information that emerges from the recent explosion of interest in the holographic paradigm is certainly no exception to this rule. Within this emerging view of the universe lies a wealth of information regarding the dynamics and consciousness of life, but in order to begin to truly appreciate it, one must already, in a sense, understand it.

Now, I don't intend for this to sound like psycho-babble, but when we try to fully experience or understand the holographic paradigm in anything other than a holistic fashion—with full inclusion of the intellect, the senses, intuition, and the accumulated experience of a lifetime—we find ourselves denied the complete view. Alas . . . Alice without her key. In a highly provocative way, the holographic paradigm reminds us that we too are parts of a master hologram and the closer we come to fully knowing and experiencing ourselves, the closer, therefore, we are to interfacing with the identity of this grand holographic information.

Since the holographic paradigm suggests a dynamic of life that is nonlinear, we can expect that conceiving it or explaining it in linear ways will probably fall somewhat short of being a true and accurate representation of the actual truth and beauty of this system. In addition, since inherent in this system is a deep appreciation for nonrational modalities of experience and expression, our difficulty in explanation is multiplied. For in this article I am unable to communicate about holography with smells, temperatures, colors, sounds, tones, vibrations, chemicals, touches or expressive gestures. Rather I am forced to deal entirely in word symbols that are contextually narrow and confining in scope. It's not unlike trying to explain a verb using only nouns . . . you can get very close without ever quite succeeding.

I am reminded of an illuminating anecdote I once read on an album cover. On this album, the rock singer explains that for one of the songs, whose title is "Lost in the Woods," it was his wish to have the refrain sung in Swahili. Before the album was actually recorded, the singer/songwriter had an opportunity to visit Africa while on a concert tour. While there, he took the opportunity to ask a bilingual tribal chieftain how he could say "lost in the woods" in Swahili. The chieftain looked at him for a while, scratched his head and simply replied, "We don't get lost in the woods."

Similarly, it is inherent in our language, belief system and thought patterns to *not* understand ourselves or our universe in a holographic or holistic way. The task then, of understanding and explaining this *new* paradigm with *old* symbols and images is a curious and frustratingly enlightening procedure in and of itself.

I have found that it has been especially helpful for me to ease into an understanding of the holographic paradigm by relating and comparing it to other more familiar, yet similar images and constructs. I have also found that the experiences in my own life which have allowed me to understand some of the dimensions of the holographic paradigm have frequently been nonlogical in nature and have occurred to me through my senses, in dreams or reveries, while experiencing a particularly strong emotion, while enjoying a masterful piece of art or through some unexpected illuminating flash of inner reorganization.

One of the simplest and most functional examples of the holographic paradigm is displayed in the expression of a mandala. "Mandala" is a Sanskrit word which refers to a particular type of circular or geometrically arranged drawing that is frequently used as a focus for meditative self-exploration. The mandala is said to be a symbol or representation of some particular aspect of the universe. Supposedly, the designer or creator of each mandala seeks first to identify some particular spectrum of experience from the entire range of life, such as relationships between people, feelings of love or hate, dance, the history of a civilization, etc. Once the spectrum of experience is selected, it is then examined deeply until the artist has distilled the entire experience into its most elemental forms and dynamics. These basic relationships are then translated into symbolic patterns which are woven together into the mandala drawing.

Now, this symbol serves a number of purposes. First, it exists as a thing on its own, a work of art, a statement of beauty. In addition, it is believed that when a person looks deep into the mandala, the person will not only experience the lines, flows and statements of the art, but in addition will begin to enter into the symbolic drama that the drawing offers. As a result, the experiencer of the mandala comes to appreciate and understand not only the passion of the original artist who served as the translator of the information, but also finds himself entering into the universal context that the mandala has deftly captured. This is a perfect example of the way in which a particular aspect of life stands as a whole unto itself as well as a storehouse of information of some grander, larger whole. In this sense, the mandala is holographic, a whole/part epiphany.

We may experience this same event while reading a poem. In the poem, the poet has endeavored to capture a key aspect of life in a word. When we read this word, we not only experience it, but as we enter into the context of the poem, we begin to also experience the poet who offers this word to us. In addition, we can travel along this word through the poet who is acting as the medium between us and some spectrum of universal experience. Through this word, we enter into a holographic relationship with a culture, an era, an energetic dynamic, a spectrum of life.

Similarly we can allow ourselves to experience our planet as a kind of mandala or energetic expression. If we like, we can perceive the lines and flows of this planet and enter into the information that it has captured within its form. By experiencing the form we can move through its symbology and understand the life or passion of this planet. Or if we choose, we might isolate one particular aspect of our planet and sense its holographic relationship to the cosmic context within which it exists.

To do this we might go to the beach in Big Sur, and remove one of the curiously twisted cypress trees from the side of the cliff in which it has been living. When we take this tree into our laboratory and attempt to understand its nature, we realize that although we have removed it from its natural context, the information about its previous environment still lives within its present form. As we look at the twisted limbs we can almost visualize the winds that have blown through them. In the coarse dry bark we can sense the long, hot, dry seasons in which this tree has existed since birth. A quick look at the roots informs us that this tree was partially rooted in loose soil and partially planted in hard rock . . . its cells teach us of gravity and the earth's core while its leaves speak of sunlight and sky and renewal.

Using this cypress tree as an example, we see that the various aspects of our lives may exist not only as whole unto themselves, but also exist in interface with other holographic contexts. Since the energetic fit between the whole and its various parts is composed of pure and honest information, we then see that each particular entity is not only expressive about itself but also contains comprehensive information about the larger contexts within which it exists.

Similarly, if we were to look closely at an individual human being, we would immediately notice that it is a unique hologram unto itself; self-contained, self-generating and self-knowledgeable. Yet if we were to remove this being from its planetary context we would quickly realize that the human form is not unlike a mandala or symbolic poem, for within its form and flow lives comprehensive information about various physical, social, psychological and evolu-tionary contexts within which it was created. Given one human being, the necessary tools for deciphering its information, and an intelligence capable of reasoning with this information, we could accurately determine the complex nature and identity of the planet through the living symbology of one of its creatures. We might even extend this discussion one step further by realizing that we could probably identify the nature of this planet if we had only one cell from this human . . . perhaps only one atom . . . perhaps one electron . . . perhaps one unit of time.

I would also like to suggest at this point, that the kind of reason-ing that must be applied to the understanding of holographic sys-tems seems to be a curious blend of deduction, induction, intuition, sensation and insight. As a result, I propose that within the frame-work of understanding this new paradigm we appreciate the emer-gence of a more complete form of reasoning which might be called "holographic reasoning."

It is also important that we remember that the holographic para-digm is not specifically psychological, mathematical, chemical, phys-ical or philosophical. Instead it is simply a system from which arise explanations for the various flows and activities we associate with life and consciousness. However, in light of this new paradigm, we are forced to reevaluate many of the purely arbitrary scientific categorizations that have been established. For in reality, there are no such things as biology or psychology or physics. They are merely constructs designed to facilitate the development and articulation of knowledge. When knowledge or information emerges which doesn't fit within the categories and schemes of these fields, it might make more sense to dispose of the fields than to disregard the new knowledge. This is certainly one of the challenges of the holographic paradigm.

What then are the basic bodies of meaning that we can extract from the holographic paradigm and how does this information allow us to understand and therefore serve ourselves and each other more sensitively and completely? In the rest of this article I would like to share some of my beliefs and notions regarding the nature and implications of this paradigm. In so doing, I intend to extract the most elemental truths upon which much of the holographic theory seems to rest. For our needs here, I prefer to do this in a relatively personal and casual fashion. Since I am only beginning to really understand the many meanings and aspects of this new paradigm, my intention is not so much to "prove" or totally explain these issues. Rather, I would simply like to discuss some of the thoughts and feelings I have been exploring and attempting to understand regarding this highly fascinating and certainly most controversial field of inquiry.

To my mind, there are several basic statements about life and consciousness that emerge simultaneously from this theory:

1) *There is actually no such thing as pure energy or pure matter. Every aspect of the universe seems neither to be a thing or no-thing, but rather exists as a kind of vibrational or energetic expression.*

As the quantum physicists look deeper and deeper into the most elemental building blocks out of which the so-called "physical world" is constructed, they begin to discover that the line between what is matter and what is energy is not a very clear line at all. Instead, the basic particles of life seem to exist somewhere in the never-never land between these two extreme states of being. The building blocks of life seem to resemble vibrational probabilities more than they do slabs of wood and sheets of metal.

Similarly, as metaphysicists look deeper and deeper into the most elemental building blocks of the so-called "non-physical" or psychological world, they are also discovering that the world of matter and energy, or body and mind, are not quite as distinct as many of us have been led to believe. Similarly, the basic particles or units of consciousness seem to exit somewhere in the energetic never-never land between these two extreme states of being. (As I will briefly discuss later in my section on "time," matter and energy only appear to exist as distinct states in the illusory context where time has been stopped, or where there is no time, or where the human mind attempts to freeze time with thoughts and cameras.)

What this point suggests is that the various aspects of the universe express themselves in the form of intermingling, yet distinct, energetic interference patterns which contain information that defines their nature, spirit, style, consistency and in fact, identity. As Buckminster Fuller once proposed, "I seem to be a verb."

2) *Every aspect of the universe is itself a whole, a full being, a comprehensive system in its own right, containing within it a complete store of information about itself.* This information doesn't necessarily exist within a central nervous system as a fact or theory, but instead may exist as energetic or vibrational information.

This point is particularly challenging for two major reasons. First, pre-holographic science has proposed that there are two general categories of matter; living and nonliving. Within this framework, so-called "living" systems are assumed to be whole and fundamentally or biologically intelligent whereas so-called "nonliving" systems are neither. However, since all aspects of the universe can be seen to exist as energetic expressions, then the rigid line between living and nonliving systems immediately disappears and we see that everything is quite alive in some very fundamental way.

The second challenging part of this point has to do with acknowledging that every aspect of the universe is knowledgeable. Once again, from the pre-holographic frame of reference we observe a kind of "human chauvinism" which asserts that if you have two arms, two legs, a brain of a certain size relative to body weight, stand erect, reproduce sexually, etc., then you are a being and may be knowledgeable. Yet within this new paradigm, everything is not only alive existing as a whole unto itself, but also is knowledgeable about itself in an informational or energetic fashion. I am not suggesting that a pebble knows about itself in the same way as I know about myself. However, even in the various animal and insect communities we observe alternate systems of self-knowledge and expression than that which humans practice. For example, the pebble might be self-knowledgeable in a way similar to a swarm of bees who use elaborate vibrational movement and energetic patterns to communicate within the swarm devoid of a central nervous system and linear communicational properties.

We might also remember that *pure size is not a determining factor in the experience of wholeness. . . .* a circle is a circle no matter how big it is. Therefore, not only are the tiniest atomic particles to be considered whole, intelligent and alive systems, but we must also view the planet earth, the solar system and the galaxy as being alive, whole and self-intelligent at a fundamental energetic level.

3) *Every aspect of the universe seems to be part of some larger whole, grander being, and more comprehensive system.* If my first two points are valid, then this particular point seems to follow quickly on their heels. For when we view every aspect of the universe, no matter how small or large, as being alive and vibrationally intelligent, we must also realize that the universe is composed of an incomprehensible number of sets, subsets and interrelated systems. As long as the universe reveals itself as boundless, we can expect that there will always be larger and grander holographic schemes within which other systems exist. As if this isn't enough, we're then faced with the staggering notion that our boundless universe might itself simply be a tiny atomic particle within some other incomprehensibly enormous holographic system.

This particular notion suggests the traditional microcosm/macrocosm phenomenon: since each system is an expression of the dynamic of its parts, each subsuming holographic system is therefore composed of many other *complete systems* that, within this larger set, are now expressed as *parts*. In addition, since we now see that each whole may contain a variety of parts, and each whole is also fundamentally self-intelligent, it then follows that each holographic system is energetically knowledgeable about all of its various parts.

4) *Since each aspect of the universe expresses itself vibrationally, and all vibrational expressions intermingle within the master hologram(s), every aspect of the universe contains knowledge about the whole(s) within which it exists. In addition, since the vibrational expression of each holographic unit is also a statement of pure information, we can expect that each particular aspect has the ability to be intimately knowledgeable about every other particular aspect within the master hologram(s).*

Therefore not only does each aspect or part of the universe exist as an individuated statement of itself, but also this same part, no matter how small or large, contains within it a complete store of information, what we might translate to mean a basic understanding, about the existential nature of the rest of the universe. Stated simply, each part is not identical to every other part, but rather, is knowledgeable in a most basic way about the other holographic systems within whose presence it exists.

This particular point is often misconstrued in several directions which I will playfully refer to as the "capitalistic" direction and the "communistic" direction. In the capitalistic misunderstanding it is believed that the "bigger the better" and therefore the larger the holographic unit the more aware and knowledgeable it is. This is untrue. Size is not the ultimate determining factor in the area of information and knowledge. In the communistic direction, many people mistakenly believe that every aspect of the universe is equal to every other aspect. This is also untrue. Each holographic unit is simply *itself*, and while it is aware of every other aspect of the universe, they are not necessarily the same.

5) *Within the holographic paradigm, time does not exist as a ticking away of moments forever traveling linearly from "now" to "just then." Instead, time might very well exist multidimensionally moving in many directions simultaneously.*

This notion reminds us that we have imprisoned time with our intellects and have connected the concept of time to our own beliefs about biological decay and therefore, the death of personality. If we step back from this illusion, we can begin to experience the multidirectionality and eerily flexible properties of time. Stated simply, each moment or aspect of time seems to exist everywhere always. In this way, time is a full and living dimension (or many dimensions) with each moment coexisting in knowledgeable and holographic relationship to every other moment.

In addition, since within this framework, time can also be considered an energetic or vibrational expression, then each aspect of time would also be alive, whole, self-knowledgeable and completely informed about every other aspect of the universe.

At this point, we are forced to completely revision the pre-holographic images and symbols that we customarily associate with the three dimensions of space and the linear progression of time, for *they simply don't fit.* Instead, space, time and energetic expression seem to be interrelated as a kind of multidimensional möbius strip forever twisting, moving and enfolding on themselves and yet going absolutely nowhere in no time at all.

The last point I would like to make regarding the holographic paradigm is that, contrary to what I have been suggesting throughout this article, this paradigm is certainly not new. If it were really new then the theories that underlie it would be false. Rather, what is new is our own ability to experience the nature and possibilities of this paradigm in such a way as to have direct meaning and application to the experience we have of ourselves and of our universe. I am reminded of a TV game that I watched when I was young. The game was called "Concentration" and it worked something like this. There was a game board that had thirty numbered squares on it. Each contestant would pick two of the numbered squares and the numbered surfaces would be removed revealing a piece of a puzzle on the next surface layer of these two particular regions on the game surface. If the two revealed pieces were significantly related—if they matched—then these surfaces were also removed and the contestant was given an opportunity to observe the two underlying sections beneath. It was on this primary surface that the ultimate puzzle lived. As more and more pieces were explored, matched and finally revealed, the contestants had more and more of the ultimate puzzle's surface available to them. If a contestant were really perceptive, he could guess the nature of the puzzle before all of the surfaces had been removed.

Similarly, it seems that the holographic identity of the universe and its parts is not unlike the ultimate puzzle in the "Concentration" game. As we learn more and more about ourselves and about the nature of life, there are fewer surfaces blocking our view of the full puzzle. Then, as the puzzle becomes more available, some people will more quickly guess or understand it than others. So it is with the holographic paradigm. No one has invented it, for it has existed forever, and no one has made it up because it is already made. The task of comprehending or knowing the full meaning of this paradigm and translating this understanding into our ongoing experience is the task that lies before us. Hopefully, this short article has in some way contributed to this end.

Holonomy[1] and Bootstrap

FRITJOF CAPRA

The purpose of this note is to point out the conceptual relationship between the holonomic models of Bohm and Pribram, and the bootstrap approach in particle physics originated by Geoffrey Chew.[2]

The basis of the bootstrap approach is the idea that nature cannot be reduced to fundamental entities, like fundamental building blocks of matter, but has to be understood entirely through self-consistency. All of physics has to follow uniquely from the requirement that its components be consistent with one another and with themselves. The bootstrap philosophy not only abandons the idea of fundamental building blocks of matter, but also accepts no fundamental entities whatsoever—no fundamental laws, equations or principles. The universe is seen as a dynamic web of interrelated events. None of the properties of any part of this web is fundamental; they all follow from the properties of the other parts, and the overall consistency of their mutual interrelations determines the structure of the entire web.

In particle physics, the bootstrap approach is presently applied to the description of hadrons, or strongly interacting particles. The "hadron bootstrap" is formulated in the framework of a theory called S-matrix theory, and its aim is to derive all properties of hadrons and their interactions uniquely from the requirement of self-consistency.

The phenomena involving hadrons are so complex that it is by no means certain whether a complete, self-consistent, mathematical theory of hadrons will ever be found. However, one can envisage a series of partially successful models of smaller scope. Each of them would be intended to cover only part of the observed phenomena and would contain some unexplained aspects, or parameters, but the parameters of one model may be explained by another. Thus more and more phenomena may gradually be covered with ever increasing accuracy by a mosaic of interlocking models. The adjective "bootstrap" is thus never appropriate for any individual model, but can be applied only to a combination of mutually consistent models, none of which is any more fundamental than the others. As Chew has put it, "A physicist who is able to view any number of different partially successful models without favoritism is automatically a bootstrapper."

Several models of that kind already exist and indicate that the program of the hadron bootstrap is very likely to be carried out in the not too distant future. The picture of hadrons which emerges from these bootstrap models is often summed up in the provocative phrase, "Every particle consists of all other particles." It must not be imagined, however, that each hadron contains all the others in a classical, static sense. Hadrons are not separate entities but interrelated energy patterns in an on-going dynamic process. These patterns do not "contain" one another, but rather "involve" one another in a certain way which can be given a precise mathematical meaning but cannot easily be expressed in words.

The bootstrap picture of an interconnected web of relations in which particles are dynamically composed of one another, each of them involving all the others, evidently shows great similarities to holonomic models. However, because of its essentially dynamic nature it goes beyond the hologram analogy. Subatomic particles are dynamic patterns which can only be described in a relativistic framework where space and time are fused into a four-dimensional continuum. The static, non-relativistic picture of the hologram is not appropriate to describe their properties and interactions. For that reason, the universe is definitely *not* a hologram, as is sometimes erroneously stated.

The limitations of the hologram analogy have clearly been recognized by David Bohm who prefers to use the term holomovement to describe the holonomic *and* dynamic nature of reality. Bohm's ideas, in fact, go beyond the present framework of the hadron bootstrap. At every stage of the bootstrap approach, we have to accept some unexplained aspects of our theory. These aspects are treated, temporarily, as "fundamental" but will be expected to emerge, eventually, as a necessary consequence of self-consistency. In a subsequent, more general framework, some of the concepts which had previously been accepted without explanation will be "bootstrapped," i.e., they will be derived from the overall self-consistency. The concept of relativistic space-time plays the role of such a "temporarily fundamental" concept in current S-matrix theory, and Bohm's work, although using a different formalism, can be understood as an attempt to "bootstrap" space-time and to use some "fundamental" concepts of quantum mechanics.

The hadron bootstrap, then, works within a more limited framework but represents nevertheless a radical innovation compared to the "fundamentalist" approaches pursued by the majority of physicists. Very recently, there have been several important developments in S-matrix theory which have brought extremely encouraging results. One of the major challenges to the hadron bootstrap had always been the demand to explain the "quark structure" of hadrons without having to assume—as most particle physicists do—that quarks are the fundamental building blocks out of which hadrons are made. A group of researchers at the Lawrence Berkeley Laboratory, led by Chew, has now succeeded in deriving results character-istic of quark models without any need to postulate the existence of physical quarks. These results have generated tremendous enthusi-asm among S-matrix theorists. We believe now that we shall be able, in the near future, to go beyond the quark model; to "bootstrap the quark," as it were.

In obtaining these results, the decisive breakthrough was made when the notion of order was recognized as a new and important ingredient of hadron physics. The quark patterns emerged as a consequence of combining the general principles of S-matrix theory with the additional concept of order. The significance of order in hadron physics is still mysterious, and the extent to which it can be incorporated into the S-matrix framework is not yet fully known. However, it is intriguing to note that the notion of order, which is now emerging as a central feature of the bootstrap approach, is also an essential aspect of Bohm's theory. To me, this is yet another indication that the approaches of Bohm and Chew may well merge in the future.

Self-Love and the Cosmic Connection

SAM KEEN

The ancient taboos against self-love spring from low self-esteem, from a degraded and mistaken notion of the nature of the human self. There has always been a battle between orthodoxy and mysti-cism. The orthodox counsel us to forget the self, obey the laws, perform the rituals, stay within the traditional social roles. The mystics claim self-knowledge is the path to liberation. "Go within" they tell us. "Further in is further out. The kingdom of God is within you. Eternity is in every grain of sand."

For the first time in a century science and religion are partners in an adventure of cosmic discovery. Mysticism and physics are mak-ing common cause. Research into the brain is confirming the wildest visions of perennial mysticism. It appears that evidence and mystical experience both support the notion that every person is a microcosm of the macrocosm.

Consider the enormity of the self each of us is invited to inhabit and love.

The mind is a hologram that registers the entire symphony of cosmic vibratory events. Karl Pribram, Itzhak Bentov and others are discovering that the mind is a neural net that encodes in a holographic manner the entire information of the universe. A star explodes and the mind trembles. Just as any cell in the body encodes all the information necessary to reproduce the entire body, so any mind recapitulates all cosmic events. What we call ESP and paranormal experience may only be our dipping into the timeless dimensions which make up the holographic structure of our minds. Science and mysticism suggest that the self may be ubiquitous. Mind knows no barriers. At the very center of the self, "eternal" events, vibratory happenings in the atomic and the astronomic dimension, resonate within our time-binding minds. As Plato said "time is the moving image of eternity."

The body is a living museum of natural history in which the entire drama of evolution is recapitulated. Studies in the development of the foetus show that from conception to birth the child must pass through all the stages of evolution. On the way to our human form we pass through the evolutionary hierarchy. Before we grow lungs we have gills. Glen Doman at The Institutes for the Achievement of Human Potential has shown in work with brain injured children, that if we do not slither on our bellies like snakes and crawl on all fours like puppies the medulla, pons, and mid-brain, the so-called reptillian and mammalarian brains, will not develop correctly.

The self is a meeting place of eternity and time, the holographic mind in the evolutionary body. Each nervous system tells the story of Bethlehem. The encoded information of the cosmos is incarnate in every historical body. A human being is a gateway to the beyond.

When the question of self is placed in the context of the mystical-scientific view of the cosmic-evolutionary self the vistas and possible adventures of self-love are staggering. How much can we learn from ourselves? How much of the encoded information that resides in our bodies and minds can be recovered and brought into awareness? What can we know of happenings in distant galaxies and of animal wisdom by tuning into our own nervous systems? Can we slip out of the prison of time and space and travel into the beyond which is the source from which all things flow? Can we travel backwards and forwards in time? Once we see that the self is not merely a captive to the phenomenal world, not a mere prisoner of this time and space, of this body, the possibilities become endless. The adventure of self-knowledge takes us to the edges of every unknown.

How far can we travel? Who knows. We are at the beginning of a new age of discovery. The marriage of science and mysticism will open new possibilities and release potentialities we can scarcely imagine. We may be able to preview some of the future by taking seriously the stories of extraordinary powers (siddhis) which were attributed to ancient yogis and mystics.

The goal of self-exploration is beyond our wildest imagination but at least the first steps on the path are clear. The journey into the cosmic-evolutionary dimensions of the self cannot begin until we have dared to go beneath the images of the self given us by our parents and peers. The first step is to break out of the persona, the character armor created by our "normal" process of psychological development. We must go beyond the threshold which is guarded by *guilt* and *shame* (the guardians of conscience which represent the values and visions of the Giants—Parents and Authorities). In the magic theater on the far side of personality we discover the many roles the "persona" was forbidden to play. Beneath character we find the repressed selves: the killer, the playboy, the victim, the saint—the many faces of Eve, or Adam. It is only when we have passed through this theater of the multiplicity of the roles of the self that we may pass beyond the second threshold to where the journey into the cosmic-evolutionary dimensions of the self begins. And that adventure is endless. At this point in my own life I cannot say anything more. I see the horizon clearly, but I have only some dreams, omens and messages from other travelers to guide me into this unknown.

Uncertainty Principle Factors in Holographic Models of Neurophysiology

KENNETH R. PELLETIER

Holographic models of human consciousness require neurophysiologists to take into account events at the same order of magnitude as is addressed in quantum physics. There is nothing inherent in any aspect of the natural sciences which excludes the consideration of the interface between neurophysiology ("matter") and the phenomenology of consciousness ("mind"). Quite the opposite; it seems increasingly necessary to postulate the presence of such nonphysical entities in the most advanced areas of science including mathematics, physics and neurology (Young, 1976). Those researchers who have attempted to penetrate the ultimate mystery of mind in interaction with matter have focused upon quantum events occurring in and among the neurons of the brain.

For example, early in the development of quantum mechanical theory it was recognized that the Heisenberg Uncertainty Principle (governing elementary "material" particles) had a direct bearing on the philosophical problem of free will. Werner Heisenberg demonstrated that this uncertainty is not simply a matter of the physical limitations of present instruments. He maintained that the imprecision in one measurement (position or momentum of an elementary particle) multiplied by the imprecision of the other can never be less than Planck's Constant ($\hbar = 6.77 \times 10^{27}$) (Heisenberg, 1971), so that the total configuration is *not* deterministic. Niels Bohr suggested that certain key points in the regulatory mechanisms of the brain might be so sensitive and delicately balanced that they should properly be regarded as quantum mechanical in nature—or "nondeterministic"—and therefore could be considered to be the physical mechanisms of an individual's free will (Bohr, 1958; Capra, 1975). Another physicist, Sir Arthur Eddington, examined the possibility that mind controlled the brain within the limits allowed by the Heisenberg Principle, although he eventually discarded the idea since he considered the range of influence to be too small to affect the physical brain (Eddington, 1935). Speculating in the context of neurological knowledge of the mid-1930s, Eddington addressed his thinking to an object as large as the neuron. Currently, however, neurophysiologists possess more detailed knowledge regarding the synaptic vesicles and "slow wave potentials" (Pribram, 1971), and Fourier transforms which seem to be the key principles by which mind is operational.

Nerve cells are tree-like in appearance, and usually one branch of the cell body is longer than the others. This is the axon that carries electrical current from the cell body to its terminal point, or "end foot," which is in close proximity to other cells. If the adjacent cell is another neuron, then this zone of interaction is called a synapse, the space between the two neurons being the synaptic cleft. Quite importantly, the space between these neurons is on the order of 200 to 300 Å which is a magnitude so minute it is in the range considered by quantum physics. In the current understanding, the transmission of nerve impulses across this cleft is initiated by a nerve impulse arriving at the end foot and causing the release of "packets" of chemical neurotransmitters from synaptic vesicles or sacs located in the presynapse. Actually, the exact process is not yet understood, for the delicately poised, highly volatile synaptic activity is only now beginning to be studied in terms of quantum physics. Graded slow-potential changes wax and wane continuously at the junctions between neurons. These potentials can be influenced by infinitesimal amounts of energy on the order of quantum events. Interestingly, in the earliest explorations of the cortex by electron microscopy, researchers expected to find something unique about synaptic organization in areas concerned with higher functions. It was assumed that those cells would bear a property which would not be found in cells of the spinal column. However, in recent years they have concluded that the basic nature of the synapse is constant throughout the nervous system (Pelletier, 1978). In fact, all synapses are alike in their essential features and in their mode of chemical transmission. There appear to be no essential differences between the parts of the nervous system which, like the spinal column, are associated with autonomic activity and those which, like the cortex, are associated with mentation, imagery and other such higher order phenomena of consciousness.

Commenting on the convergence between quantum physics and innovations in neurophysiological measurement, the neurologist John C. Eccles has pointed out that the synaptic vesicle is an approximately spherical structure of 400 Å diameter, and that Eddington thought the uncertainty principle was applicable to an object of this size, having calculated the uncertainty of the position of such an object to be about 50 Å in one millisecond. This value is extremely significant since 50 Å might be the order of magnitude of the latitude in which consciousness might operate in interaction with the neurophysiological mechanisms of the brain within the limits allowed by uncertainty. In rough terms, that 50 Å might be a measure of "free will" or "mind influence." According to Eccles, "It is therefore possible that the permitted range of behavior of a synaptic vesicle may be adequate to allow for the effective operation of the postulated 'mind influences' on the active cerebral cortex" (Eccles, 1970). Experimental research by Eccles and other neurologists has yielded data permitting great refinement of the concept of ephemeral mind acting upon static matter; theirs is a model of ineffably subtle interactions among infinitesimal energy fields occurring in quantum space.

Advanced hypotheses concerning brain function no longer employ hardware metaphors of the brain as a machine or even a sophisticated computer. Rather, the brain is thought to function by virtue of "spatio-temporal fields of influence." Again as Eccles had noted:

> . . . these spatio-temporal fields of influence are exerted by the mind on the brain in willed action. If one uses the expressive terminology . . . the "ghost" operates a "machine," not of ropes and pulleys, valves and pipes, but of microscopic spatio-temporal patterns of activity in the neuronal net woven by the synaptic connections of ten thousand million neurones, and even then only be operating on nuerones that are momentarily poised close to a just-threshold level of excitability. It would appear that it is the sort of machine a "ghost" could operate, if by ghost we mean in the first place an "agent" whose action has escaped detection even by the most delicate physical instruments (Eccles, 1970).

A "ghost" that has escaped and might elude detection by physical instrumentation within the limits of the uncertainty principle would certainly be a cause of despair if inquiry into the nature of consciousness were to be limited to physical observation of events in the brain. Fortunately, the mind is able to reflect upon itself and thus to transcend this limit and provide another approach through the systematic study of the phenomenology of consciousness.

Holonomic Knowing

BOB SAMPLES

Without question the emergence of the holographic brain and holographic universe represents the most exciting paradigm shift in modern times. To blend ideas about how the brain creates consciousness and how that consciousness is wedded to the universe is an awesome task. Yet this is precisely what Karl Pribram and David Bohm have done.

In this paper I will explore but a small facet of the implications of these ideas . . . the implications I see in knowing, learning and creating in the process of education. At first, it seemed refreshing when the data base emerged from neurophysiological research with regard to the lateralization of functions in the cerebral cortex. That is, the notion of left & right hemisphere functions as being quite different. These ideas have become very popular in the arena of public education. Workshops, seminars and public lectures are widely attended by educators. However, a more reflective view of the popularity of this idea suggests a well-known cultural affection for the comfortable dichotomies of Newtonian visions of the past. Left/right brain functions mirrored a social commitment to dualistic and dichotomous thought

I have written extensively about these ideas and celebrated the possibility that by honoring metaphoric (right brain) as well as rational (left brain) thought and modes of knowing, education and psychology might well experience a quantum jump into more holistic domains. It is clear now that my appeals for holism, as well as those of other educators, psychologists and neurophysiologists, were lost in the reflexive acceptance of the ideas regarding the lateralized cortex as a new Newtonian management principle. In short, the left/right brain dichotomy was more appealing politically than the pleas for holism. Left/right brainedness deteriorated quickly in the educational marketplace to slogans and instruments for zealotry.

Hemisphere specialization does not represent a paradigm shift. The holographic model of the brain does. For too long brain function has been metaphorically linked to mechanical circuitry. The computer metaphor seems to represent the supposed "ultimate" statement about the brain. Even in the lateralized models the separation of specialties was quickly translated to digital computer (left hemisphere) and analogue computer (right hemisphere).

The gift of the holographic model is that its metaphors are more appropriately linked to ecology. That is, as each person gains experience which becomes encoded into the brain, a multidimensional energy field is set up. This pattern of energy (i.e., the thought) is simultaneously generated throughout the brain. Another researcher, Ralph Abraham, refers to these energy configurations as macrons.

A macron can be thought of as a highly specific pattern of energy in three dimensions. Abraham suggests that a thought is a macron generator. Furthermore, he suggests that macrons set up a kind of energy ecology in the brain that favors the fixation of certain neurochemical configurations. If a person repeats a particular thought macron it establishes what he calls long-term memory. If the macrons are not repeated then short-term memory exists.

Aside from such speculations, it is of interest to note that the proposed macrons are highly regular in their basic geometric configuration. Also macrons in other than brain contexts are capable of being mathematically analyzed.

Pribram's work creates a model of the brain that is compatible with the basic ideas of the macron. But even more exciting is the way the hologram represents the most sophisticated physical system for the storage, retrieval and transformation of data (i.e., experience). Yet I am still apprehensive of the limitations of using physical metaphors for biological systems. However I am willing to rest with the realization that the hologram might be the best physical metaphor available to explain an infinitely more complex biological system . . . the brain. In an awkward way, we are still victims of the Newtonian paradigm, as Newton still owns the research.

The awesome cleverness of Pribram's research stands as its own beacon. His decision to use the mathematics of Fourier Transformations creates in itself a brilliant metaphor. The graphic expression of the results of such a transformation is a mandala—an expression in two dimensions of radial symmetry within the confines of mathematical relationships. Another attribute of the Fourier "mandalas" is that the entire pattern can be regenerated from any shard of the data bound within the "graph." This makes the mechanisms of expressing the analysis of data metaphorically compatible with the model.

To those of us interested in human thought, Pribram, Bohm, Abraham, and—with less attention to left hemisphere rationality—a clan of others, are giving a kind of permission for holism. My own work exploited results rather than theory. For more than a decade with funding from the National Science Foundation, my colleagues and I explored the tendency of people of all ages to perform more effectively in rational tasks if the more holistic forms of knowing were honored. The models of lateralized brain offered hopeful yet temporary sustenance. To far too many it became a gimmick rather than a model.

Pribram's work rises above Newtonian habits and toward a "normal" or "natural" context for holism. He provides us with the realization that experience is patterned into the whole brain and not localized in the reductive geographies of the cortex that were previously favored. With this neurophysiological liberation, we in the educational and psychological professions are encouraged by theory to give up our reductive practices. Behaviorism can be seen as a treatment of symptoms and not causes. It can be seen as the enforcement of pre-selected macrons on mind while reducing the options for self-selection.

Pribram's entrance into the new paradigms must be incomplete. So it is with explorers at the edge of knowledge. Einstein saw beyond the present but he never grasped the future. What Pribram gives us is a model of mental inclusion rather than exclusion. He increases the legitimacy of an array of mental-media in the process of living life. He also pushes us beyond the parochialism of conventional ways of processing experience.

Holonomic knowing is holistic. It must honor the nonrational as well as the rational. It is clear that the macronic holograms of Karl Pribram give us wider horizons, greater depths and higher reaches. The lateralized brain gave us permission to acknowledge and honor diversity in the modes of knowing. The holographic brain insures the simultaneous legitimacy of the interconnectedness of that knowing.

It basically means we can legitimately weave in and out of all the mental media and processing modes with far less trepidation. It is now clear that the possibility of holistic unity in thought is part of the basic structure and function of the brain. Reductive visions of thought and neurophysiology gave us a Yes But! mentality. Karl Pribram gives us Yes And. . . .

Holonomy and Parapsychology

STANLEY KRIPPNER

It has often been observed that parapsychology has a factual base on which there is yet to be built an explanation. Over the years, a number of writers have posited physical explanations for parapsychological phenomena, usually having to do with electromagnetic fields or various energetic forces. However, the puzzling ability of extrasensory perception and psychokinesis to transcend ordinary time and space boundaries produces problems for those who espouse explanatory models based on energy.

Perhaps ESP and PK could be better subsumed under the proposed holographic model of reality as described by David Bohm and Karl Pribram. One need not speculate how information can quickly travel from point A to point B if that information is already at point B. One need not speculate how a force at point Y can exert an effect on point Z if the information needed to activate the object is already present at point Z. If the brain is a hologram interpreting a holographic universe, ESP and PK are necessary components of that universe. Indeed, holographic theorists would have to hypothesize the existence of ESP and PK had not parapsychologists carefully documented their existence over the years.

As the details of the holographic theory are worked out, it is my feeling that "units of information" will need to be defined and their distribution discerned in the brain and throughout the universe. In so doing, C.G. Jung's concept of synchronicity may take on new importance. According to Jung, synchronicity refers to a noncausal relationship which links two events together in a meaningful way. Each of the synchronistically related events, of course, may have its own causal progenitors, but their linkage produces a "meaningful" coincidence that makes sense. And it is the element of meaning which draws our attention to those units of information which are involved in ESP and PK phenomena.

Perhaps all events are so closely related that it is folly to divide the universe into its parts. Yet, humans attempt this division, in part, for survival purposes. When an event appears to transcend this division, the observers of the events are often disturbed—not realizing that they made the rules of the game that they are playing, a game which reflects surface reality rather than the Grand Hologram which is the true nature of things.

This insight has been appreciated for centuries by many Eastern philosophers, and it is of interest that Pribram was a friend of Alan Watts, just as Bohm is a friend of Krishnamurti. But the Eastern widsom did not lend itself to the development of the technological expertise which has enabled the West to gain renown as the arbiter of reality. It is now time to bring Eastern and Western thought together; the holographic model may be the proper vehicle for this purpose.

The Simplified and Revised Abridged Edition of Changing Reality by Marilyn Ferguson

JOHN SHIMOTSU

Is what we see really there? Or is it just what we think we see? And if it is not there, why do we think we see it? What we think is real, our reality, may be different from actual reality. To understand our reality, we must understand the brain and its functions, for the brain is the organ that computes what we think and sense.

Perhaps one of the greatest mysteries yet to be solved is how the brain works. A very current and shocking theory on this is being proposed by Dr. Karl Pribram, a neuroscientist at Stanford. Dr. Pribram has been involved in many of the major current theories in brain research. His current proposal is a model that covers all the areas of the brain's functions. His model is a holograph, and it combines brain research with theoretical physics, covers the areas of normal and paranormal perception, and takes things out of the supernatural and explains them as a part of nature.

To understand his theory, first we must know what holography is. Holography is a form of photography. In this process the wave field of light scattered by an object is recorded on a plate as a pattern. When this photographic record is placed in front of a laser beam, the original wave pattern is regenerated. A three-dimensional image appears, and any piece of the hologram will reconstruct the entire image.

Perhaps, like the hologram, our brain deals in decoding, storing and showing images. To see, hear, or use other senses, our brains, like the hologram, perform complex mathematical computations on the frequencies of information. And maybe as the light waves travel through the hologram, nerve impulses travel through a network of fine fibers in the cells in the brain.

Then Dr. Pribram stated that maybe the world is a hologram. If this is true, there is no such thing as solidity, and it is merely an illusion. That means that we see things as a child sees an animated cartoon, with illusions.

For a long time, man has been looking at things through lenses that change things so that we can see them. We wish to see a sample so that we can understand what it is. But in doing so, we are not viewing what is actually there. The brain may very well be our lens, and we may be viewing a reality that has been limited so that we can understand it.

Dr. Pribram also suggested that if we saw reality without our mathematical computations performed by the brain, we would know a world in the frequency domain, without time or space, just events. He says that our brain's computations construct physical reality by explaining frequencies from a dimension beyond time and space. The brain is a hologram, explaining a holographic universe.

Because our brains are a part of the big hologram, they have access, under certain conditions, to all the information in the principles of control. If there is no time or space, there is no here or there; psychic occurrences and the supernatural can occur in nature.

Dr. Pribram explains paranormal actions in this way: things are really not solid, so when we think in a certain manner (as some Hindus and others do) we have the power to change what we think is real. People like Uri Geller have a reality that is different from ours because in his reality the things we think are impossible are possible.

Then you may ask, "If this is true, why do we all see the same thing?" One answer is that our brains register a relative reality because they have been set by our culture, and so the mathematical computation will be similar. If a person is intoxicated, that will distort his computation so that he sees a different reality.

A good example of this is you. Why can't you perform actions that we consider paranormal or supernatural? I think it is because you do not think you can. You may say you wish to, or may sincerely want to, but that will not change what you subconsciously think. Our culture says that those actions would not be possible, so that is what you think is real. To change your reality, you would have to alter your innermost thoughts.

Dr. Pribram's entire proposal on the holographic universe is fascinating. It could be the biggest revolution in brain research. What is theory today may be fact tomorrow.

The Holographic Paradigm and the Structure of Experience

JOHN WELWOOD

So far, most discussions of the holographic paradigm have been at a general, conceptual level, describing transformations in the brain or organizations of subatomic particles. What has been missing is an appreciation of how the structure of ordinary experience may be organized on holographic principles. I would like to discuss the holographic structure of ordinary experience in this paper, as well as consider an inherent limitation of the holographic paradigm in regard to experiential knowledge.

Holograms are defined primarily as ways of storing information in terms of a network of interference patterns, which represent the interaction of energy frequencies, such as light waves. These interference patterns are recorded in the hologram in a way that does not literally resemble the objects they represent. Rather, these interference patterns make up a "holographic blur," which has no recognizable form, but which contains numerous bits of information about the whole pattern in every part of it.

Felt Meaning as Holographic Compression

The structure of a hologram provides an analogy for what we experience when we refer to our "inner experiencing," which Gendlin (1962) has described in terms of "felt meaning." If you ask yourself how you feel now, what you get when you first refer inwardly to your felt sense of your present situation, is a blurry whole. Or try referring to your inner felt sense of a person in your life. What is your overall feeling about your father, your whole sense of him? Let yourself feel the whole quality of your relationship to him, without concentrating on specific thoughts or images. Notice that this whole sense has no definite form, but is a very global "feel quality." If what came to mind first was a particular image, see if you can let it broaden out into a blurry whole felt sense.

Gendlin has pointed out that felt meaning represents our interaction with the world. We feel our situations in this global way before we can articulate or delineate them. Felt meaning is like a network of interference patterns formed in our relating to the world. What is felt in the body implies the world (e.g., your stomach tension "contains" a particular world situation in it).

Felt meaning can be seen as an experiential manifestation of holographic compression, where many bits of information function all together as a whole. For example, go back to your felt sense of your father. Now notice that not only can you have this global sense of him apart from any particular image, memory, emotion or thought about him, but also your felt sense actually includes all of the ways you have ever experienced or interacted with him. This felt sense is like a holographic record of all the aspects of your relationship to him (interference patterns). All of your joys, hurts, disappointments, appreciations, angers—all of your whole experience with him is holographically compressed in this one felt sense. The felt sense is blurry in that it includes all of this *implicitly*. This implicit is not focal or sharply defined, but always functions as a global background.

When we attend to an implicit felt sense in this way, we are using a scanning type of attention that does not single out specific focal objects one at a time. This global type of *diffuse attention* allows us to sense a holographic blur all at once, without imposing a preconceived grid, filter or focus on it. When we attempt to focus or pinpoint it, then we begin to make aspects of it *explicit* (explication).

David Bohm (1973) points out that:

> the word "implicit" is based on the verb "to implicate." This means "to fold inward" (as multiplication means "folding many times"). So we may be led to explore the notion that in some sense each region contains a total structure "enfolded" within it (p. 147).

Bohm's reference here to the *implicate order* of the physical universe applies equally well to the implicit nature of experiencing. All of your experiences with your father have been "folded inward" in your felt sense. How you act and respond to him from moment to moment will largely be affected by this global felt background sense (which, however, is not static but keeps changing).

It seems that much of our everyday experience works in this holistic way. As Gendlin (1973b) puts it:

> What goes through is much more than what we "have" [explicity]. . . . Any moment is a myriad richness, but rarely do we take time to "have" it. . . . Going through a simple act involves an enormous number of familiarities, learnings, senses for the situation, understandings of life and people, as well as the many specifics of the given situation. All this goes into just saying "hello" in a fitting way to a not very close friend. We go through, we are all this, but we "have" only a few focal bits of it. *The feel of doing anything involves our sense of the whole situation at any moment*, despite our not focally reflecting on it as such (p. 370, my italics).

Moreover, our sense of the "whole situation at any moment" goes beyond the particular event happening now. It also includes the way in which our past functions implicitly in our present relating, our orientation toward the future, and many other dimensions as well. As Bohm (1973) says of the holographic storage of light waves: "Indeed, in principle, this structure extends over the whole universe and over the whole past, with implications for the whole future (p. 148)." He further suggests that not only particle interactions or brain functions, "but also our thoughts, feelings, urges, will and desire" have their ultimate ground in the implicate order of the larger universe (1977).

William James expressed this holographic compression in his own colorful way:

> In the pulse of inner life immediately present now in each of us is a little past, a little future, a little awareness of our own body, of each other's persons, of these sublimities we are trying to talk about, of the earth's geography and the direction of history, of truth and error, of good and bad, and *of who knows how much more?* (1967, pp. 295-96, my italics).

This "who knows how much more?" covers the many ways in which the organism processes information that we are not aware of or even have categories to understand. In this phrase, James opens the door to the domains of transpersonal psychology and who knows what kind of disciplines that may develop to illuminate the subtle and complex patterns of information processing beyond the span of normal consciousness.

Explication: Direct Reference and Unfolding

Gendlin (1964) has outlined a series of experiential steps for making the implicit explicit, for bringing the holographic blur into focus. If you ask yourself, or rather ask of your felt sense, "What is the main quality of my relation to my father?" you have created a frame or lens to focus the felt sense further. How does this work? Perhaps a word will now arise (e.g., "heavy"), or you may feel a bodily change (e.g., a flutter in the stomach, a sigh), or a certain image may appear that expresses this feel of your father. Gendlin calls this framing of the implicit *direct reference:* "a use of words to set off, separate out . . . some aspect of experience which can thereby be called 'this' or 'that' experience, or 'an' experience" (1973a, p. 293).

Applying a frame to the implicit is somewhat analogous to deblurring a blurred photograph by highlighting the major contours or spatial frequencies, so that particular shapes can emerge from the blur. In photography, this can be done through a Fourier transform, one of the mathematical formulas for the convolution and deconvolution of certain types of holograms. Thus the felt implicit, as the way the organism holistically feels patterns of relationship, is analogous to the way in which a Fourier transform encodes spatial frequencies into a hologram. Explicating the implicit is like a re-transformation or deblurring of the transform back into a recognizable form. The first step of explication, direct reference, allows a pattern to emerge from the blur.

The words we then use to describe what emerges are not "snapshots" or literal reproductions of the blur, any more than the three-dimensional projected image of an apple resembles the holographic record of the apple as it is stored on a photographic plate in the form of a complex pattern of ripples. Our descriptions of experience do not "read off" what is there, but are rather further transformations of it: "To delineate the situations involves simplifying and further organizing what is already very complexly patterned" (Gendlin, 1973a, p. 293).

Gendlin (1964) has described these explication transformations as a "focusing" process that opens up the implicit and "carries it forward," thus making concrete differences in the way we live. The first two steps in focusing blurry feelings are *direct reference* and *unfolding*. Unfolding may occur when we take whatever has emerged from direct reference and refer it back to the felt implicit. If you got a "heavy" feeling from direct reference, you might ask yourself, "What is this heaviness? What is so heavy?" and let your whole body sense respond. You may now get a chain of images or sentences, which could be still further drawn out and explicated. If you took this as far as possible, you could probably write a whole novel about your relation to your father. By continuing to explicate your implicit felt sense, each new explication serves as a focus to allow new aspects of the implicit blurry whole to emerge. Your whole novel (all 500 pages of it!) was holographically compressed in the very first blurry felt sense that you had. As Pribram (1971) points out in regard to optical holograms: "Some ten billion *bits* of information have been usefully stored holographically in a cubic centimeter" (p. 150).

Psychotherapy; Intuition

Psychotherapy, which may be seen as "a search for the few statements—about five percent—that do have . . . a directly felt effect" (Gendlin, 1973a, p. 309), is one way of transforming the implicit in ways that affect a person's life. Statements having this transforming effect are those that resonate with the implicit and allow it to unfold, either gradually or in a sudden "opening up":

> With a great physical relief and sudden dawning, the individual suddenly knows. He may sit there, nodding to himself, thinking only words such as "yes, I've got it" quite without as yet finding concepts to tell himself what it is he "has got." . . . It is a great and physically experienced tension reduction when the directly felt referent "unfolds" in this way (Gendlin, 1964, p. 118).

The unfolding itself clarifies and changes stuck patterns, hidden associations and meanings (interference patterns) that have been enfolded in the implicit, and that have exerted a compulsive effect on behavior.

Interestingly, this way of listening to the implicit and letting it unfold without imposing preconceived forms on it, which is so effective in therapy, is precisely the same process that Bohm (1973) recommends to physicists for discovering a new order amid the present chaos of data in the field:

> What then will be the new kind of description appropriate to the present context? . . . such a question cannot be answered immediately in terms of definite prescriptions as to what to do. Rather, one has to *observe the new situation very broadly and tentatively and to "feel out" what may be the relevant new features* [direct reference]. From this, there will arise a discernment of the new order, which will articulate and *unfold* in a natural way (and not as a result of efforts to make it fit well-defined and preconceived notions as to what this order would be able to achieve) (p. 146, my italics).

Bohm makes the precise distinction here so essential in psychotherapy to distinguish creative "working through" from "intellectualizing" or going around in circles.

Once the implicit has opened up—whether in therapy or in evolving a new theory in physics—it is never quite the same again. Once you have unfolded the problem in your relationship to your father, that relationship (and your life) is never quite the same. The zig-zag dialectic between transformative explication (which need not be verbal) and felt meaning changes or "carries forward" experiencing, resulting not only in therapeutic progress or personality change, but also in creative discoveries of all kinds.

From this discussion, it becomes clear that intuition is an integral part of everyday experience, rather than a special "altered state of consciousness" (cf. Weil, 1972). Let us define intuition as direct access to the implicit, which operates by scanning a holographic-type blur with a diffuse attention that does not impose preconceived notions on it—Bohm's "to observe the new situation very broadly and tentatively and to feel [it] out." Specific intuitions usually come to us as diffuse wholes, which we may have difficulty explicating at first or providing reasons for. We simply "know" something through contacting our diffuse felt sense of the situation. Much scientific and philosophical argumentation and reasoning is often a working back from a conclusion arrived at intuitively, adding the logic or proof steps afterward.

Our depth of attunement to implicate orders seems to range through a continuum from everyday intuition to profound mystical insight. Mystical experience seems to be a more total form of this holistic vision that sees through one's particular situation to the whole of the life process, the implicate order of the universe itself. For some people, working with the felt implicit in a therapeutic way is a first step in unlocking their deeper connectedness with all of life.

Perhaps the moment-to-moment intuition that globally scans the implicate order underlying thought and feeling goes so often unrecognized precisely because it does not focus on explicate forms that can be grasped or fixed in memory. William James (1890) called these seemingly "empty" moments in the stream of consciousness the "transitive tracts." They appear as pauses or split-second transitional moments during which one scans a whole felt meaning complex (see Welwood, 1976). How else do we know what to say from moment to moment, except by these split-second references to the blur of the implicate order? One of James's great contributions was to point out the essential, predominant role of the transitive moments in the stream of consciousness:

> It is, in short, the reinstatement of the vague to its proper place in our mental life which I am so anxious to press on the attention. . . . What must be admitted is that the definite images of traditional psychology [i.e., explicit forms] form but the very smallest part of our minds as they actually live (pp. 254-55).

Bohm (1973) echoes these very words in speaking of modern physics:

> We are proposing that in the formulation of the laws of physics, primary relevance is to be given to the implicate order, while the explicate order is to have a secondary kind of significance (p. 148).

The Unconscious as Implicate Order

Thus we are continually processing many kinds of interactions or interference patterns, and can only pay attention to a very few. The organismic processing that we do not attend to becomes part of an unconscious, background, holographic blur. This background blur, which has an implicit structure to it, is surely what the concept of the unconscious refers to. However, the traditional model of the unconscious in depth psychology makes it appear as though the unconscious has an explicit structure to it, as though drives, wishes, repressions or archetypes exist in explicit form, as though the unconscious were a kind of autonomous alter ego. I have discussed this question elsewhere (Welwood, 1974, 1977). Here I can only suggest that what is unconscious is the implicate order of experience, rather than a set of autonomous or explicit "contents." What is unconscious are holistic patternings, which may be explicated in many different ways and at many different levels of the organism/environment interrelationship.

Conclusions

The holographic paradigm has many features that may make it an acceptable and stimulating new scientific model or metaphor for humanistic, phenomenological and transpersonal psychologists. As Pribram (1977) has pointed out, experientially and clinically based concepts are often

> plagued by considerable vagueness, which gives rise to unresolvable conflict of opinion. The sharpening that occurs when data from other disciplines become available to support and clarify a distinction is therefore a necessary preliminary if the conceptions are to become more generally useful in scientific explanation (p. 226).

The holographic paradigm may be able to provide a cross-disciplinary language for discussing realms of human experience that have traditionally been ignored by "hard-headed" psychologists. Moreover, if the universe works on holographic types of principles where the whole is implied in every part, it makes sense that different sets of data will reveal similar kinds of patterns, and that modern physics and neurophysiology have a familiar *deja vu* quality, echoing the ancient wisdom of the mystical traditions and the modern findings of phenomenology.

However, in our enthusiasm about the power of this new scientific model, we should not lose sight of the fact that it is still only a model, a conceptual form, which obviously can never substitute for the direct knowing and experiential realization discovered through intuition and in its fullest form through radical awakening or enlightenment. It would be a mistake to believe that any new scientific paradigm could serve as a Western equivalent of spiritual wisdom, as though the intellectual method of science could provide a modern path of enlightenment. The holographic paradigm may resemble certain Eastern esoteric ideas, such as the teachings of totality, nonobstruction and mutual interpenetration set forth in the Buddhist *Avatamsaka Sutra*. However, we should not assume that a resemblance in conceptual content implies that they have an equivalent import, for their contexts are entirely different. The difference is between "ideas that help us to discover the truth for ourselves as opposed to concepts that organize what has already been discovered either by ourselves or others" (Needleman, 1975, p. 112). Jacob Needleman argues that one danger of the intriguing "strange concepts" and "new paradigms" of science is that they may maintain and intensify our fascination with the "contents of the mind"—our own thought patterns—rather than motivate us to see through our mind patterns altogether to the nameless reality beyond them. He very cogently points out how modern man takes up ideas that are associated with the disciplines of the spiritual path

> *without himself following these disciplines, thus turning the awakening force of great ideas into fuel for the engines of egoism.* . . . We see, however, that we are afraid to distrust our thoughts. And so, imperceptibly and swiftly, explanations gather together and fill the emptiness created by the reception of a great idea. What is called a "new paradigm" or a "breakthrough" is then celebrated. But it may only be a new turn of the wheel of man's bondage to the isolated intellect (p. 92, my italics).

Moreover no conceptual paradigm can ever validate the direct experiential knowing of reality that the paradigm may seem to "account for." Direct intuition, clear insight is self-validating, although we often rely on conceptual schemes in order to communicate it or persuade others of its validity. One important role that the holographic paradigm may have is to suggest to those who trust only conceptual knowledge that it is possible to know things in a different way. But it can neither provide nor validate that different way.

What moves us to accept a new paradigm, finally? Experimental data alone can never fully establish the truth of a paradigm, for the paradigm itself orders and makes sense of the data. Are we not moved to embrace a paradigm when it somehow resonates with the richness of what we already implicitly know? In this sense, is it not perhaps our intuitive sense of the implicate order of things that actually validates a new paradigm and encourages us to adopt it?

Comments on the
Holographic View of Reality

ITZHAK BENTOV

In everyday life our senses describe to us our reality. When we reduce the visible three-dimensional reality to two dimensions by means of photography, the picture of that reality is quite recognizable. Not only do we see the shapes, but we also see their colors. Hence, photography stores information about our reality in a convenient, comfortable, recognizable form. There is a one-to-one correspondence between the objects we see and the objects represented on the photograph.

In holography all this is changed. There is no one-to-one correspondence between the holographic image and reality, as perceived by the eyes. The hologram of a flower, no matter how lovely, will appear as a tangle of interfering wave fronts, because reality is presented to us in a different order.

What happens between the retina of the eye and the visual cortex in the brain is similar to this process. The eye acts as a camera, and the image which appears on the retina has a one-to-one correspondence to the object we see. However, the image gets processed in such a way that the neighboring dots on the retina end up at entirely different places when they reach the visual cortex. Thus, we have a more or less "random" pattern of dots on the visual cortex.

Pribram's work shows that these single "dots" or neurons in the cortex emit "waves," which interfere or interact with each other, thus forming a hologram of information. In other words, the order or reality of the eye is different from the order or reality of the cortex.

To generalize this, we can say that we have two kinds of order or realities: the one-to-one image, which is evident to the senses, and the holographic order. It appears that the one-to-one image order derives from or is based on the holographic one, which is more basic. The holographic reality is based on the dynamic relationsihp or interaction of wavefronts, which causes a diffusion of information throughout a structure, but at the same time, each element of the surface or volume of that structure contains all the information comprised in the whole structure. An example of this is our own body, where each cell contains the information about the whole body.

Pribram talks about waves of electrochemical reactions in the neurons of the brain. But what are the neurons made of? They are made of atoms, and atoms are composed of subatomic units, which can be viewed as either particles or waves. When viewed as waves, the atom can be described as a structure dependent on the interaction of its components, hence the interaction of electromagnetic waves.

Bohm describes two realities, the "enfolded" and the "unfolded." The "enfolded" reality or order is the holographic reality, which Bohm considers as more basic than the one-to-one reality apparent to the senses.

Pribram postulates a neural hologram, made by the interaction of waves in the cortex, which in turn is based on a hologram of much shorter wavelengths formed by the wave interactions on the subatomic level. Thus, we have a hologram within a hologram, and the interrelatedness of the two somehow gives rise to the sensory images.

It would not be unfounded to assume, therefore, that there is reality underlying these two, which would be an even more basic reality and which Bohm describes as being an "invisible flux that is not comprised of parts. It is inseparable interconnectedness."

Thus, we now have a hierarchy of realities, going from individuated separate units to "inseparable interconnectedness." In order to see how it affects us, I would suggest that we use them as analogy to our human condition. We can consider the "inseparable" reality as being the absolute, transcendent state, the unity-of-all-there-is of the Eastern concepts of reality, which is the state of infinite interconnectedness. We may add that within this Source all individuals are contained in potential form.

On the level of reality just below that of unity, interconnectedness

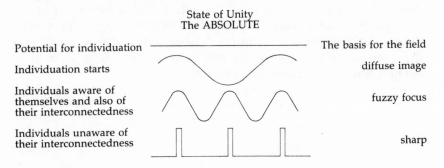

State of Unity
The ABSOLUTE

Potential for individuation — The basis for the field

Individuation starts — diffuse image

Individuals aware of themselves and also of their interconnectedness — fuzzy focus

Individuals unaware of their interconnectedness — sharp

predominates, but nuclei of individuals are evident (see diagram). On the level below that, individuals are aware of themselves, but also very aware of their interconnectedness. On the bottom level the awareness of interconnectedness is lost. Individuals consider themselves totally separate. This is the reality given to us by our normal senses. It is the level of one-to-one relationship.

It is high time for science, which lately has been going in the direction of finding out more things about less and less, and losing the sense of interconnectedness of things, to turn around and ask a few questions about how the whole system works. Pribram and Bohm are doing just that.

Cautions

WILLIAM IRWIN THOMPSON

The collaboration of the physicist David Bohm with the neurologist Karl Pribram is an exciting one. Considering that David Bohm is also working with the Indian philosopher Krishnamurti, there is even greater interest in seeing what direction this will take. The concept of the hologram and the enfolded order is an exciting metaphor that seems to cross several different fields from the physics of Bohm to the economics of Hazel Henderson. Since this vision of the relationship of the one and the many is, in some ways, a development of the theories of the prehensive unification of space in the philosophy of organism developed by Alfred North Whitehead, I think it is important to consider the idea with a balanced enthusiasm. I hope the public will not do to the metaphor of the hologram what they did to the model of the lateralization of the brain. Ornstein's ideas were overgeneralized *ad nauseum*. And this encouraged a good deal of "misplaced concreteness," in which highly complex psychologic psychic states were simply located in physiological processes. Pribram and Bohm are doing good work, but I hope we will give them the necessary space to do that work and not jump in with an overgeneralized advertising campaign.

The New Science and Holonomy

WILLIS HARMAN

In the transform mathematics of holographic theory, a pulse of energy which in the physical domain seems to occur at a particular instant in time, in the frequency domain is "timeless," "eternal." That domain is "beyond time and space." Thus the holographic theories appear to make more plausible psychic and mystical phenomena that transcend usual space-time relationships. But these theories still would interpret the primary datum, consciousness, in terms of something else ultimately quantifiable. There will be, someday, a new science, complementary to the kind we have, in which wholes are seen as wholes, and consciousness is more nearly cause than effect. These holographic theories are not yet of that new science, but rather of the old, in which the attempt is made to explain away consciousness rather than to understand it.

A Multidimensional View

WILLIAM A. TILLER

Of the many individuals who include a holographic representation of the universe in their "World Picture," Pribram[1] has labored long and well to clarify the central issues involved and has focused his attention largely on the sensory apprehension of this representation at the physical level of consciousness. The present author, who has been attempting to develop a model of reality that synthesizes both current physical understanding of the universe and understanding arising from psychoenergetic experiments in the parapsychological, religious, health, etc. areas, has opted for a multidimensional representation of consciousness and possible structures of the universe for its manifestation. Without such an extension beyond the purely physical perception frame, the scope of any "new paradigm" will be severely limited.

To illustrate what is meant by this, consider the entrance of Einstein's ideas on Relativity into the domain of classical physics. The theoretical work of Einstein showed that time and the three dimensions of space are intimately connected, such that they form a space-time manifold in our experiential frame of reference. He showed that, in certain domains of our experimental variables such as very high velocities, very large energy densities and very large mass densities, the observable behavior of nature meaningfully departs from expectations based upon a linear extrapolation of our common experience; i.e., clocks slow down, measuring sticks shorten, everything becomes heavier, etc. Experiments of the last two decades have confirmed that these very nonlinear and totally unexpected phenomena do, in fact, occur.

Today, a number of investigators are considering the consequences of the space-time-X, space-time-X-Y and space-time-X-Y-Z type perception frames where the variables X, Y, and Z are other significant qualities of the human perception mechanism on a parallel footing with space and time. It is postulated that, as a consequence of self-integration of various types, individuals may manifest and manipulate the X-quality to such a degree that the four-dimensional space-time frame is coupled to a fifth-dimensional space-time-X manifold—so that, again, essentially nonlinear effects relative to space-time expectations appear. It may seem as if our scientific laws are being contravened by many of the psychoenergetic phenomena; however, this is not so. Rather, it is that these phenomena have their origins in a higher dimensional frame of perception of the universe and are not fully constrained by a four-dimensional space-time description. In the foregoing, we may wish to replace X by "coherence of intention."

We may now properly ask how the universe might be structured to allow an individual's coherence of intention to affect the world of his/her physical perception. In this author's model,[2,3] the following postulates are made:

(1) Space is imbedded in the domain of Spirit.
(2) This is a six-dimensional Euclidean space rather than just the three-dimensional Euclidean space that one perceives at the purely physical level of consciousness.
(3) Space is a hexagonal close-packed lattice of active nodal points rather than a continuum.
(4) The lattice consists of three sub-lattices, each of which is a reciprocal lattice to the other. The mind sub-lattice is the finest of the three (grid size $\sim 10^{-25}$ cm). Next comes the negative space-time[4] sub-lattice (grid size $\sim 10^{-15}$ cm), and the positive space-time[4] sub-lattice is the coarsest of the three (grid size $\sim 10^{-5}$ cm).
(5) All substance arises from the nodal points as waves traveling in this lattice.

One of the conclusions of such a model is that, since these are reciprocal lattices of each other, when waves traveling in the mind sub-lattice are diffracted at that level, the constructive interference beams pass through the nodal points of the negative space-time and positive space-time sub-lattices generating correlative patterns at those levels. Thus, there is a connectivity and integration of patterns between these three levels. In addition, this information has a direct space pattern and an inverse or frequency space pattern, with the mind domain being the primary frequency domain.[3]

To illustrate the holographic features of the model, think of a coherent energy beam coming from the Divine level of the Self. It impinges upon the frequency patterns of substance that have been built at the Mind level of the universe and projects them onto a screen, really onto two screens, the negative space-time frame grid points and the positive space-time frame grid points. Thus, the information about what we are collectively doing in the universe at the Mind level is stored on these two grids in the form of holograms. Substance interacts with these grid points via a special coupling agent[3,4]; i.e., physical substance interacts with the positive space-time grid and conforms to the potentials written there while etheric substance interacts with the negative space-time grid and conforms to the potentials written there. This model proposes that when we make an action at the physical level, we are doing so at this level because our substance is trying to conform with the changing pattern stored on the positive and negative space-time grids.

Because things happen so much faster in the negative space/time frame, we conform at that level (the etheric level of substance) before we conform at the physical level. The physical is like a shadow, like puppets dancing on their strings. Generally, we only use our physical eyesight to observe this physical milieu. However, some appear to have developed the capability of perceiving things at the etheric level of substance or of perceiving the patterns directly from the grids. The more evolved they become, the more developed is this third-eye kind of sensing leading to what has been called precognitive awareness.

To see how the coherence of an individual's intention affects the universe via this model, consider first how an individual responds to events entering his/her consciousness in daily life. The response is in the form of thoughts, attitudes and actions. The thoughts and attitudes are waves that enter the mind sub-lattice and superpose with those patterns already there. If the individual's intensity and coherence is high, the degree of change will be high. This change at the mind level is thus instantly transferred to the positive and negative space-time grid points which produce eventual changes at the substance level. These latter changes prepare a new set of events which conform more closely to the attitudes and thoughts that served as the initial generator. Once again response is made to the new events via thoughts, attitudes and actions, and so the cycle is iterated. In this way, we create our own future and experience that creation whether or not we are consciously aware of doing so. In a completely similar fashion, if we have a high coherence of intention, the energy density of our mental visualizations creates such a perturbation in the mind sub-lattice that large potential changes occur at the negative and positive space-time grids and changes quickly occur at the substance level of our perception in accordance with our visualization. Unfortunately, most of us are not sufficiently coherent to do this very well at the present stage of evolution. This is how changes are produced in our "World of Appearances and Form."

This model[2-4] has many interesting consequences that, because of space limitations, cannot be dealt with here. It allows one to rationalize virtually all the ESP phenomena; i.e., precognition, remote viewing, materialization/dematerialization, etc. It allows one to understand how multiple, simultaneous existences could be possible. It allows one to understand a scale of consciousness that extends from that of rocks and minerals to that of bacteria, plants, animals and humans. From it, one can begin to understand what was meant by the statement made a long time ago that "the brain is in the mind but not all of the mind is in the brain." The present modeling proposes that the mind is not spatially limited because the information is represented in the frequency domain of one grid cell ($\sim 10^{-75}$ cc) and periodicity reproduces it everywhere. On the other hand, the brain, at the physical level, is a spatially localized, individualized thing that overlaps only some of the grid points of the mind sub-lattice.

The Holographic Model,
Holistic Paradigm,
Information Theory and Consciousness

JOHN R. BATTISTA, M.D.

We are experiencing a growing recognition of the limitations of the analytic model based on the digital computer. Quantum physics has led us to recognize the interconnectedness of all events, and psychology has become increasingly aware of the inability of the analytic model to account for the intuitive and transpersonal dimensions of consciousness.

The work of Karl Pribram (1971, 1975, 1976) and David Bohm (1971, 1973) has generated a rapidly growing interest in the application of holographic concepts to our understanding of consciousness and the universe. Thus a new holographic model is being developed which emphasizes the interdependent, parallel and simultaneous processing of events.

We need to avoid making the same mistake with the holographic model that we did with the analytic model—to try and explain everything with it. That kind of approach would make little sense because many phenomena (like telephone communication) seem best conceptualized analytically while other phenomena (like transpersonal states of consciousness) seem best understood holographically.

Pribram (1975) uses the holographic and analytic models in this complementary sense. Basically, he believes that the brain functions both as an analytic (digital) and holographic (analog) computer. He accepts that the brain functions analytically in the sense that data are processed sequentially according to a set of specific programs, the output of which is fedback onto input for the purpose of comparison. For example, Pribram (1975) has hypothesized that the inferior temporal cortex effects vision by programming the functions of the primary visual projection system. This allows him to explain data showing that lesions to the inferior temporal cortex will greatly impair the ability to make visual discriminations. Similarly, such a model could explain motivated perception, as when a hemotologist who is scanning a bone marrow for cancer cells "sees" only the cancerous cells. Alternately, Pribram argues that the brain is holographic in that data are processed as a whole as the result of interactions occuring in and between synaptic clefts. This allows him to explain the image-like nature of perception and the ability to maintain sensory capacities despite massive insults to the sensory system. Thus, it is Pribram's use of both the holographic and analytic models that has allowed him to develop a more encompassing and integrating theory of the brain than those theorists who have exclusively employed an analytic model.

However, if the analytic and holographic models are complimentary rather than competitive, this implies that there may be a more encompassing theoretical structure that is capable of integrating both of these models. My attempt to discover this structure led me to examine the basic assumptions which underlie both the analytic and holographic models. This examination revealed that both the analytic and holographic models are based on a set of holistic assumptions and led me to conclude that information theory is a theoretical structure capable of integrating both of them.

All models and theories are based on assumptions. I use the term paradigm to refer to the set of these underlying and often unrecognized assumptions. Paradigms can be differentiated by the way in which they answer three basic questions of the philosophy of science:

1) What is? or what is the nature of reality?
2) How do we know what is? or what constitutes knowledge?
3) What accounts for change and stability in what is?

The answer to the first question constitutes the paradigm's ontology; to the second its epistemology; to the third its dynamics or means of explanation. Table 1 provides a comparison of the three main paradigms of Western thought as I view them: vitalistic, mechanistic and holistic. Our discussion will be limited to a consideration of the holistic paradigm but the interested reader is referred to a previous article (Battista, 1977) for a fuller discussion of the mechanistic and vitalistic paradigms.

Table 1

Vitalistic, Mechanistic and Holistic Paradigms

Parameters	Vitalism	Mechanism	Holism
Ontology	Dualistic	Dualistic	Monistic
Epistemology	Subjective	Objective	Interactive
Methodology	Phenomenological	Empirical	Analogical
Causality	Teleological	Deterministic	Probabilistic
Analysis	Metaphysical	Reductivistic	Structural
Dynamics	Nullentropic	Entropic	Negentropic

According to the holistic paradigm the entire universe is interconnected and hierarchically organized. Matter and energy, living and nonliving, mind, body and spirit all refer to different levels of the same, unified system. We know about this universal system because of our interaction with it. Uncertainty is an inherent part of our relationship to the system because the system is a process and we are a part of the process we are attempting to know. To the extent we can reduce this uncertainty we generate information about the world process. Knowledge thus exists in relationship rather than in an "objective" world or in "subjective" experience. The world is not classically determined in a simple, linear billiard ball manner; rather, each level of the universal system operates on every other. Events are thus partially determined from above (more complex and encompassing levels) and from below (less complex and encompassing levels) as well as from the same level of complexity. Thus, we can never know the absolute cause of anything, or whether an event is totally determined.

In a general way, these assumptions have received a wide acceptance. In fact, it seems fairly clear that we are now in the process of a paradigmatic shift in which all fields are being revisioned in light of these assumptions (Bateson, 1972; Harman, 1974; Lifton, 1975).

However, it may not be so clear why I believe that both the holographic and analytic models are holistic. I imagine some people may think that holographic model and holistic paradigm are synonymous, and that the analytic model is really an example of the now outdated mechanistic paradigm from which we need to free ourselves.

It seems to me that the key to grasping the holistic and complementary nature of the holographic and analytic models lies in an understanding of the concept of *information*. Although information is commonly thought of an an entity or thing carried by a signal or input, this mechanistic interpretation is actually false. In information theory, "information" is defined in terms of a *relationship* between an input and a receiving device. From this perspective, it is impossible to talk about information independent of some receiver. A book contains no information for someone who can't read. It is this relational aspect of information that makes it a holistic rather than mechanistic concept. An input is said to have carried a certain amount of information when it reduced the uncertainty associated with the receiving or measuring device. The selective value of the input refers to the *meaning* of the information, while the *amount* of information is a measure of the degree of uncertainty reduction that results from the input itself (MacKay, 1972).

For example, if a man is conversing with a woman and wishes to know if she is married, notices a diamond ring on the 4th finger of her left hand, and concludes that she is married, the *meaning* of the ring—its "selective value"—to the man is that she is married. The *amount* of information carried by that perception depends on the degree of uncertainty that the man initially had about whether the woman was married. The uncertainty of a finite set (H) is represented mathematically as:

$$-\sum_{R=1}^{n} p_R \lg p_R$$

(Khinchin, 1957). In this case there are two possible alternatives (p_R's)—married or unmarried, and the probability of whether the man believes the woman to be married will determine the amount of information carried by its perceptions of the ring. Thus the perception of the ring will carry more information if the man thought the probability the woman was married was 50% than if he was already 90% sure she was married. In the first case, he is largely uncertain as to the woman's marital status, and thus the perception of the ring greatly reduced his uncertainty—this is why "information" and "reduction of uncertainty" are synonymous. In the second case, he is not in a state of very much "uncertainty," so the ring carried much less information for him.

What does this concept of information have to do with the analytic and holographic models? The essential point is that both the analytic and holographic models refer to processes for generating information—and information itself is a *holistic* concept, as I earlier explained. In the analytic model information results from the selection of a particular outcome from a set of possibilities. In the holographic model information results from an analog mechanism that allows two states to interact with each other. Thus, although the analytic and holographic models refer to distinct means of generating information, they both rest on holistic assumptions and can be considered as complimentary holistic models. Furthermore, because the analytic and holographic models both refer to the generation of information, information theory is revealed to be an underlying structure that can integrate both the analytic and holographic models. It is interesting to note in this regard that Gabor, the inventor of the hologram, was also one of the three independent originators of the concept of information (MacKay, 1972).

This conclusion about the relationship between information theory and the holographic and analytic models is important because if we accept Pribram's view that the brain functions both holographically and analytically, it implies that a general theory of consciousness needs to be based on holistic assumptions and needs to utilize information theory. I have attempted to develop such a theory (Battista, 1978), using three basic concepts.

1) Consciousness is information.
2) The different forms of consciousness refer to different hierarchical levels of information.
3) The intensity of consciousness at any level is a function of the amount of information at that level.

This theory is important because it clarifies the relationship between consciousness and brain states, explains the conditions under which consciousness occurs, and makes predictions about consciousness in nonhumans and the universe as a whole. The only point that I wish to emphasize here is that this information theory of consciousness can integrate the holographic and analytic models of specific forms of conscious experience into a general theory of consciousness by providing a hierarchial structure which can relate the different forms of consciousness to each other.

We have learned from the pioneering work of Tart (1972) that the problem of consciousness is not a unitary one, but must encompass each specific state of consciousness. Although there is no standard nomenclature of states of consciousness any complete theory of consciousness must address a wide variety of states of consciousness, including sensation, perception, emotion, cognition, intuition, self-awareness and unition (transpersonal consciousness).

I have little doubt that we will find both the holographic and analytic models useful in understanding these states. For example, the sensory system appears to be analytic in character in that each sensory neuron responds to a particular frequency pattern in the environment and translates that pattern into a sequential rate of neuronal discharges. Alternately, perception, as mentioned previously, may involve both holographic and analytic processes. The situation with emotions remains unclear, but the well-known work of Schacter and Singer (1962) showing that a particular state of arousal is compatible with a number of different emotions depending on the environmental circumstances under which it occurs suggests that some analytic mechanism is involved. Work on cognition and intuition is commonly conceptualized in terms of two different information processing structures, one found predominantly in the dominant hemisphere, the other in the nondominant hemisphere. The dominant hemisphere structure processes information in an analytic (linear, sequential) manner and is thought to be involved in cognition. The nondominant hemisphere may process information in a holographic (holistic, transformational) manner and is thought to be involved in intuition and dreaming.

Anderson (1977) and Bentov (1977) have both made excellent cases for the role of a holographic mechanism in transpersonal states. Basically, they contend that all of the potential information about the universe is holographically encoded in the spectrum of frequency patterns that constantly bombard us. Through meditation one quiets the brain so that it can become sympathetically in tune with (entrained to) this universal frequency pattern. When this occurs, the encoded information about the universe becomes holographically decoded, and the individual experiences a state of unitive consciousness with the entire universe. I find this model appealing for three reasons. First, the common experience of meditators having a deeper meditation with a group of experienced meditators is compatible with this model because such a group could set up a more powerful localized field with which to become entrained. Second, the EEG findings of a number of investigators (Banquet, 1973; Gellhorn & Kiely, 1972; Domash, 1976) showing the synchronization of the entire cerebral cortex during such states lends support to the idea of a holographic mechanism involving the entire brain. Third, such a model could explain the experience of knowing everything at once in such unitive states.

The value of an information theory approach is that it can integrate each of these specific models of consciousness into an integrated general theory of consciousness. This is possible because the holographic and analytic mechanisms can be understood as devices for generating information and the different states of conscious experience can be related to each other in terms of hierarchial levels of information. Table 2 provides an outline of the relationship between specific states of consciousness and levels of information. This relationship is more fully discussed in a previous paper (Battista, 1978).

Table 2

Information and Consciousness

State of Consciousness	Level of Information
Sensation	Information 1
Perception	Information 2, i.e., information about information 1 (the meaning of sensation).
Emotion	Information 3, i.e., information about information 2 (the meaning of perception).
Awareness	
a. Cognition	Information 4a, information about information levels 2, 3, 5, 6, 7 (reflective knowledge of the other forms of awareness).
b. Intuition	Information 4b, information about information levels 2, 3, 5, 6, (nonreflective knowledge of the other forms of awareness).
Self-awareness	Information 5, information about information 4 and 6 (knowing the nature of one's own awareness).
Unition	Information 6, information about information 5 and 7 (experience of the process of awareness itself).
Absolute	Information 7, an integrated awareness of all the levels of awareness (pure awareness).

It is now possible to review the essential points in this paper from a somewhat different perspective. Basically a distinction has been made between scientific models, paradigms and theories. A scientific model is an analogy which attempts to explain one thing in terms of another. Theories rely on a set of abstract constructs which are used to represent and explain phenomena by the development of a set of verifiable hypotheses about them. Paradigms refer to the set of implicit basic assumptions which underlie models or theories.

There has been increasing dissatisfaction in the twentieth century with the set of mechanistic assumptions which underlie our traditional scientific theories such as Newtonian physics. The first holistic model to be developed (the analytic model) was based on the digital computer and emphasized the independent, linear, sequential processing of information. This holistic model seems to have arisen first because it bears some resemblance to the old mechanistic energy-drive models utilized in traditional physics. However, this model is actually holistic in that it utilizes concepts of information, uncertainty, organization, probability and entropy rather than energy, drive, force, mass and determination. As this analytic model became more and more widely applied, its limited applicability became more and more apparent. In order to explain those phenomena not well explained by the analytic model, e.g., the quantum interconnectedness of the universe, the panoramic nature of perception, the existence of transpersonal states of awareness, a new holistic model is emerging. This new model, the holographic, stresses the interdependent, parallel and simultaneous processing of information.

Confusion has developed because it has been unclear that both the analytic and holographic models are holistic. Thus, there has been the tendency to see the holographic and analytic models as competitive rather than complementary.

However, both the analytic and holographic models are part of the emerging development of a general holistic theory based on information theory. Therefore, the overall value of the holographic model lies in its ability to complement the analytic model and reveal to us a new means by which information can be generated. This model will have wide applicability and certainly may have great importance in helping us to explain the universe as a whole, perception, intuition, memory, unition, etc. However, the limitation of the holographic model lies in the fact that it is a model rather than a theory. The theory of holograms lies in information theory and information theory is needed to explain and predict *what* is occurring, much as the holographic and analytic models are needed to explain *how* something is occurring.

Formal holistic theories need to be constructed using information-system concepts. As this occurs, the holographic and analytic models can hopefully be integrated into a richer and more encompassing understanding than could be obtained from the use of either one alone.

Experiencing Holography

LEONARD J. DUHL, M.D.

I listened to Karl Pribram in a variety of ways. I saw him dance like an elf playing with ideas, concepts and thoughts by presenting images before hungry receptive listeners. I heard, too, the science—

only some of which I could follow—and it, too, flowed through me as movement and energy. Like an artist he resonated with the audience.

As he talked I listened to the words, felt his presence as he drew images around me. I could react to these, not by responding in a dialogue, but by setting off my own visions that I could sculpt into multiple dimensions. In some ways this was nothing new, for many experiences and ideas have led me toward similar paths. In others, it was a model of teaching and learning.

My prime concern has been for change, both of individuals and society. I have so often grappled with the simple issue that the reality, the map of the world, and the organizing concepts were apparently so unchangeable and the only changes possible were within strict accepted rules. Do others see as I do? The pieces were there and yet they seemed to fall together so differently. Slowly, it became clear that by allowing oneself the space of being able to see differently, that what was fixed, unchanging and given began to crumble and new patterns emerged. There was a new reality: a creative process.[1]

The questions then became whether to change realities or to follow Pribram; and how to program oneself to tap into the realities that already exist, which would open the doors toward a way to mediate with the accepted reality, and thus to change. One often gets programmed via external or internal crises, for without them we rarely give up the comforts of the known. The beginning of re-learning is a felt crisis.

If re-programming is *not* inventing a new reality but leading one to see realities that exist but are unseen, the issue is in the process of self-change; not external cure; not alternative ways of doing; not authoritarian direction alone but perhaps an authoritative direction of a developmental learning process which teaches one how to re-perceive. Change then becomes re-creation,[2] and re-creation the process by which we learn to see alternative realities.

On one hand, I am a therapist; on the other, a social planner. But most of all I feel myself to be a teacher-guide who aids in openness, offers alternative images, and authoritatively states that they could exist. There are processes available to get there, but no one offers the solutions or cures to any one or any situation. The answer then is to assist one "to remember," to search within, and to assist and permit others to do the same.

Where I become stymied is in realizing that change of this kind is often a luxury, for within current realities basic necessities often have to be met first. Then the change to which one aspires is the achievement of that grounding (nutrition of all kinds, and growth) which gives one enough sense of self-esteem to go on and trust a process of reality change. Certainly this is not always true, for jumps in growth can be made which re-create alternative realities; but for most of the world, long-accepted paths are still followed.

Pribram offers us a way of knowing. Aha! we can say. When I say, "The Emperor has no clothes," I am right, as is the one who says, "They are new and beautiful." The concept of right/wrong can disappear. It becomes right for what end? In what hologram there then are "right" answers for us all and, indeed, answers that can connect us into a universal group, since on one level of that hologram is all of existence. Science now offers "proof" for the Western mind that other realities do exist and that within us is the bridge between all these realities. There can be respect then for difference and uniqueness ("Let a thousand flowers bloom" can be a social policy) which is held together by a socio-spiritual fabric.

I circle back in my own dance to social change where the real wisdom is not legislation, programs, money or the administrative policy details in which we are so caught. Rather, there is a societal learning[3] whereby we each (individually and, most important, collectively) can know new perceptions which do not have to be created, but drawn forth through different kinds of planning, political and governance processes.

The whole nature of social change becomes transformed. The images, perceptions and alternative realities (images) that we can learn to "see," reprogram us. Through a form of "bottoms-up" planning process, we change the institutions, structures and laws. Leadership[4] for change becomes a community-wide social and individual learning, healing and holy task, for in it is the responsibility of re-awakening in us all the ultimate potential of the seeds which we are. It is holy because it is a process of mediating between all parts of the hologram and because so much, despite our new insights, remains unknown and can be felt only with a primitive child-like awe of an unknown wisdom.

Symbolically, we climb the magic mountain to bring a nourishment of new light to the seed. Rather than becoming an unwanted weed, it is created into a beautiful flower.

Thank you, Karl Pribram.

NOTES AND REFERENCES

Holonomy and Bootstrap

1. The term "holonomic" was introduced by George Leonard to refer to entities "in the nature of a hologram"; see G. Leonard, *The Silent Pulse*, Dutton, New York, 1978.
2. For a detailed discussion of the bootstrap, including references to Chew's original papers, see F. Capra, *The Tao of Physics*, Shambhala, Berkeley, 1975; chapter 18.
3. For a detailed review, see F. Capra, "Quark Physics Without Quarks: A Review of Recent Developments in S-matrix Theory," Lawrence Berkeley Laboratory report LBL-7596, May 1978; submitted to American Journal of Physics.

Uncertainty Principle Factors in Holographic Models of Neurophysiology

Bohr, N. *Atomic Physics and Human Knowledge*. New York: John Wiley and Sons, 1958.

Capra, F. *The Tao of Physics*. Berkeley, California: Shambhala, 1975.

Eccles, J.C. *Facing Reality*. New York: Springer Verlag, 1970.

Eddington, A.S. *New Pathways in Science*. Cambridge, England: Cambridge University Press, 1935.

Heisenberg. W. *Physics and Beyond*. New York: Harper & Row, 1971.

Pelletier, K.R. *Mind as Healer, Mind as Slayer: A Holistic Approach to Preventing Stress Disorders*. New York: Delacorte and Delta, 1977.

Pelletier, K.R. *Toward a Science of Consciousness*. New York: Delta, 1978.

Young, A.M. *The Reflexive Universe*. New York: Delacorte, 1976.

The Holographic Paradigm and the Structure of Experience

Bohm, D. "Quantum Theory as an Indication of a New Order in Physics. Part B. Implicate and Explicate Order in Physical Law." *Foundations of Physics*, 1973, 3, 2, 139–68.

Bohm, D. "Interview." *Brain/Mind Bulletin*, 1977, 2, 21.

Gendlin, E.T. *Experiencing and the Creation of Meaning*. New York: The Free Press, 1962.

Gendlin, E.T. "A Theory of Personality Change." In P. Worchel & D. Bryne (Eds), *Personality Change*. New York: Wiley, 1964.

Gendlin, E.T. "Experiential Phenomenology." In M. Natanson (Ed.), *Phenomenology and the Social Sciences*. Evanston: Northwestern University Press. 1973a.

Gendlin, E.T. "A Phenomenology of Emotions: Anger." In D. Carr & E. Casey (Eds), *Explorations in Phenomenology*. The Hague: Martinus Nijhoff, 1973b.

James, W. *Principles of Psychology*. New York: Henry Holt, 1890.

James, W. *The Writings of.* . . . Edited by J. McDermott, New York: Random House, 1967.

Needleman, J. *A Sense of the Cosmos*. New York: Anchor, 1975.

Pribram, K. *Languages of the Brain.* Englewood Cliffs, N.J.: Prentice-Hall, 1971.

Pribram, K. "Observations on the Organization of Studies of Mind, Brain, and Behavior" In N. Zinbert (Ed.), *Alternate States of Consciousness.* New York: The Free Press, 1977.

Weil, A. *The Natural Mind.* Boston: Houghton Mifflin, 1972.

Welwood, J. "A Theoretical Reinterpretation of the Unconscious from a Humanistic and Phenomenological Perspective." Unpublished doctoral dissertation, University of Chicago, 1964.

Welwood, J. "Exploring Mind: Form, Emptiness, and Beyond." *J. Transpersonal Psychol.,* 1976, 8, 89–99.

Welwood, J. "Meditation and the Unconscious: A New Perspective." *J. Transpersonal Psychol.,* 1977, 9, 1–26.

A Multidimensional View

1. K. H. Pribram, *Languages of the Brain.* Prentice-Hall, Inc., New Jersey, 1971.
2. W. A. Tiller, "Future Medical Therapeutics Based Upon Controlled Energy Fields," *Phoenix,* 1, 5 1977.
3. W. A. Tiller, "A Lattice Model of Space and Its Relationship to Multidimensional Physics," *Proceedings of the A.R.E. Medical Symposium,* Phoenix, Arizona, January 1977.
4. W. A. Tiller, "The Positive and Negative Space-Time Frames as Conjugate Systems," in *Future Science,* eds. S. Krippner and J. White. Doubleday-Anchor, 1976.

The Holographic Model, Holistic Paradigm, Information Theory and Consciousness

Aurobindo (Sri). *The Life Divine,* New York: Dutton, 1949.

Anderson, R. "A Holographic Model of Transpersonal Consciousness," *Journal of Transpersonal Psychology,* 1977, 9, 119–128.

Banquet, J. "Spectral Analysis of the EEG in Meditation," *Electroence-phalography and Clinical Neurophysiology,* 1973, 35, 143–151.

Bateson, G. *Steps to an Ecology of Mind.* New York: Ballantine Books, 1972.

Battista, J. "The Holistic Paradigm and General System Theory." *General Systems,* XXII, 1977, 65–71.

Battista, J. "The Science of Consciousness." In K. Pope & J. Singer (Eds.), *The Stream of Consciousness: Psychological Investigations into the Flow of Private Experience.* New York: Plenum Press, 1978.

Bentov, I. *Stalking the Wild Pendulum: On the Mechanics of Consciousness.* New York: E.P. Dutton, 1977.

Bohm, D. "Quantum Theory as an Indication of a New Order in Physics. Part A. The development of new orders as shown through the history of physics," *Foundations of Physics,* 1, 1971, 359–381.

Bohm, D. "Quantum Theory as an Indication of a New Order in Physics. Part B. Implicate and explicate order in physical law," *Foundations of Physics,* 3, 1973, 139–168.

Domash, L. "The Transcendental Meditation Technique and Quantum Physics," In D. Orme-Johnson (Ed.), *Scientific Research on Transcendental Meditation,* Vol. 1. Weggis, Switzerland: Maharishi European University Press, 1976.

Gellhorn, E., and Kiely. W. "Mystical States of Consciousness: Neuropsychological and Clinical Aspects," *Journal of Nervous and Mental Disease*, 1972, 154, 399–405.

Harman, W. "The New Copernican Revolution." In C. Muses & A. Young (Eds.), *Consciousness and Reality*, New York: Discus, 1974.

Heidegger, M. *Being and Time*. New York: Harper & Row, 1962 (1927).

Kant, I. *Critique of Pure Reason*. New York: Doubleday, 1966 (1781).

Khinchin, A. *Mathematical Foundations of Information Theory*. New York: Dover, 1957.

Lifton, R. "From Analysis to Form: Towards a Shift in Psychological Paradigm," *Salmagundi*, 28, 1975, 43–78.

MacKay, D. *Information, Mechanism and Meaning*. Cambridge, Mass: M.I.T. Press, 1972.

Piaget, V. *The Construction of Reality in the Child*. New York: Basic Books, 1954.

Pribram, K. *Languages of the Brain*. Englewood Cliffs: Prentice Hall. 1971.

Pribram, K. "Toward a Holonomic Theory of Perception." In S. Ertel (Ed.), *Gestalttheorie in der modernen psychologie*. Darmstadt: Steinkopff, 1975.

Pribram, K. "Problems Concerning the Structure of Consciousness." In G. Globus (Ed.), *Consciousness and the Brain*. New York: Plenum Press, 1976.

Rahula, W. *What the Buddha Taught*. New York: Grove Press, 1959.

Roberts, T. "Beyond Self-actualization," *ReVision*, 1, 1978, 42–46.

Schacter, S., and Singer, J. "Cognitive, Social and Physiological Determinants of Emotional State." *Psychological Review*, 69, 1962, 379–399.

Sperry, R. "A Modified Concept of Consciousness," *Psychological Review*, 76, 1969, 532–536.

Sperry, R. "Mental Phenomena as Causal Determinants in Brain Function." In G. Globus (Ed.), *Brain and Conscious Experience*. New York: Plenum Press. 1976.

Taimni, I.K. *The Science of Yoga*. Wheaton, Illinois: Theosophical Publishing House, 1961.

Tart, C. "States of Consciousness and State-Specific Science," *Science*, 1976, 1972, 1203–1210.

Experiencing Holography

1. Vargiu, James. Creativity. *Synthesis*, 3–4, pp. 17–53, 1978.
   Koestler, Arthur, *The Act of Creation*. New York: Macmillan Publishing Co., 1964.
2. Duhl, Leonard J. "The Process of Re-creation: The Health of the 'I' and the 'Us'," *Ethics in Science and Medicine*, Vol. 3, pp. 33–63. Pergamon Press, 1976.
3. Michael, Donald L. *On Learning to Plan and Planning to Learn: The Social Psychology of Changing toward Future-Responsive Societal Learning*. San Francisco: Jossey-Bass, 1973.
4. Duhl, Leonard J. "The Promotion and Maintenance of Health: Myth and Reality," Prepared for presentation at the Conference, "Health Promotion Through Designed Environment," held at Ottawa, Canada, October 5–7, 1976.

CONTRIBUTORS

JOHN R. BATTISTA, M.D., *teaches in the department of Psychiatry at the University of California, Davis.*

ITZHAK "BEN" BENTOV *is a biomedical inventor, a meditator, and author of* Stalking the Wild Pendulum: On the Mechanics of Consciousness.

LEONARD J. DUHL, M.D., *is a psychiatrist, clinician and a health planner deeply involved in holistic health.*

KEN DYCHTWALD, PH. D., *psychologist, author of* Bodymind, Revisioning Human Potential: Glimpses into the 21st Century *and numerous articles on issues of health, growth and human transformation, is Codirector of the SAGE Project, Founding President of the National Association for Humanistic Gerontology, and serves as a consultant and adjunct instructor in psychology and health related sciences at several universities.*

WILLIS HARMAN, *an advisor to* ReVision, *is the associate-director of the Center for the Study of Social Policy at the Stanford Research Institute. He is the author of* An Incomplete Guide to the Future.

SAM KEEN, *contributing editor to* Psychology Today, *is an author, poet, lecturer and pioneer in consciousness research.*

STANLEY KRIPPNER, *an advisor to* ReVision, *teaches at the Humanistic Psychology Institute. He is one of the foremost authorities and researchers in the field of parapsychology and author of numerous articles and books on the subject.*

KENNETH R. PELLETIER, PH.D., *is an Assistant Clinical Professor in the Department of Psychiatry, University of California School of Medicine, San Francisco, and Director of the Psychosomatic Medicine Clinic, Berkeley, California. He is co-author of* Consciousness: East and West *(New York: Harper & Row, 1976), author of* Mind as Healer, Mind as Slayer: A Holistic Approach to Preventing Stress Disorders *(New York: Delacorte and Delta, 1977), and* Toward a Science of Consciousness *(New York: Delta, 1978).*

BOB SAMPLES *is author of* The Metaphoric Mind.

JOHN SHIMOTSU *is in tenth grade.*

WILLIAM IRWIN THOMPSON *is the founder and director of Lindisfarne, an educational community. He is a cultural historian and author of* At the Edge of History. Passages About Earth, Evil and World Order *and* Darkness and Scattered Light.

WILLIAM TILLER *teaches in the Department of Materials Science at Stanford University and is an explorer of the physics of consciousness.*

JOHN WELWOOD, PH.D., *is an associate editor of* ReVision *and an editor for* The Journal of Transpersonal Psychology.

7

PHYSICS, MYSTICISM, AND THE NEW HOLOGRAPHIC PARADIGM

A Critical Appraisal

by

Ken Wilber

We are currently undergoing a paradigm shift in science—perhaps the greatest shift of its kind to date. It is for the first time that we have stumbled upon a comprehensive model for mystical experiences, which has the additional advantage of deriving from the forefront of contemporary physics.

—Lawrence Beynam (1978)

IN ORDER TO UNDERSTAND how the new scientific paradigm fits into the overall scheme of things, it is necessary to have an overall scheme of things to begin with. The perennial philosophy has always offered such a scheme, and, for purposes of convenience, it is one I will use here.

In what follows, I will summarize the *philosophia perennis*—leaving, however, enough details to work with—and then apply this philosophy to an elucidation and critique of both the "holographic paradigm" and the "new physics," touching briefly on each of the key points involved.

The most striking feature of the perennial philosophy/psychology is that it presents being and consciousness as a hierarchy of dimensional-levels, moving from the lowest, densest and most fragmentary realms to the highest, subtlest and most unitary ones. In Hinduism, for example, the lowest level is called the *annamayakosa*,

which means the level made of food—that is, the physical body and
the material cosmos. The next level is *pranamayakosa*—the sheath
made of biological functions, life-breath, emotions, bioenergy and so
on. Both of these levels, in Mahayana Buddhism, are referred to as
the five *vijnanas*—the realm of the five senses and their physical
objects.

The next highest level, according to Hinduism, is the *manomayakosa*,
"the sheath made of mind." In Buddhism, this is called the *mano-
vijnana*—the mind that stays (myopically) close to the five senses.
This is approximately the level we in the West would call intellect,
mind, mental-ego, secondary process, operational thinking, etc.

Beyond mind, according to Hinduism, is the *vijnanamayakosa* (what
Buddhists call *manas*). This is a very high form of mind, so high, in
fact, that it is better to refer to it by a different name—the most
common being "the subtle realm." The subtle is said to include
archetypal processes, high-order insights and visions, ecstatic intuition, an extraordinary clarity of awareness, an open ground consciousness that reaches far beyond the ordinary ego, mind and
body.

Beyond the subtle lies the causal realm (Hinduism: *anandamayakosa*;
Buddhism: tainted *alayavijnana*). This is a realm of perfect transcendence, so perfect that it is said to reach beyond the conception,
experience and imagination of any ordinary individual. It is a realm
of formless Radiance, of radical insight into all of manifestation,
blissful release into infinity, the breaking of all boundaries, high or
low, and of absolutely panoramic or perfectly mirrorlike wisdom
and awareness.

Passing through the causal realm, consciousness reawakens to its
absolute abode. This is Consciousness as Such, and not only is it the
infinite limit of the spectrum of being, it is the nature, source and
suchness of each level of the spectrum. It is radically all-pervading,
one without a second. At this point—but not before—all levels are
seen to be perfect and equal manifestations of this ultimate Mystery.
There are then no levels, no dimensions, no higher, no lower,
no sacred, no profane, so matter-of-factly so that Zen describes it
thus:

As the wind sways the willows
Velvet beads move in the air.
As the rain falls on the pear blossoms
White butterflies lilt in the sky.

The above summary would give us approximately six major levels—physical, biological, mental, subtle, causal and ultimate (listed below as Table 1). Now many traditions greatly subdivide and extend this model (the subtle, for instance, is said to consist of seven levels). But aside from that it is important to understand that *all* major perennial traditions agree with that general hierarchy, and most of them agree right down to details. Further, this hierarchy is not a nicety of philosophical side-issues; for these traditions, it is the fundamental core of the perennial wisdom insofar as it can be stated in words. It is fair to say, then, that any account of the mystic's "world view" that leaves out this type of hierarchy is seriously inadequate.

According to the perennial traditions, each of these various levels has an appropriate field of study. The study of level–1 is basically that of physics and chemistry, the study of nonliving things. Level–2 is the realm of biology, the study of life processes. Level–3 is the level of both psychology (when awareness is "turned in") and philosophy (when it is "turned out"). Level–4, the subtle, is the realm of saintly religion; that is, religion which aims for visionary insight, halos of light and bliss, angelic or archetypal intuition and so on. Level–5, the causal, is the realm of sagely religion, which aims not so much for higher experiences as for the dissolution and transcendence of the experiencer. This sagely path involves the transcendence of all subject-object duality in formless consciousness. Level–6, the ultimate, awaits any who push through the final barriers of levels 4 and 5 so as to radically awaken as ultimate consciousness.

Table 1

1. *Physical*—nonliving matter/energy
2. *Biological*—living, pranic, sentient matter/energy
3. *Mental*—ego, logic, thinking
4. *Subtle*—archetypal, trans-individual, intuitive
5. *Causal*—formless radiance, perfect transcendence
6. *Ultimate*—consciousness as such, the source and nature of all other levels

Notice that these different disciplines, like the levels which they address, are hierarchic. That is, just as each level of the spectrum transcends but includes its predecessor, so each higher study envelops its junior disciplines—but not vice versa. Thus, for example, the study of biology uses physics, but the study of physics does not use biology.

That is another way of saying that the lower levels do not and cannot embrace the higher levels. The primary dictum of the perennial philosophy is that the higher cannot be explained by the lower or derived from the lower. (In fact, as we will see, the lower is created from the higher, a process called "involution.")

Even though the various dimensional-levels are hierarchic, this does not mean they are radically separate, discrete and isolated from each other. They are indeed *different* levels, but different levels *of* Consciousness. Therefore, it is said that the various levels mutually interpenetrate one another. Here is an excellent description:

> These "worlds" [or dimensional-levels] are not separate regions, spatially divided from one another, so that it would be necessary to move in space in order to pass from one another. The higher worlds completely interpenetrate the lower worlds, which are fashioned and sustained by their activities.
>
> What divides them is that each world has a more limited and controlled level of consciousness than the world above it. The lower consciousness is unable to experience the life of the higher worlds and is even unaware of their existence, although it is interpenetrated by them.
>
> But if the beings of a lower world can raise their consciousness to a higher level, then that higher world becomes manifest to them, and they can be said to have passed to a higher world, although they have not moved in space (Shepherd, 1977).

The various levels, then, are mutually interpenetrating and interconnecting. *But not in an equivalent fashion.* The higher transcends but includes the lower—*not* vice versa. That is, all of the lower is "in" the higher, but not all the higher is in the lower. As a simple example, there is a sense in which all of the reptile is in man, but not all of the man is in the reptile; all of the mineral world is in a plant, but not vice versa, and so on. "The more highly evolved," explains Wachsmuth, "always contains in itself the attributes of the earlier, yet always develops as a new entity, an activity clearly distinguishable from that of the other" (1977).

Thus, when the mystic-sage speaks of this type of mutual interpenetration, he or she means a *multidimensional interpenetration with nonequivalence*.

The explanation, by the mystic-sages, of this multidimensional interpenetration forms some of the most profound and beautiful literature in the world.* The essence of this literature, although it seems almost blasphemy to try to reduce it to a few paragraphs, is that "in the beginning" there is only Consciousness as Such, timeless, spaceless, infinite and eternal. For no reason that can be stated in words, a subtle ripple is generated in this infinite ocean. This ripple could not in itself detract from infinity, for the infinite can embrace any and all entities. But this subtle ripple, awakening to itself, *forgets* the infinite sea of which it is just a gesture. The ripple therefore feels set apart from infinity, isolated, separate.

This ripple, very rarefied, is the causal region (level-5), the very beginning, however slight, of the wave of selfhood. At this point, however, it is still very subtle, still "close" to the infinite, still blissful.

But somehow not really satisfied, not profoundly at peace. For in order to find that utter peace, the ripple would have to return to the ocean, dissolve back into radiant infinity, forget itself and remember the absolute. But to do so, the ripple would have to die—it would have to accept the death of its separate self sense. And it is terrified of this.

Since all it wants is the infinite, but since it is terrified of accepting the necessary death, it goes about seeking infinity in ways that prevent it. Since the ripple *wants* release and is *afraid* of it at the same time, it arranges a *compromise* and a *substitute*. Instead of finding actual Godhead, the ripple pretends itself to be god, cosmocentric, heroic, all-sufficient, immortal. This is not only the beginning of narcissism and the battle of life against death, it is a *reduced* or *restricted* version of consciousness, because no longer is the ripple *one* with the ocean, it is trying itself to *be* the ocean.

Driven by this Atman-project—the attempt to get infinity in ways that prevent it and force substitute gratifications—the ripple creates ever tighter and ever more restricted modes of consciousness. Finding the causal less than perfect, it reduces consciousness to create the subtle (level-4). Eventually finding the subtle less than ideal, it reduces consciousness once again to create the mental (3). Failing there, it reduces to the pranic, then material plane, where, finally, exhausting its attempt to be god, it falls into insentient slumber.

Yet behind this Atman-project, the ignorant drama of the separate

---

*What follows is, approximately, a combination of the *Lankavatara Sutra*, *The Tibetan Book of the Dead* and Western existentialism. For a more detailed account, see *The Atman Project* (Wheaton: Quest, 1980).

self, there nonetheless lies Atman. All of the tragic drama of the self's desire and mortality was just the play of the Divine, a cosmic sport, a gesture of Self-forgetting so that the shock of Self-realization would be the more delightful. The ripple *did* forget the Self, to be sure—but it was a ripple *of* the Self, and remained so throughout the play.

Thus, this movement from the higher into the lower—which is involution—is at once an act of pure creation and effulgent radiance (on the part of Atman), and a tragic tale of suffering and epic unhappiness (on the part of the self-ripple attempting the Atman-project). The ultimate aim of evolution—the movement from the lower to the higher—is to awaken *as* Atman, and thus retain the glory of the creation without being forced to act in the drama of self-suffering.

During the course of our universe's history (and science helps us here), we have evolved from level–1 (which began approximately 15 billion years ago with the Big Bang) to level–2 (which occurred several billions of years later when matter awakened into some realization of life) to level–3 (which so far has been reached fully by humans only). Evolution is, as it were, half completed. "Mankind," said Plotinus, "is poised midway between the gods and the beasts."

But in the past course of human history, some men and women, through the evolutionary discipline of higher religion, succeeded in pushing their own development and evolution into level–4: that of saintly religion and the first intuition of a transcendental reality, one in essence, lying above and beyond the ordinary mind, self, body and world. This "beyond" was poetically called Heaven; this oneness was called the one God. This intuition did not fully occur until around 3000 B.C., with the rise of the first great monotheistic religions. (Prior to that time, there were only polytheistic realizations—a god of fire, a god of water, etc. This is really shamanistic magic, stemming from a simple manipulation of level–2, emotional-sexual energies and rites.) By the time of 500 B.C., however, certain evolutionary souls pushed their development into the causal—Christ, Buddha, Krishna, the great axial sages. Their insights were drawn out and extended to produce what the Tibetans called the *Svabha-vikakaya* path—the path of level–6, or already realized Truth, the path of Zen, Vajrayana, Vedanta. What remains is for the world to follow suit, via evolutionary or process meditation, into the higher realms, culminating at infinity.

According to the perennial philosophy, not only does this whole process of involution and evolution play itself out over centuries, it repeats itself moment to moment, ceaselessly and instantaneously. In this moment and this moment and this, an individual starts out at infinity. But in this moment and this moment and this, he contracts away from infinity and ends up reduced to the level of his present adaptation. He *involves* to the highest point he has yet *evolved*—and all the higher realms are simply forgotten, repressed, rendered unconscious. This is why all meditation is called remembrance or recollection (Sanskrit *smriti*, Pali *sati*, as in *satipatthana*, Plato's *anamnesis*, Sufi *zikr*—all are precisely translated as "memory" or "remembrance").

This whole panoply of higher levels generating the lower moment to moment, and of the dazzling interpenetration of each level with the others, and of the extraordinary dynamics between the levels, all occurring in a field of effulgent radiance—all this is meant when the mystic-sage speaks of multidimensional interpenetration with non-equivalence.

The fact that the mystic-sage speaks so often of the difference between levels, and emphasizes those differences, does not mean he neglects the relationships between the elements on a *given* level. In fact, the mystic is precise in his understanding of the community of elements constituting each level. Since all of the elements are "made of" the same density of consciousness—since they are all *of* the same level—they are all perfectly interpenetrating and mutually interdependent, in an *equivalent* fashion. That is, no element of any *given* level is higher, or more real, or more fundamental than the others, simply because they are all made of the "same stuff" (which means, same density of consciousness).

To be sure, there are certain hierarchies within each level, but they are nonstatus hierarchies, such as that of size. For example, a planet is bigger than a rock, a solar system is bigger than a planet, a galaxy bigger than a solar system. That is a heirarchy of size, not ontological status, because they are all equally of the material plane. Just so, all hierarchies within each dimension are of *equivalent* elements.

Thus, on the physical plane, no elementary particle is "most fundamental" (they all seem to bootstrap). On the nutritional plane, no vitamin is ultimately more essential (take away any one and you're equally dead). In the moral sphere, no virtue is greater than another—they all seem to involve each other (as Socrates knew and as Maslow discovered for B-values). In the subtle, all archetypes are equivalent reflections of the Godhead, just as all *Sambhogakayas* are equivalent aspects of the *Dharmakaya*.

The point is that all the elements of a given level are roughly equivalent in status and mutually interpenetrating in fact. All in one and one in all—holographically, as it were. But, by virtue of hierarchy, any element from a senior level is higher in ontological status than any element of a junior dimension (e.g., the virtue of compassion is *not* equivalent with vitamin B–12). This mutual interconnectivity of the elements of any *single* level is *one-dimensional interpenetration with equivalence*. It is a type of *holo-archy* existing within each level of *hierarchy*. Thus, the simplest way to summarize the mystic's world view would be:

1) Holo-archy within each level
2) Hierarchy between each level

With this background information, we come to the new paradigm.

PHYSICS AND MYSTICISM

One of the frequently mentioned doctrines of mysticism is that of "mutual interpenetration," as presented, for instance, in the Kegon school of Buddhism, Meher Baba's *Discourses*, the Five Ranks of Soto Zen, etc. By "mutual interpenetration" the mystic means *both* forms of interpenetration discussed above: one-dimensional and multidimensional, holo-archic and hierarchic, horizontal and vertical.

Think of the six levels of consciousness as a six-story building: the mystic means that all the elements on each floor harmoniously interact, *and*, most importantly, each of the floors interact with each other. As for this multileveled interaction, the mystic means that the physical elements interact with the biological elements which interact with the mental which interact with the subtle which interact with the causal which pass into infinity, each level superseding its predecessor but mutually interpenetrating with it. And thus, speaking of *all* these levels the mystic says, to use Meher Baba's words, "They all interpenetrate one another and exist together."

Now it happens that the modern-day physicist, working with the lowest realm—that of material or nonsentient and nonliving processes—has discovered the *one-dimensional* interpenetration of the material plane: he has discovered that all hadrons, leptons, etc. are mutually interpenetrating and interdependent. As Capra explains it:

> Quantum theory forces us to see the universe not as a collection of physical objects, but rather as a complicated web of relations between the various parts of a unified whole. . . . All [physical] particles are dynamically composed of one another in a self-consistent way, and in that sense can be said to "contain" one another. In [this theory], the emphasis is on the interaction, or "interpenetration," of all particles (1977).

In short, speaking of these subatomic particles and waves and fields, the physicist says, "They all interpenetrate one another and exist together." Now a less than cautious person, seeing that the mystic and the physicist have used precisely the same words to talk about their realities, would thereby conclude that the realities must also be the same. And they are not.

The physicist, with his one-dimensional interpenetration, tells us that all sorts of atomic events are interwoven one with the other—which is itself a significant discovery. But he tells us, and can tell us, nothing whatsoever about the interaction of nonliving matter with the biological level, and of that level's interaction with the mental field—what relationship does ionic plasma have with, say, egoic goals and drives? And beyond that, what of the interaction of the mental field with the subtle, and of the subtle with the causal, and the reverse interaction and interpenetration all the way back down through the lower levels? What can the new physics tell us of that?

I suggest that the new physics has simply discovered the one-dimensional interpenetration of its own level (nonsentient mass/energy). While this is an important discovery, it cannot be equated with the extraordinary phenomenon of multidimensional interpenetration described by the mystics. We saw that Hinduism, as only one example, has an incredibly complex and profound theory of how the ultimate realm generates the casual, which in turn generates the subtle, which creates the mind, out of which comes the fleshy world and, at the very bottom, the physical plane. Physics has told us all sorts of significant things about that last level. Of its predecessors, it can say nothing (without turning itself into biology, psychology or religion). To put it crudely, the study of physics is on the first floor, describing the interactions of its elements; the mystics are on the sixth floor describing the interaction of all six floors.

Thus, as a blanket conclusion, even as an approximation, the statement that "The world views of physics and mysticism are similar" is a wild over-generalization and is based, as one physicist recently put it, "on the use of accidental similarities of language as if these were somehow evidence of deeply rooted connections" (Bernstein, 1978).

Further, physics and mysticism are not two different approaches to the same reality. They are different approaches to two quite different levels of reality, the latter of which transcends but includes the former. That is to say, physics and mysticism do not follow Bohr's complementarity principle. It is not generally understood that complementarity, as used in physics, means two *mutually exclusive* aspects of, or approaches to, one interaction. Physics and mysticism are not complementary because an individual can be, at the same time and in the same act, a physicist *and* a mystic. As we said, the latter transcends but includes the former, not excludes it. Physics and mysticism are no more two mutually exclusive approaches to one reality than are, say, botany and mathematics.

This whole notion of the complementarity of physics and mysticism comes from ignoring levels 2 through 5. It then appears that physics (level–1) and mysticism (level–6) are the only two major approaches to reality. From this truncated view of reality springs the supposed "complementarity" of physics and mysticism. This claim is not made for sociology and mysticism, nutrition and mysticism, or botany and mysticism; no more so physics and mysticism.

What *is* new about the new physics is not that it has anything to do with higher levels of reality. With a few minor exceptions (which we will soon discuss), it does not even attempt to explain or account for level-2 (let alone 3–6). Rather, in pushing to the extremes of the material dimensions, it has apparently discovered the basic holoarchy of level-1, and that, indeed, is novel. There, at least, physics and mysticism agree.

Yet even here we must be careful. In the rush to marry physics and mysticism, using the shotgun of generalization, we tend to forget that quantum reality has almost no bearing whatsoever in the actual world of macrosopic processes. As physicist Walker puts it, in the ordinary world of "automobiles and basketballs, the quanta are inconsequential." This has long been clearly recognized by physicists. The quantum level is so submicroscopic that its interactions can for all practical purposes be ignored in the macro world. The intense interactions between subatomic mesons, which sound so mystical, are not observed at all between macro-objects, between rocks and people and trees. As Capra carefully explains it, "The basic oneness of the universe . . . becomes apparent *at the atomic level* and manifests itself more and more as one penetrates deeper . . . into the realm of *subatomic particles*" [my italics] (1977).

But it is precisely in the ordinary realm of rocks and trees that the mystic *sees* his mutual interpenetration of all matter. His basic oneness of the universe does not "start at the atomic level." When the mystic looks at a bird on wing over a cascading stream and says, "They are perfectly one," he does not mean that if we got a super microscope out and examined the situation we would see bird and stream exchanging mesons in a unitary fashion. His unitary vision is an immediate impact expressing his personal realization that "All this world in truth is Brahman."

That is to say, even the agreement between mystic and physicist on level–1 must be looked upon either as somewhat tenuous or as a fortunate coincidence. Ask almost any physicist if the connections between, say, a macroscopic tree and river are as intense and unitary as those between subatomic particles, and he will say no. The mystic will say yes.

That is a fundamental issue and shows, in fact, that the physicist and mystic aren't even talking about the same world. The physicist says: "The ordinary Newtonian world is, for all practical purposes, separate and discrete, but the subatomic world is a unified pattern." The mystic says: "The ordinary Newtonian world is, as I directly perceive it, one indivisible whole; as for the subatomic realm, I've never seen it."

The issue here is crucial, because, as Jeremy Bernstein, professor of physics at the Stevens Institute, explains (1978), "If I were an Eastern mystic the last thing in the world that I would want would be a reconciliation with modern science." His point is that it is the very *nature* of scientific discoveries that they ceaselessly change and alter, that last decade's scientific proof is this decade's fallacy, and that no major scientific fact can escape being profoundly altered by time and further experimentation. What *if* we said that Buddha's enlightenment just received corroboration from physics? What then happens when, a decade from now, new scientific facts replace the current ones (as they must)? Does Buddha then lose his enlightenment? We cannot have it both ways. If we hitch mysticism to physics now, mustn't we ditch it then? What does it mean to confuse temporal scientific facts with timeless contemplative realms? "To hitch a religious [transpersonal] philosophy to a contemporary science," says Dr. Bernstein, "is a sure route to its obsolescence."

THE IMPLICATE ORDER

The same types of difficulties surround the popular use of the concept, introduced by David Bohm, of an "implicate order" of matter. The public at large, and many psychologists in particular, look upon the implicate realm as if it transcended physical particles and reached somehow into a higher state of unity and wholeness. In fact, the implicate realm does not transcend matter—it subscends matter and expresses a coherence, unity and wholeness of the entire physical plane, or level–1. It does indeed go beyond explicate matter, but in a subscending or underlying manner, not a transcending one. As a matter of fact, the concept explicitly *excludes* any higher realms such as mind and consciousness.

This is made very clear by Bohm himself. First of all, Bohm is clearly opposed to trying to introduce mind or consciousness into the formalism of quantum mechanics (QM), as some physicists would like to do. As he and Hiley put it in a recent paper, "We show that the introduction of the conscious mind into physics . . . is motivated by certain quite general considerations that have little to do with quantum mechanics itself. This approach is contrasted with our own investigations using the quantum potential. . . . Our aim is, in fact, to *describe this order without bringing in the observer in any fundamental role*" [my italics] (1975). The conclusion of Bohm's work is that there seem to be certain quantum phenomena that "present us with a new order or a new structure process, that does not fit into the Newtonian scheme" (1975).

This new order, in general terms, is the implicate (holographic or holomovement) realm. But Bohm is at pains to emphasize that there is nothing mystical or transcendental about the implicate order. His theory, and it is very elegant, is that explicate matter rests upon a sea of implicate physical energy of extraordinary magnitude and potential, and that the equations of quantum mechanics "are describing that [implicate order]" (1978). In one sense, then, the implicate realm goes way beyond explicate matter: "Matter is like a small ripple on this tremendous ocean of energy. . . . This implicate order implies a reality immensely beyond what we call matter. Matter itself is merely a ripple in this background" (1978).

But in the final analysis, this implicate sea, although "finer" than explicate matter, is still of the realm of *physis* or nonliving mass/energy in general. This is obvious because 1) Bohm has already *excluded* higher realms, such as mental consciousness, from quantum mechanics, and 2) the equations of QM are said to "describe the implicate order." The unfolding from the implicate realm is, he says, "a direct idea as to what is meant by the mathematics of (quantum mechanics). What's called the unitary transformation or the basic mathematical description of movement in quantum mechanics is exactly what we are talking about" (1978). Now QM equations do not define biological life, or level–2; they do not describe mental life, or level–3; they do not describe subtle or causal or absolute realms either. They describe something going on in the realm of *physis* and nowhere else. Besides, Bohm clearly states that "the implicate order is still matter."

It is Bohm's credit that, in his theoretical writings, he makes it very clear that he is not trying to introduce consciousness or mind into the QM formalism, or trying thereby to "prove" higher states of being with equations that are clearly descriptive not even of animal life (level–2) but rather of nonsentient processes. For it is certainly true that if the implicate realm rests on an elegant interpretation of the facts generated by QM, then it just as certainly has no fundamental *identity* with any of the levels of 2 through 6. In short, the implicate order, as I would state it, is the unitary deep structure (holo-archy) of level–1, which subscends or underlies the explicate surface structures of elementary particles and waves.

At the same time, Bohm himself is perfectly aware that the notion of a nonlocal implicate order of *physis* is still far from the only possible interpretation of QM, and far, in fact, from being the absolute case anyway: "At present," he says, "it is necessary to resist the temptation to conclude that everything [in the physical realm] is connected to everything else regardless of space and time separations. The evidence to date indicates that the nonlocal effects [what the public has come generally to call holographic or implicate order events] arise under very special conditions and any correlations that have been established tend to be broken up rather quickly so that our traditional approach of analysing systems into autonomous sub-systems is, in general, quite valid" (1975).

The important point is that the mystic's insight does not rest on what these physicists finally decide.*

IMPLICATE ORDER APPLIED TO PSYCHOLOGY

Simply because the implicate order has validation only on the level of *physis*, doesn't mean it can't be applied, as a metaphor (not model), to higher levels—it can (and Bohm himself has increasingly been speculating in this direction). But certain precautions might be observed.

First, the implicate/explicate metaphor, because it provides only two major dimensions (three at most, by tossing in a realm "beyond both"), offers only the vaguest representation of the Great Chain of Being, which, as Huston Smith has demonstrated, must possess at least four and preferably five levels if it is to claim anything resembling completeness (we already summarized the six-level Hindu/Buddhist version of this Great Chain). Talking loosely of "gradations of the implicate realm," in order to stretch out the metaphor to cover the Chain is acceptable; but unless we can specify the precise nature of these "gradations," nothing has been gained. And naturally, we cannot imagine we have the authority of physics in doing so.

On the other hand, if we collapse the Great Chain of Being in order to fit the implicate/explicate metaphor, we lose that great precision and comprehensiveness of the traditional hierarchy of consciousness. John Welwood, for instance, has presented a nice version of the Chain of Being consisting of such levels as the thinking mind, the situational ground of body (level-2), the personal ground of mind (level-3), the transpersonal ground (levels 4–5), and the open ground (level 6). But in order to correlate it in any way with the implicate/explicate metaphor, he had to collapse his model into only three levels with a consequent and substantial loss

*I am, in this paper, leaving out the most radical and pervasive difference between mysticism and any sort of physical or holographic paradigm, because it is also the most obvious. Namely, 1) The comprehension of holographic principles is an act of mind, whereas the comprehension of mystical truth is an act of trans-mental contemplation, and 2) if holographic theories are actually said to describe transcendent truths, or to be the same as actually transcending, a violent fallacy known as category error occurs [for which, see Wilber (1979)]. Some have even suggested that a simple learning of the holographic paradigm would be the same as actual transcendence, in which case these hypothetical theories are not just wrong, they are detrimental.

of precision, and no discernable gain in clarity. Again, this is perfectly acceptable and useful up to a point. (In this case, Welwood was writing in a simple introductory style, and succeeded nicely therein [1979].) But if we push the metaphor beyond rough generalizations and introductory hyperbole, nothing is gained; on the contrary, certain specifiable fallacies result.

Second, some writers use the implicate order as a metaphor not of subscendence but of transcendence. That is, the implicate realm is used as a metaphor of *higher-order* wholeness or unity, referring, presumably, to such levels as the subtle or causal. This, too, is a useful generalization—up to a point. The difficulty is that, as originally explained by Bohm for the realm of *physis*, the explicate and implicate "entities" are mutually exclusive. The "ink-drop" particle is either unfolded and manifest (explicate) or it is enfolded and unmanifest (implicate). It cannot be both at the same time (not, anyway, without wrecking the original demonstration).

All of which is fine for the dimension of *physis*. But truly higher levels are not mutually exclusive with lower ones—the higher, as we said, transcend but include the lower. Look even to a simple example: when level–2 (bio-life) first arose and transcended matter, it did not disperse the explicate order of matter—it neither annihilated it nor dispersed it into enfolded potentiality. It transcended but included it in a perfectly explicate fashion as an aspect or part of itself. This is evolution, or explicate enveloping, not involution, or implicate dispersal. One of the most beautiful illustrations of this is the human brain: the reptilian brain is enveloped by the limbic brain which is enveloped by the neocortex, all of them perfectly explicate but subsumed, representing and retaining the evolution or unfolding of reptile to mammal to human.

The point is that, unless it is done with extreme care and precision (and it can be done using this metaphor),* the use of the metaphor

---

*I have, in *Atman Project* (Wilber, 1980), attempted to do so along the following lines: The point often overlooked is that if there are gradations of implicate order, there are also gradations of explicate order as well, and, in fact, they parallel one another throughout evolution. "Implicate," when used as a metaphor, is almost always given a connotation of being more real, more fundamental, and more basic than the explicate world of manifest entities. In fact, however, they alternate. What is implicate at one level of consciousness becomes explicate at the next. That is, each level is implicate to its predecessor but explicate to its successor. Prana, for example, is implicate to matter and explicate to mind, just as mind is implicate to prana and explicate to subtle. Evolution is a series of making explicate that which was formerly implicate. As each higher structure unfolds, or explicates, it subsumes, or implicates, the lower. This whole process is carefully described in the *Atman Project*. But when

of implicate order tends to end up generating a description of involution, which is a regressive movement. The resultant implicate
metaphor is a "melt-down model": the absolute, instead of perfectly
transcending and subsuming distinctions, merely obliterates and
disperses them. But grace, as St. Thomas knew, perfects nature, it
does not blur it.

MIND AND QUANTUM MECHANICS

Unlike David Bohm, and unlike the great majority of physicists,
there are a handful of avant-garde physicists who not only want to
inject "mind" into the equations of QM, but insist on it as well.
Wigner, Walker, Muses and Sarfatti are producing elaborate mathematical explanations that purport to show the crucial role of consciousness in the formulations of QM. It is these types of formulations,
above all else, that have brought the physicist wandering into the
backyard of the mystic—or at least the parapsychologist.

The impetus for these formulations lies in what is called the
"measurement problem," and the measurement problem is short-
hand for some very sophisticated and elaborate mathematical equations and certain paradoxes they generate.

The problem itself concerns this type of dilemma: the mathematics
of QM can determine, with great precision, the *probability* that a
certain quantum event will occur in a certain environment (at a
certain place or at a certain time), but it can never predict *the* precise
environment itself. It can say, for instance, that the chance of the
finding a quantum particle in area A is 50%, in area B, 30%, and in
area C, 20%. But it cannot, under any circumstances, say that a
particular event *will* occur in area A (given the above probability
distribution). Thus, the particular event is not looked upon as a

---

the terms "implicate/explicate" are used in that fashion, there is precisely nothing
new about them; that is the very core of the *philosophia perennis*, from Hegel to
Aurobindo. That is not, however, the way these terms are presently used. As for the
terms "implicate" and "explicate," then, I generally try to avoid their use in describing this overall process and its hierarchial context of multidimensions, because the
perennial philosophy goes far beyond anything contained in the present-day use of
these notions of implicate/explicate. And when these notions *are* brought into line
with the *philosophia perennis*, as in the above summary, they end up bearing only
minimal resemblance to the meaning originally given them by physicists.

Finally, there is a vast difference between subscendence and transcendence, and
when "implicate order" is taken to mean *both*, certain glaring fallacies result. The
easiest way to avoid this is to use the notion of "implicate order" in precisely the
way it was proposed: a subscendent unity of the plane of *physis* level-1.

single entity or occurrence, but rather as a "tendency to exist," which, in this example, would be *defined* by an equation (or probability amplitude) that says, in effect: 50% A/ 30% B/ 20% C.

Now the odd thing is that the event, when it occurs, *does* occur in just *one* area. It is almost (not quite) as if a statistician were trying to predict which of three doors you are likely to walk through, and, for various reasons, he winds up with the results: 50% chance of door A, 30% door B, 20% door C. He cannot predict exactly which door it will be, just the percentages. But when you finally walk through the door, you go through only *one*—50% of you doesn't go through door A, 30% through B and 20% through C.

But beyond that, the analogy breaks down. The statistician had reasons to believe that you exist before your walk through any of the doors—he can go look at you, for one. But the physicist has no such assurances about his quantum particles, because there is *no way* he can go look at the particle (for our less than accurate purposes, let's just say it's too small to see perfectly). The *only* way he can look at the particle is by using certain instruments—that is, by *measuring* it in some sense. But to measure the particle he has, as it were, to get it through the doors of his instruments. And there is the problem: to find out what's behind the door, the physicist has to use a door. In all cases, his phenomena can be detected only as they walk through various doors, and the equations describing these "walks" are purely probabilistic: say, 50/30/20.

The physicist therefore faces a conceptual problem: prior to measurement, *all* he can say about a quantum event is that it *is* (not has) a certain tendency to exist (e.g., 50/30/20). The event itself, if left alone (not measured) will "propagate through space-time" according to the Schroedinger wave function, which, if squared, gives the probability of finding the event in a certain environment (50/30/20). But prior to the actual measurement, there is *no way whatsoever* to know precisely in which region the particle will occur. Yet, when it is finally detected, it does occur in *one* region only (say B) and does not spread out through the three doors. This is called the collapse of the state vector or wavepacket, because when measurement determines that the particle is in B, the probability of it being in A or C collapses to zero. The collapse of the state vector means that the event *jumped* from being a "tendency to exist" (50A/30B/20C) to a "real occurrence." (B)

Hence the problems. Does measurement itself "cause" the collapse of the wavepacket? Does the actual particle even exist at all prior to measurement? If we say it does exist (which seems common sense), how can we know for sure, since there is *no* way to tell, and since our mathematical equations, which otherwise describe perfectly this realm, tell us only 50/30/20? If we deny the equations, how can we deny the fact that they otherwise work so well?

Aside from a large number of philosophers who maintain (not without certain justifications) that what collapses the wavepacket is not mind or matter but bad metaphysics, there are several different schools of thought on this "measurement problem," offered by the physicists themselves:

1. The Copenhagen Interpretation—The vast number of physicists follow this school, which maintains that the collapse of the wavepacket is at bottom purely random. There is no need for an explanation. Since there is no way to get behind the door, there is no behind the door.* QM is a complete explanation as it stands, and there is no need or possibility to "look behind the scenes" and try to figure out whether the event is there or not prior to measurement. In all fairness, it should be said that there are many good, if not absolute, reasons for adopting this view. It should also be said, as is often pointed out, that Einstein himself violently rejected this view (with the exclamation "God does not play dice with the universe!"), even though every objection he forwarded to this interpretation was brilliantly parried by Bohr and others, using Einstein's own theories. At the same time, I repeat that this (and the following) are species of extremely popularized explanations. But within that disclaimer, the Copenhagen Interpretation says that the probability 50/30/20 is all we can know and all there is to know; which door the particle goes through is purely random.

2. The Hidden Variable Theories—These theories maintain that there are indeed specifiable factors lying "behind the scenes" of the collapse of the wavepacket. These subquantal processes are described by presently hidden variables, but it is possible that they will eventually become technically accessible. In the crudest of terms, this theory says that quantum events are not purely random, and that the particle goes through a particular door for a "hidden" reason, a reason that the particle "knows" and that we should be able to find out. Bohm and his colleagues, working with the quantum potential (and implicate order), belong to this school, as, presumably, did Einstein. Bell's theorem, which has received much popular atten-

---

*This is crudely stated, but it is also the basis of the charge of bad metaphysics.

tion, is often used by some advocates of this school to point to the apparent nonlocal (not confined to a local region of space causality) "transfer" of information between widely isolated regions of space. Bell's theorem is generally taken to mean that, if QM is otherwise correct, and if there are some sort of hidden variables, then those hidden variables are nonlocal—a type of "instant" causality not separated by time or space. Bohm and his colleagues take this as an example of a possible implicate order; Sarfatti takes it as an example of faster-than-light "communication"; others (such as Einstein) take it as nonsense.

3. The Many Worlds Hypothesis—This is proposed by Everett, Wheeler and Graham (EWG). According to the Copenhagen Interpretation (theory #1), when the 50A/30B/20C particle is measured and is found to occur in region B, then the other two possibilities (A and C) collapse—they simply do not occur (just as, for instance, if you toss a coin and it comes up heads, the possibility of it being tails collapses to zero). Now according to EWG, *all* of the mutually exclusive possibilities contained in the wave function *do* occur, but in different branches of the universe. At the moment the particle hits B in this universe, two other universes branch off, one of which contains the particle hitting A, and one of which contains the particle hitting C. Or, as soon as I catch "heads" in this universe, I *also* catch "tails," but in an entirely different universe. Neither "I" knows the other. This has been developed in a very sophisticated mathematical fashion.

It's easy, upon hearing that type of theory, to sympathize with Francois Mauriac: "What this professor says is far more incredible than what we poor Christians believe." But the real point is that it is already obvious that what is called the "new physics" is far from a consensus as to the nature of subatomic reality, a fact that will eventually lead us to certain suggestive conclusions. In the meantime, we move on to the fourth major theory generated by the "measurement problem."

4. The Matter/Mind Connection—This theory has many different forms, but, in keeping with our popularized presentation, we can say that the theory in general suggests the following. If measurement itself collapses the wave pocket, then isn't measurement in some way *essential* to the manifestation of this material event? And *who* is doing the measurement? Obviously, a sentient being. Is not *mind*, then, an influence on—or even creator of—matter?

This general view, in one form or another, is held by Wigner, Sarfatti, Walker and Muses. "In my opinion," says Sarfatti, "the quantum principle involves *mind* in an essential way. . . . mind creates matter" (1974). Walker equates the hidden variables, assuming they are there, with consciousness; Muses plugs consciousness into the quantum vacuum potential. But Beynam sums it all up as: "It is consciousness itself that collapses the state vector." It is this theory we want now to examine, because this is said to be *the* connection between physics and parapsychology/mysticism.

To begin with, is there anything in the perennial philosophy which would accord with the general statement, "Mind creates matter"? The first-approximation answer is definitely affirmative. Matter is held, by all traditional philosophies, to be a precipitate in the mental field. But they express it more precisely. It is not directly mind (level–3) which creates matter (level–1), but prana (level–2) which does so. Mind creates prana; prana creates matter.

Thus, the physicists would be more precise, according to tradition, if they said not "mind' but "prana," "bio-energy," or "biological sentience" was directly senior to matter. Von Weizsacker has already done so explicitly (using the word "prana"), and so have several others. This would not be a problem for these physicists, because the characteristics they already ascribe to "mind" as being necessary for the wavepacket collapse are actually characteristics of prana. That is, these physicists usually don't say "concepts," "ideas" or "logic" collapses the state vector. Rather, they use such terms as "biological systems" (Sarfatti), "sentient being" (Walker), "sensation" (Wigner), and these are distally characteristic of mind but proximally characteristic of prana (or any living system). Mind could also collapse the vector, but *via* prana. This would also fit Sarfatti's suggestions, because all biological systems would *contribute* to random quantal Brownian movement, but a disciplined mind (not present in animals) might *control* it.*

All of which sounds as if this version of QM is right in accord with the mystic view, at least as far as levels 1 and 2 are concerned (i.e., level–2 creates level–1). Yet again we must be very precise here, because premature conclusions are much too easy to draw.

First of all, when the mystic says that matter is created by prana, he does not mean that prana itself must be present in a manifest

*It should be said that, while I will end up disagreeing with this school of QM as to the nature of the *generation* of matter from mind, I do not rule out that they may have some important and brilliant things to say about the *influence* of mind on matter, *after the fact* of matter's generation from mind. This is a very dilute agreement, but an agreement nonetheless, and certain very select areas of parapsychology (not mysticism at large) might find resonance with these theorists.

fashion (and from this point on, for ease of recognition, I will use "mind" instead of "prana," remembering the important qualifications given above). That is, mind does *not* create matter by perceiving it, or sensing it, or "measuring" it—which is, as we saw, the form of the theory held by the QM physicists under discussion. Rather, matter simply precipitates out of mind whether mind is paying attention or not. In fact, during involution, mind generates matter and then "disappears" from the scene altogether. It doesn't stay around to watch matter and thereby generate it.

In this fashion, the traditional philosophy avoids entirely the otherwise ridiculous dilemma: if mind creates matter by perception or actual contact (as participator-observer), then what occurred, say, ten billion years ago when there was only matter and no minds? Science is rather certain that biological life appeared only billions of years *after* matter. Prior to that time, there was no life, no mind. If mind has to measure or observe matter in order for the latter to exist (or have its wavepacket collapsed), we arrive at absurdity. We aren't even working with a ghost in the machine, but a nonexistent shadow of a nonexistent ghost in an all too real machine.

This view—that mind generates matter by the effect of the "participator-observer"—is like saying the chicken (mind) *sees* the egg (matter) and thereby creates it. No chicken to see the egg, no egg. The traditional view says that the chicken (mind) lays or gives birth to the egg (matter) and thereby creates it; what the chicken does after that is its own business—the egg continues to exist, perceived or not. In fact, during involution, the chicken is, well, buried. What it leaves behind is a reduced version of chicken-ness, a reduced version of mind called matter (the egg). But the egg-matter has enfolded in it the potential to actualize ("hatch") a new chicken, or mind itself, which is just what happens in evolution. But in no case does the chicken create the egg by watching it.

It is for similar reasons that most physicists themselves reject this version of the QM interpretation. As David Bohm himself explains: "The introduction of the conscious mind into physics by Wigner is motivated by certain quite general considerations that have little to do with quantum mechanics itself." And speaking of this tendency to hastily conclude that observation by mind is needed to produce matter (measurement), Bohm answers succinctly: "Indeed this is often carried to such an extreme that it appears as if nothing ever happens without the observer. However we know of many physical processes, even at the level of quantum phenomena, that do occur without any direct intervention of the observer. Take for example the processes that go on in a distant star. These appear to follow the known laws of physics and the processes occur, and have occurred, without any significant intervention on our part" (1975).

In short, the perennial philosophy would agree that matter is created out of mind (prana), but through an act of precipitation and crystallization, not perception and measurement. But QM can account, *if* at all, for *only* the latter theory, and therefore the agreement of QM and mysticism on this point is purely coincidental.* Should, therefore, this particular interpretation of QM prove incorrect (and I agree with Bohm and others that it will), it would not affect one way or the other the world view of the mystic-sage.

But my point does not concern whether any of the above four QM interpretations is right or wrong. And there are even others we haven't really discussed at all—superluminal connections, simple statistical interpretations, quantum logic interpretations. These issues are extremely complex and difficult, and it will take decades to work out their implications. However, what we can do now is reach certain immediate conclusions:

1. The "new physics" is far from a grand consensus as to the nature of even subatomic reality. To hook transpersonal psychology/ mysticism to the consensus of the new quantum physics is not possible, because there is no consensus. Those connections that have been drawn between physics and mysticism are of the pick and choose variety. The actual details of the various QM interpretations are, as we have seen, largely mutually exclusive. Simply to take a detail from one interpretation, then another, a little bootstrap here, a little implicate order there, is, in the words of physicist Bernstein, "a travesty and a disservice" to the theories involved.

2. Even if we could draw several tight parallels, to hook transpersonal psychology to physics is still "the surest route to oblivion." To paraphrase Eckhart, if your god is the god of today's physics, then when that physics goes (tomorrow), that god goes with it.

3. The most important point is that no matter which version of

---

*When Bishop Berkeley (even though he wasn't a purist vis à vis the perennial philosophy) said that to be was to be perceived, he meant ultimately perceived by God, or absolute Consciousness. But, as he knew, being and perception are *one* in absolute Consciousness; i.e., it is not that entities exist *because* they are perceived by consciousness, but that their existence *is* consciousness. They are not created by being seen by God, they simply are God at heart. In other words, Berkeley did not mean being *by* perception (or consciousness), but that being *is* consciousness. Consciousness doesn't create a thing by looking at it; it simply *is* that thing, and specific "perceptions" are irrelevant.

QM theory is finally accepted, this will not profoundly affect the mystic's vision or world view. First of all, in no case could it *invalidate* the mystic world view. When Newton's "fractured world view" was "truth," this did not invalidate the mystic vision. If the Copenhagen Interpretation is the "truth," this will not invalidate the mystic vision. If *any* of the QM interpretations are true, this will not invalidate the mystic vision. And therefore, as any epistemologist will tell us, in no case could an interpretation *validate* the mystic world view. If there is no conceivable physical test that would disprove the mystic view, and there isn't, then there is no conceivable one which could corroborate it either.

4. It is sometimes said that the new physics at least *accords* with the mystic world view. I think we can easily agree that certain aspects of some interpretations of mathematical quantum formalisms, when placed into everyday English, sound similar to aspects of the mystic's view, not of the world (levels 1–6), but of level–1. The mystic's insight, however, does not find its validation nor explanation in that possible accord. But if this accord helps "legitimize" mysticism in the public's eye; if it at least does not cause its proponents to radically deny mystical states as hallucinatory; if it opens the way to a fuller acceptance of mystical experience—then, by all accounts, we will indeed have the new physics to thank.

Beyond that point, however, take Bernstein's warning with you: thank the new physics for agreeing with you, but resist the temptation to build your transpersonal models upon the shifting sands of changing level–1 theories.

THE HOLOGRAPHIC BRAIN

While the holographic/implicate theories of physics deal unequivocably with level–1, the theories of holographic brain processes deal, apparently, with level–3, or mind and memory. In tandem, then, these theories would cover, more or less, levels 1–3.

But beyond that, it is suggested by some that *if* the mind were holographic, then this could also account for higher, transpersonal experiences via the mind melting down into the holographic blur beyond explicit distinctions. This holographic blur is called a "frequency realm," where, supposedly, objects in space and time "do not exist." The holographic blur or frequency realm is described as: "No space, no time—just events (or frequencies)."

Let us pass by the difficulties of having *events* existing without *any sort* of space or time; let us also ignore the fact that physical objects (space-time *things*) are needed to produce holograms in the first place. Aside from that, how might this holographic-mind fit with the perennial philosophy?

To start with, it is fundamentally the storage of memory-information that is said to occur on the principles of optical holography. The mechanisms of holography are explained by mathematical transforms, one of whose intriguing properties is that—in mathematical terms anyway—space and time seem at one stage to be left out, and the desired temporal results are retrieved through a read-out function of frequency information. This has led to the notion of a frequency realm—the notion that space/time objects come out of "no space, no time frequencies."

I have no doubt that that is basically true—that memory is holographically stored, just as is said. I also think that the research demonstrating that is brilliant. But beyond that, how this relates in any fashion to transcendent states is far from clear. To be sure, there are similarities of language—the holographic blur ("no space, no time") sounds like a mystical state. It also sounds like passing out. There is a world of difference between pre-temporal consciousness, which has no space and no time, and trans-temporal consciousness, which moves beyond space and time while still embracing it. "Eternity," after all, "is in love with the productions of time." This in no way proves that the holographic blur is not a transcendent state; it demonstrates that one cannot judge so on the basis of language correlations.

Nonetheless, it is said that a shift to a "perception of the holographic blur" would produce transcendent states. Since it is memory which is holographically stored,* what would it actually mean to shift to a perception of the storage bin of personal memory? Would this be nirvana, a direct consciousness which transcended but included all manifestation?

By the accounts of the theory itself, I do not see that it would or could result in anything but an experience of one's own memory storage bin, properly blurred and without benefit of linear readout. How one could jump from a blur of one's own memory to a crystal consciousness that transcends mind, body, self and world is not

---

*The "perception" of the physical frequency realm is discussed later in conjunction with William Tiller's critique of the holographic paradigm.

made clear at all. It is a wild theoretical leap to move from "personal memory is holographically stored" to "therefore all minds are part of a transpersonal hologram."

I think instead that we are allowing certain superficial similarities of language to rule the day of reason. The above is example enough, perhaps, but beyond that there exists the whole notion of a "transcendent frequency realm beyond space and time"—which is said to be the implicate holographic blur. This notion, it seems to me, gains credence only from the oddities of the mathematics involved, which translate "things" into "frequencies" and thus allow a slip of language to pass for transcendent truths. The "frequency realm" transforms are assumed to refer to *experiential realities* in a way that is not only unbelievable, but frankly self-contradictory.

The transform of "things" into "frequencies" is not a transform of space/time into "no space, no time," but a transform of space/time objects into space/time frequencies. Frequency does not mean "no space, no time"; it means cycles/second or space per time. To read the mathematics otherwise is more than a quantum leap; it is a leap of faith.

This "theory has gained increasing support and has not been seriously challenged. An impressive body of research in many laboratories has demonstrated that the brain structures see, hear, taste, smell and touch by sophisticated mathematical analysis of temporal and/or spatial frequencies [hence the primacy of frequency realm]" (*ReVision*, 1978). I do not challenge the theory; I repeat, and mean, that I am straightforwardly impressed. I am not impressed, however, by speculations that call *"temporal* and/or *spatial* frequencies" by the name "no space, no time." And it is in just that semantic slip that this theory *sounds* transcendentally alive.

Needless to say, this semantic sleight-of-hand, which replaces personal blur with transpersonal unity, helps neither the brilliant work of these brain researchers—Pribram for example—nor the difficult task of transpersonalists attempting to explain transcendence.

Aside from the above, we have still another strand of argument which has been proposed. For this strand, let us assume anyway that the mind *in general* is holographic in its operations. Would this fit with the perennial philosophy, and beyond that, would it possibly account for higher levels of consciousness?

I am afraid that, even given this generous lead, we fare no better. First of all, the fact that the deep structure of the mental field is holographic would not in itself account for transpersonal levels, or levels 4–6. The reasons, according to the perennial traditions, are that 1) *every* level is a holo-archy, not just mind, and 2) the experience of any level's holo-archy does not take one *beyond* that level, but merely opens up deeper insights *into* that level. Just as the holo-archy of level–1 does not imply nor demand level 2, 3, 4, 5 or 6, so the holo-archy of level–3 doesn't automatically account for any of the levels above it (levels 4, 5 or 6).

Likewise, the actual experience of the holo-archy of level–3 would not necessarily—nor even likely—involve levels 4, 5 or 6. The ordinary surface mind (level–3) experiences itself as separate and somewhat isolated from other minds. To experience the holo-archy of level–3 would be, at most, to experience a strong resonance with, and even over-lapping of, other minds. It would produce a direct experience of actual interpersonal empathy.

But interpersonal empathy is not transpersonal identity. In states of transpersonal awareness (beyond certain introductory practices), whether mind is present or not, explicit or implicit, standing out or holographically blurred—all of this is irrelevant. The higher realms transcend but can easily include mind, and whether mind itself arises doesn't matter. The *existence* of higher states cannot be explained in terms of something that may or may not happen to a lower state, whether that state is unfolded and projected or enfolded and blurred. You might as well say you can explain level–2 by sufficiently blurring level–1. This disguised reductionism led Willis Harman to comment, "These holographic theories still would interpret the primary datum, consciousness, in terms of something else ultimately quantifiable [i.e., in terms of lower physical level measurements]. These theories are not yet of the new science, but rather of the old, in which the attempt is made to explain away consciousness rather than to understand it."

Finally, we might heed William Tiller's suggestions: "The holographic [theory of brain perception] has focused largely on the sensory apprehension of this representation at the physical level of consciousness [level–1]. [We might do better] to opt for a multi-dimensional [hierarchical] representation of consciousness and possible structures of the universe for its manifestation. Without such an extension beyond the purely physical perception frame, the scope of any 'new paradigm' will be severely limited."

Tiller hints at two points. First, the "frequency realm" said to be so transcendent is really "precendent": it's just the chaotic "blooming buzz" of physical level–1 frequencies before the brain can sort them into higher-order organization. An actual experience of *that* "primary reality" would be, in fact, pure regression, not transcendence. Second, holo-archy cannot account for hierarchy, and thus the whole theory, as a paradigm, falls flat in the most important area of explanation.*

CONCLUSIONS AND ASSESSMENTS

There are several beneficial repercussions coming from the "new physics" and the "holographic paradigm," even if we conclude, as I think we must, that the latter constitutes nothing close to a comprehensive or even adequate paradigm. But among the benefits are:

1. The interest of influential physicists in metaphysics. This has taken two different forms. First, the willingness to postulate unmeasurable and undetectable orders of *physis* lying behind or subscending explicate energy/mass. This is Bohm's quantum potential/implicate order. Second, the willingness of physicists to acknowledge the necessity of ultimately including references to levels higher than *physis* in their accounts of *physis*. As Wheeler put it, "No theory of physics that deals only with physics will ever explain physics" (quoted in Sarfatti, 1974). And Sarfatti: "Therefore, *meta*-physical statements are absolutely vital for the evolution of physics" (1974), whereupon Sarfatti introduces the notion of "mind creating matter." But even if that were true in the fashion proposed by Sarfatti, the perennial philosophy would remind him to add: "And you then need meta-mental to explain mind, which brings you to the subtle; and you then need meta-subtle to explain that, and so on in such fashion until, like an asymptotic curve that approaches an axis but never reaches it until infinity, you arrive at Consciousness as Such."

2. The reductionistic fury of mechanistic science seems to be fi-

---

*I am not questioning the fact that perception and memory occur as suggested in this hypothesis. I am not challenging the hypothesis on that ground at all. I am questioning whether, beyond that, this hypothesis could have anything to do with transcendent realities. My tentative, personal conclusion is that it only *appears* to have something to do with actual transcendence because of the oddities of the math involved and because of a less than precise manipulation of language. Particularly questionable is the jump from "each personal memory is equally distributed in every cell of the individual brain" to "therefore each individual mind is part of a transpersonal hologram." The holographic paradigm is described as "one in all and all in one"—where "one" means "individual memory/cell" and "all" means "all individual brain cells." From that accurate statement a quick substitution is made: "one" comes to mean "one individual" or "one person" and "all" comes to mean, not all other personal brain cells, but all other persons, period.

nally winding down, and physics is opening itself—and by impact
of authority, many other fields as well—to open systems of unending
novelty and creativity. This is especially evident in the work of I.
Prigogine, whose theory of dissipative structures is as beautiful as it
is profound. Dissipative structures are simply a mathematical way to
allow for the evolution of higher, more organized states from less
complex structures. Dissipative structures are not actually explanations of life or mind, as is sometimes said, but rather descriptions of
what has to happen to matter in order for higher realms to unfold.
To actually identify the essence of a higher level as simply being a
dissipative structure is like saying the *Mona Lisa* is simply a concentration of paint. The importance of dissipative mathematics is that it
clearly shows and fully allows for higher-order patterns of emergence.

3. The whole movement of new physics and the new paradigm at
least demonstrates that there is profound, serious and rapidly growing interest in perennial concerns and transcendent realities, even
among specialists and fields that a decade ago could not have cared
less. No matter that some of what is said is premature, *that* it is said
is extraordinary.

4. Books such as the *Tao of Physics* and *The Dancing Wu-Li Masters*
and publications such as Marilyn Ferguson's *Brain/Mind Bulletin* are
introducing vast numbers of people not only to the intrigue of
Western science and physics, but also to aspects of Eastern wisdom
and thought, and in ways that simply would not have been possible
before.

My point, therefore, in criticizing certain aspects of the new paradigm is definitely *not* to forestall interest in further attempts. It is
rather a call for precision and clarity in presenting issues that are,
after all, extraordinarily complex and that resist quick generalization.
And I say this with a certain sense of urgency, because in our
understandable zeal to promulgate a new paradigm, which somehow touches bases with physics at one end and mysticism at the
other, we are liable to alienate both parties—and everybody in
between.

From one end of the spectrum: already certain mystically or
transpersonally oriented researchers—Tiller, Harman, W.I. Thompson, Eisenbud—have expressed disappointment in or total rejection
of the new paradigm.

From the other end: already many physicists are furious with the
"mystical" use to which particle physics is being subjected. Particle
physicist Jeremy Bernstein recently unleashed a broadside on such

attempts, calling them "superficial and profoundly misleading" (1978). And no less an authority than John Wheeler—whose name is always mentioned in the "new paradigm" and in a way he finds infuriating—recently released two scathing letters wherein, among several other things, he brands the physics/mysticism attempts as "moonshine," "pathological science" and "charlatanism." "Moreover," he states, "in the quantum theory of observation, my own present field of endeavor, I find honest work almost overwhelmed by the buzz of absolutely crazy ideas being put forth with the aim of establishing a link between quantum mechanics and parapsychology" (1979)—and transpersonal psychology, for that matter. He has asked, and Admiral Hyman G. Rickover has joined him, to have all sanctions of the American Association for the Advancement of Science removed from any endeavor tending toward transpersonalism, a sanction that Margaret Mead, ten years ago, fought so hard to obtain.

The work of these scientists—Bohm, Pribram, Wheeler and all—is too important to be weighed down with wild speculations on mysticism. And mysticism itself is too profound to be hitched to phases of scientific theorizing. Let them appreciate each other, and let their dialogue and mutual exchange of ideas never cease. But unwarranted and premature marriages usually end in divorce, and all too often a divorce that terribly damages both parties.

REFERENCES

Beynam, L. "The Emergent Paradigm in Science." In *ReVision*, 1, 2, 1978.

Bernstein, J. "A Cosmic Flow." *American Scholar*, Winter-Spring, 1979.

Bohm, D. and Hiley, B.J. "Some remarks on Sarfatti's proposed connection between quantum phenomena and the volitional activity of the observer-participator." Pre-print, Department of Physics, Birbeck College, University of London, 1975.

———. "A Conversation with David Bohm—The Enfolding-Unfolding Universe." Conducted by Renée Weber. In *ReVision*, 1, 3/4, 1978.

Capra, F. *The Tao of Physics.* Boulder: Shambhala, 1975.

Gardner, M. "Quantum Theory and Quack Theory." In *New York Review of Books*, May 17, 1979.

ReVision, 1, 3/4, 1978. "A New Perspective on Reality." Reprint from the *Brain/Mind Bulletin*.

Sarfatti, J. "Implications of Meta-physics for Psychoenergetic Systems." *Psychoenergetic Systems, 1,* 1974.

Shepherd, A.P. *A Scientist of the Invisible.* Quoted in White, J. and Krippner, S. *Future Science.* New York: Anchor, 1977.

Wachsmuth, G. "The Etheric Formative Forces." In White, J. And Krippner, S. *Future Science.* New York: Anchor, 1977.

Welwood, J. "Self-knowledge as the Basis for an Integrative Psychology." *Journal of Transpersonal Psychology, 11,* 1, 1979.

Wilber, K. "Eye to Eye." *ReVision,* 2, 1, 1979.

———. *The Atman Project.* Wheaton: Quest, 1980.

8

THE PHYSICIST AND
THE MYSTIC—IS A DIALOGUE
BETWEEN THEM POSSIBLE?

A Conversation with David Bohm
Conducted by Renée Weber
Edited by Emily Sellon

WEBER: Could we begin by clarifying the difference between the holomovement, the holograph and the implicate order?

BOHM: Holomovement is a combination of a Greek and Latin word and a similar word would be holokinesis or, still better, holoflux, because "movement" implies motion from place to place, whereas flux does not. So the holoflux includes the ultimately flowing nature of what is, and also of that which forms therein. The holograph, on the other hand, is merely a static recording of movement, like a photograph: an abstraction from the holomovement. We therefore cannot regard the holograph as anything very basic, since it is merely a way of displaying the holomovement which latter is, however, the ground of everything, of all that is.

The implicate order is the one in which the holomovement takes place, an order that both enfolds and unfolds. Things are enfolded in the implicate order, and that order cannot be entirely expressed in an explicate fashion. Therefore, in this approach, we are not able to go beyond the holomovement or the holoflux (the Greek word might be *holorhesis*, I suppose) although that does not imply that this is the end of the matter.

In any discussion of this sort, people often are led to speak of the totality, of a wholeness which is both immanent and transcendent, and which, in a religious context, is often given the name of God. The immanence means that the totality of what is, is immanent in matter; the transcendence means that this wholeness is also beyond matter.

WEBER: In a past issue of *ReVision* (Volume 2, No. 2, 1979) [See Chapter 1] Ken Wilber says that the perennial philosophy has universally assumed that the world is hierarchically structured, each higher level containing the lower, but not vice versa. On that ground he rejects the theory of the hologram, according to which the part contains the whole.

BOHM: First of all, the hierarchial position seems to reject the notion of the immanence of the whole. To my mind, the ancient tradition includes both immanence and transcendence. Certainly the Buddha, and a great many other philosophical and religious teachers as well, would have agreed to this.

WEBER: Spinoza only emphasized immanence.

BOHM: Perhaps. However, the totality can be described as *both* immanence and transcendence in one sense, and *neither* immanence nor transcendence in another, since it is beyond the possibility of description. Words are, after all, limited; they are merely a sign which points to an actuality that cannot be completely symbolized by this means.

WEBER: Wilber claims that the new physics has only discovered the unity of the part with the part, and not the part with the whole. In this sense, can science be said to bear out mysticism?

BOHM: This is a very complex subject, and most modern scientists don't address themselves to such questions. Therefore they would neither agree nor disagree. I have said that I thought mysticism's positive meaning could be that the ground of our existence is a mystery—a statement which Einstein himself accepted. It was he who said that what is most beautiful is the mysterious. To my mind, the word mystic should be applied to a person who has actually had some direct experience of the mystery which transcends the possibility of description. The problem for the rest of us is to know what that may mean.

Insofar as the mystic chooses to talk about his experience, he has left the domain of the mysterious and entered the world of ordinary experience. If he tries to make contact with others, that is valuable, but in this case he has to follow the rules governing the domain of the ordinary, that is, he has to be reasonable, logical and clear. If he fails in this, what he says will make no connection with our ordinary experience and will therefore have very little meaning for us—unless he can somehow transmit to others the essence of his experience, which is very difficult to do. Insofar as he is content to do less than that, he must respect the rules of ordinary communication. He may hope to say something which can shed light on ordinary experience or even improve it. If that is the case, the possibility could arise of a dialogue between the person who is commonly called a mystic (although the word is a poor one) and the person who is primarily interested in the behavior of matter, in ordinary human relationships and ordinary levels of consciousness, such as thought and feeling.

The problem in establishing such a dialogue is that, first of all, the mystic has difficulty in talking to the ordinary man because he is forced to use a language which is inadequate to his task. The mechanistic language commonly used in the description of matter, for example, is geared to what is for him a low level of experience. The first point, therefore, is that we need a language which will bridge the gap between these disparate levels of experience. Second, communication will be difficult if not impossible if the mystic insists on remaining on his high level and looking down on the other fellow as having essentially nothing to say—his role being merely to listen and learn. This arrangement would hardly result in a dialogue, and I doubt that either party would benefit from it.

However, I do not think all mystics would make such an assumption. For instance, Lama Govinda has called for a real dialogue between science and mysticism, and makes it clear that different mystics have very different ways of looking at things. Pir Vilayat Khan, who represents the Sufi mystical tradition, has also indicated that not all mystics are unanimous in their perception. He has said that when one rises to the level of transcendence—to the totality— and then returns, ordinary life is seen differently. But he also said that in the Middle Eastern traditions, that is, Judaism, Christianity and Islam, what happens on the ordinary level has real significance— historical events genuinely affect the eternal, whereas the significance of human history tends to be denied in the Indian tradition. For this reason, absolute unanimity should not be attributed to what is known as the mystical tradition or the perennial philosophy. There are many individual differences, and mystics, like scientists, are bent on discovering new things, with consequent difficulty in communication.

WEBER: One issue on which this question seems to turn is the Bernstein criticism, namely, if mysticism attempts to prove its case through physics, it is clinging to straws, because physics is related to time and mysticism is not. Do you disagree with this statement?

BOHM: I would say that mysticism, like physics, is neither in time nor out of it; it is both. There is nothing which is wholly time-bound or wholly time-free. Physics is changing very quickly, and I think mysticism may be, too. However, to answer your question more directly, I think it would be just as foolish for mystics to try to prove their case from physics as it would be for physicists to prove their case from mysticism. Neither can be proved. Physics can't be proved in any absolute sense because it is based on all sorts of assumptions, many of which are still unknown. Gödel's theorem alone would suggest that for every assumption we are aware of, there must be countless others not known to us. Some of these may be false, some true. So since there is no way to prove physics, and just as surely, no way to prove mysticism, I think it is a mistake to try to prove anything with absolute certainty. Nevertheless, I think something valuable could arise out of a dialogue between the two, in the sense that each can learn from the other. And at the same time, each may discover that some of its own presuppositions are nonsensical and should be dropped, and that might permit them to go on to something new, which will not separate them irrevocably.

WEBER: Does the new physics encourage the supposition that there might be a natural affinity between the two sets of concepts about the world held by physics and by mysticism?

BOHM: Relativity and, even more important, quantum mechanics have strongly suggested (though not proved) that the world cannot be analyzed into separate and independently existing parts. Moreover, each part somehow involves all the others: contains them or enfolds them. In this sense, a common language may be said to have been established, and a common set of basic concepts, for this is the one point on which all mystics have agreed. This fact suggests that the sphere of ordinary material life and the sphere of mystical experience have a certain shared order and that this will allow a fruitful relationship between them.

WEBER: What is your response to the comment that modern science only addresses the notion of unity *within* a given hierarchial level—that is, the level explored by particle physics, which is below ground, as it were, on the lowest level of the hierarchy—but that this does not imply a unity of matter and consciousness?

BOHM: By itself, physics neither implies nor denies anything about consciousness. What it does do is encourage us to look at the evidence in new ways. These ways do not necessarily stem entirely from one's professional position, requiring, that is, that I must view a question *only* as a physicist.

WEBER: Yet in your own case, your theories are of particular interest precisely *because* you are a physicist and therefore have greater insight into the interdependent and dynamic world whose cosmology is being developed.

BOHM: Perhaps, but this does not prevent me from considering other implications. I do just this in the last chapter of my latest book, *Wholeness and the Implicate Order* (Routledge and Kegan Paul, 1980), not only for life but also for consciousness, in an effort to show that a common language might prevail for all these domains. I am not trying to deduce life and consciousness from physics, but rather to see matter as a part of a relatively independent sub-totality which includes life. Leaving out life, we get inanimate matter; leaving out consciousness, we get life; leaving out something unspecified which lies beyond, we get ordinary consciousness and so on. I don't call this a hierarchy, but rather a series of levels of abstractions, which is somewhat different, since if you abstract something you cannot call it lower or higher (as in a hierarchial system), but merely different.

WEBER: But what do you do with the claim that as you go up the levels of organization you attain a greater degree of inclusiveness, whereas the reverse isn't true? For example, an animal has both life and sentience as well as material organization; but a stone, which has materiality, lacks the other characteristics.

BOHM: We don't know the stone, though, do we? If we were to talk about one cell or one virus particle, that would be equivalent to talking about a stone with respect to the whole material universe. If we contemplate nature as a whole—vast mountains, seas, growing fields and forests—we can have an experience of the whole which people call mysticism. Somehow, something is revealed to us which we do not perceive by merely looking at a single living being. We apprehend the immanence of the totality as well as its transcendence. One might say that the transcendence is "higher" than the immanence, but they both have to be present. What is important, to my mind, is the relationship, first, between the immanence and the transcendence and, second, between both of these and ordinary life. Each of the notions of an immanent totality or a transcendent totality is an abstraction; it leaves out ordinary life. The notion of ordinary life is equally an abstraction which excludes the other two. One of our difficulties is that all these ideas are abstractions which produce a relatively independent subtotality which can be discussed, to some extent, in its own right.

WEBER: But none of these can be divorced from reality, from the whole, can they? It's possible that the issue revolves around the following: the whole can be in each part, but different parts can not necessarily be in each of the other parts.

BOHM: The whole is present in each part, in each level of existence. The living reality, which is total and unbroken and undivided, is in everything.

WEBER: But is it equally in everything? That is the crucial question.

BOHM: Perhaps not equally. But if reality is present in different ways or degrees, that doesn't mean we can categorize such inequality as graded in a unique manner into a "higher" or "lower." C.S. Lewis had a nice way of putting it, which I would like to adapt for use in this context. The "higherarchy" is above and the "lowerarchy" is below. The point is that, in considering inanimate matter, to say it is dead, to say it has no intelligence, is merely abstraction. Matter is implicitly the whole, that which *unfolds*, whatever the medium may be. I look at the process of evolution as the unfoldment of the potential of matter, which at bottom becomes indistinguishable from the potential of mind.

This is not to say that I equate mind and matter, or reduce the one to the other. They are, rather, two parallel streams of development which arise from a common ground that is beyond both, and cannot be described at this stage. Perhaps that "beyond" is where the mystic experiences transcendence and immanence together as one whole.

Matter is related to what we pick up with our senses and perceive as relatively stable and recurrent, and subject to certain kinds of laws. Mind is more subtle, but we do not have any knowledge of mind without matter, or matter disassociated from mind or life. For example, in a growing seed, almost all the matter and the energy come from the environment. According to the implicate order, the seed is continually providing inanimate matter in the environment with new information that leads it to produce the living plant or animal. Who is to say then that life was not immanent, even before the seed was planted? In the same way, it is held that the more complex an animal the greater its display of intelligence, but the intelligence must also be immanent in the matter that constitutes the animal. If the immanence is pursued more and more deeply in matter, I believe we may eventually reach the stream which we also experience as mind, so that mind and matter fuse. We call the ultimate heights of mind transcendence; we find in the depths of matter the immanence of the whole of that which is. Both are needed, and to my mind the mysticism which would devalue cosmic consciousness and hold only to the transcendent experience is absurd.

Indeed, many people experience this vast totality in nature, without even thinking of it as mysticism. Something of that totality is revealed to us when we perceive matter in its vastness and depth as displayed in the earth and the sky and the universe itself—matter in which life and intelligence are immanent and implicit.

WEBER: When you speak of matter in this way, are you speaking as a physicist or as a philosopher—or is that the wrong question?

BOHM: I think that is the wrong question. A physicist has a certain kind of contact with matter; a philosopher thinks of matter in a more general way. But if you simply look at nature, you are contacting an aspect of matter which is not abstract, which somehow conveys the whole. Almost anyone who has seen mountains and the sea or the sky at night has that feeling. It is just as valid a way of learning about reality as any other.

WEBER: You have certainly broadened and redefined the concept of matter beyond its conventional use.

BOHM: Well, if the one hand we say that mind stands far above matter, but if on the other hand, we say there is no mind that we know of without matter, then it can be argued that mind is immanent in matter and in that sense, matter is more comprehensive. Therefore I assume the "lowerarchy" below and the "higherarchy" above; we need both to reveal the whole more completely.

WEBER: Would this link higher, self-reflective organisms such as ourselves with such things as a leaf, a rock, a tree?

BOHM: Yes, with the entire material universe. To my mind, this view would produce a much better civilization than that which emphasizes a graded hierarchy of conscious life, in which that which is "above" has the greater degree of reality. If we say that all matter is in some way holy, then we rid ourselves of the special sacredness we have imputed to certain things, such as the temple or the church.

WEBER: We obliterate the line between the profane and the sacred. It was Spinoza who said that matter is God as extension. Do you agree?

BOHM: Yes, it presents a different but complementary point of view. One of the weaknesses of some of the religions is that they have exalted spirituality and devalued matter. Yet the Zuni religion says that every person is a brother because the Earth is his mother and the Sun his father. This grounding has been lost in Christianity, which makes the brotherhood of man depend entirely on his descent from God the Father. But the brotherhood of man can be seen concretely in the sense that everyone springs from the same earth, depends on it for life, and returns to it at death. Brotherhood exists not only in spirit but also in matter, confirming the ancient hermetic view: "As above, so below." One of the earlier forms of mysticism would have stated it: "As in spirit, so in matter," a position which can also be developed from modern physics.

WEBER: In what way?

BOHM: In the old physics, matter (which was the only reality) was completely mechanical, leaving no room for mind. But if, according to the new physics, everything is enfolded in everything else, then there is no real separation of domains. Mind grows out of matter. And matter contains the essence of mind. These two are really both abstractions from the whole: relatively invariant sub-totalities created by our thought. Therefore, if we probe matter deeply enough, we will find a reflection of the same qualities which are revealed when mind is similarly probed.

WEBER: It raises the question whether the physicist contributes anything to the problem of how mind and matter interact and are unified.

BOHM: In order to discuss the interaction of mind and matter, we must first discuss what matter is, and what mind is. Insofar as the physicist offers a theory of matter, he contributes at least to one side of the discussion. If we were to say that the physicist can contribute nothing, that would imply that the mystic can tell us everything about matter, which is obviously not the case, even if he may have some mystical experience of it. So if the mystic wants to discuss how mind and matter are related, he will finally come to use the physicist's language. Otherwise he will have to fall back on the kind of poetic imagery which is inadequate language for a dialogue.

What I am suggesting is that in the macroscopic world, such a thing as a tree is built out of the implicate order—indeed, *is* the implicate order, which makes possible its living qualities. If we perceive the tree in this way, rather than as a bunch of dead particles into which the property of life is somehow infused when the seed is planted, then its aliveness ceases to be such a mystery.

WEBER: Life is then a continuum; everything is alive?

BOHM: Everything is alive. What we call dead is an abstraction.

WEBER: This brings up another question. Have you not urged in your writings that we ought to keep consciousness out of our descriptions in physics?

BOHM: That is not quite accurate. I am not in principle against trying to bring consciousness and physics together, but thus far the evidence upon which most of the attempts are based is not very good. Consciousness has been on the whole introduced in an arbitrary fashion unconnected with physics.

For example, Descartes said that we have extended substance, which is matter; this would be the explicate order. He made it clear that thinking substance is not of the same order, since we have clear and distinct thoughts which are not spread out in space. He was thus implying a kind of implicate order. He couldn't see how two such different categories could be related, so he postulated that God was ultimately behind the relationship. Descartes thus pointed to a serious problem: two things of such different order are very difficult to relate. It is both arbitrary and inconsistent to say that mind, which is in the implicate order, affects physics, which is in the explicate order. You cannot suddenly inject consciousness variables into physics. A more consistent approach would be to say that both mind and matter participate in the implicate order, and therein lies the basis of a relationship. I have made the suggestion that the unfoldment of thought, from the implicit to the explicit, is similar to the unfoldment of matter. I have also suggested that we experience the implicate order more directly than we experience the explicate order, both inwardly in our perception, and outwardly in our perceptual movement.

A great deal of our difficulty comes from the fact that we accept the idea that not only matter, but all of our experience as well, is in the explicate order, and then suddenly we want to connect this up with consciousness, which is of a totally different order. Before we worry about paranormal or mystical experience we should consider the nature of ordinary, everyday experience. I say that it is totally misunderstood, that it is actually part of the implicate order. Therefore, the difference between ordinary experience and mystical experience is not fundamental, but one of degree.

If the paranormal exists, it can only be understood through reference to the implicate order, since in that order everything contacts everything else and thus there is no intrinsic reason why the paranormal should be impossible. The important thing is to establish it reliably. Furthermore, mystical experience goes still deeper into the implicate order, into the wholeness of mankind, both immanent and transcendent. So if people could understand the nature of ordinary experience better, they would see that mystical experience is really a heightening, and intensification, a deepening, of something that they participate in. In fact, many of the mystics have said that one of the effects of their experience is that they see the world of ordinary experience quite differently. The implicate order provides the commonality deep within matter, energy, life, consciousness. The explicate order of the so-called ordinary world of experience unfolds and displays the implicate.

WEBER: It's not clear what you mean by the term "display."

BOHM: Well, the explicate order can be called that which displays. This is not to devalue it, since it is absolutely necessary both for life and for sanity, but rather to find its proper relationship to the whole. The implicate would not be able to function without the explicate. Suppose you have a computer whose very complex operation in the microchips is displayed on a screen as a perceptible diagram or set of words. That display instantly communicates to you what has been computed, and you act upon that information. I think the brain acts similarly through the imagination. The complex chain of logical reasoning and its conclusions is displayed in an image which is an immediate guide to activity. This image is an outward display. If we ask what it is that is guided by this display, I say it can be nothing but the implicate.

Our most immediate experience of the implicate order is movement itself. We do not actually know how we manage to move. We have a wish to go somewhere, and the imagination displays the activity we want to accomplish, but it doesn't tell us how to achieve it; this remains mysterious to us. In the light of that display, we manage to move, but we could not really describe how we did it. There is evidence that there is an intelligent internal life-energy which can perform action once something is displayed to it. There was a case in which a thin wire was attached to a single nerve in a person's hand, and then connected to a loudspeaker which displayed the function in the nerve by a click. Once the individual had that display, he could produce the click at will, although he couldn't say how, and eventually he even learned to play a tune on it. The point is that when activity is displayed, we can bring some order to it, but without display we can do nothing about it.

WEBER: Displayed means made manifest. It also means feedback.

BOHM: The word "display" literally means "unfold." "Play" is the same root as *plicare,* and "display" means to fold apart. Thus the television image displays the information content, the signal, in a way which the senses can pick up immediately. Similarly, in a series of words which are logically connected, meaning is instantly displayed in an image in the mind, and action follows, just as it follows information from the senses. Thought can display a pattern, a content, similar to what the senses might produce, although of course the pattern is different. Nevertheless, that display indicates to the life-energy what has to be done, as does the display produced by sense experience.

WEBER: I take it the intelligent life-energy you are speaking of is far from the biologically organized life-energy referred to by Descartes and others, which can be constructed mechanistically.

BOHM: Life-energy is more than just biological organization; it reaches into intelligence. Guided by a display, it can do almost anything, but without a display it has nothing to do. In ordinary life, we operate in terms of the imaginal world which displays. For example, if you close your eyes, you can display this room to yourself if you have observed it carefully. There are similar displays of relationship and of the characteristics of things, such as solidity. Indeed, all of our consciousness is a display of past information fused with present sensory data. That display is the unfolded world— all that we know about the explicate order.

WEBER: Yet you are saying that this is not all we know, because we know something of the implicate order as well. We're in touch with it.

BOHM: Yes, we have reached the stage at which the implicate order is also being displayed, or at least some symbolization of it. So the implicate order is getting to know itself better; it is reaching another level of consciousness, which is to say, another point in the evolution of consciousness. As consciousness gets to know itself more and more deeply, so it knows more of what it is doing. At present, such knowledge is mostly confined to the outward domain, because it is here that most of the display is seen.

WEBER: I suppose a mystic is further attuned to the inner display of consciousness, deeper within the implicate order.

BOHM: That's right, much deeper. Nevertheless, it is not totally different from what happens in ordinary experience. It is a continuum.

WEBER: Do you think that quantum mechanics bears this out?

BOHM: Yes, insofar as it says that there is an implicate order and there is an infinite sea of energy, and that this unfolds to form space, time and matter.

WEBER: So, from what you are saying, there is a coherence in physics with what is called the mystical point of view, not only in form but in content.

BOHM: It has not been established, but we can say that it is a plausible or reasonable avenue to explore. As I have said, physics and mysticism could try to find a common language and see if they really have some points in common. One of the issues that might be explored is the connection between mystical experience and common experience, and the possibility that common experience has features that are not usually attended to.

WEBER: You are really saying that there is no "common experience," and that we only designate it as such out of our blindness and ignorance?

BOHM: That's right. And if this view is accepted, the mystic could more easily communicate, since his experience would not be totally foreign to ordinary experience.

WEBER: Then if the notion of an implicate order as a matrix for ordinary experience were more widely understood, that would provide a direction.

BOHM: I think it would be very valuable in that people in all walks of life could participate, and that might actually begin to change their lives.

WEBER: In other words, the implicate order could furnish the unifying ground for both the mystic and the physicist. There is a converging identity of the realms which each describes.

BOHM: One can at least say it is consistent to suppose there is such an identity, even if it cannot be proved. Certainly, matter, energy and consciousness have a common ground which is unknown.

WEBER: Unlike the physicist, the mystic gives what might be called spiritual or moral properties to the unity he experiences; he calls it meaningful, orderly, good.

BOHM: The physicist would at least agree that it's orderly.

WEBER: But the mystic makes a stronger claim: he says that everything in his experience is charged with an inner meaning which precludes all doubt. It just is, and being what it is, that is enough.

BOHM: Well, the scientist could also say that nature is what it is, and that this is enough. Some physicists, like Einstein and Newton, have in fact felt this underlying unity and meaning, so it's not impossible for a physicist to experience it. That it's not more usual is possibly because science has been affected by a point of view which tries to be value-free. This is of course mere prejudice, because obviously what is implied is that the only value to be admitted is scientific truth. Scientists have chosen that as the supreme value, but it is certainly open to argument whether scientific truth is adequate to such a role. Someone else could ask, "Why not make pragmatism your supreme value?" I think if you leave out the notion of the Good, you will find it hard to justify your striving for truth. Implicit in the notion of scientific truth is the idea of the Good: that truth is good in itself or good for what it can do—or both.

WEBER: Therefore, scientists don't want just to be pragmatists; they want to discover the truth in nature.

BOHM: They want to do the good—or what they regard as the good, for they may have a different view of what the good is; this is always debatable. The mystic says that the good can be experienced: that it is wholeness, harmony. The trouble is that this unity doesn't communicate to ordinary experience, and that's why it is so important to understand what ordinary experience does have in common with this mystical experience of wholeness.

WEBER: Apropos of scientific truth, you mentioned earlier that there is no way to prove physics—that even our proofs operate on certain assumptions which themselves are not capable of being proved.

BOHM: There are always relative proofs, but no absolute proofs. In other words, we cannot be absolutely certain that the universe is always and everywhere the way we think it is.

WEBER: Yet you have also said that quantum mechanics is very precise. Is that not somewhat confusing, if science cannot really prove anything?

BOHM: As I indicated earlier, science cannot prove that it is absolutely true. Science takes the form of the universal, which would be what is always true; yet it is actually limited, and in the course of time we will discover those limits. Thus, Newton said that the laws governing the motion of matter are universal, that matter would always move in the same way, but then relativity and quantum mechanics came along and proved otherwise. Indeed, science has always stated that the laws it has discovered are universal, only to find later that they are limited and particular after all. Then the law is seen to be fairly general, but not universal.

WEBER: But there is a difference, is there not, between saying that something cannot be proved absolutely, for all time, and saying that nothing can be proved, which is what you seem to imply?

BOHM: Well, the word "proof" as used in this context usually signifies the logical or factual demonstration of something beyond question; i.e., absolutely. A proof that is relative (and therefore dependent on something else that has not been proved) is, at bottom, no proof at all. Therefore I say we can confirm scientific laws, but we cannot prove them. We confirm a law by showing we have found a large area in which it works, but later on we may discover some areas where it doesn't work at all.

WEBER: You say that this characteristic attends all science?

BOHM: And all rational thought whatsoever.

WEBER: This leads to my next question, for here you sound like Hume, the arch-skeptic. If it's true that nothing is absolute, can we know anything?

BOHM: Not with absolute certainty. We have to be careful. In my view, knowledge is always a proposal. I would differ from Hume when he says that knowledge is nothing but the summary of past experiences in logical order. Our knowledge goes beyond our past experience, but it only does so as a proposition or proposal which has to be tested on every occasion that it is used. Generally speaking, our knowledge does go beyond past experience, but it does not have an absolute character. It is always and at each stage a proposal.

WEBER: All right, treating it as a proposal, then, we can know something?

BOHM: We can know that certain propositions are likely to be confirmed in a fairly large area beyond the one we are addressing. If we say that the proposition that Newton's law holds will be confirmed in a certain area, this does not exclude the possibility that it may not be confirmed in some other area. We have confidence in it, however, with respect to a certain area which is familiar to us.

WEBER: So, to some degree, we can know?

BOHM: Knowing is said to be a proposition which, generally speaking, will be a correct guide to action. That is, it is confirmed by its correct functioning, by being tested against reality again and again, on many different levels and in many different situations.

WEBER: Can we also know that we know?

BOHM: Yes, but again, in the sense that this is a proposition which is continually being tested. It is certainly not clear how well we know that we know. Many people delude themselves in thinking they know that they know—that they are fully self-conscious—whereas they are actually often in a semi-daze.

WEBER: I wonder if the restrictions you have talked about with respect to science are less inhibiting in other modalities, such as direct experience, mysticism, meditation and so on.

BOHM: The minute you bring any experience into words and memory, it has to be taken as a proposition or proposal if it is to have further significance. If a person talks about mystical experience, he is presumably talking not only about that particular moment but also about something that may be relevant at other times and places. And that is always, in my view, a proposition or proposal.

WEBER: It then enters the domain of logic and language. Maybe that's why, throughout history, the language of mysticism has been silence.

BOHM: I think mystics haven't found a way to develop a consistent language for their experience, and therefore it hasn't been communicated to any great extent.

WEBER: Do you think such a language *can* be found?

BOHM: My proposal is that perhaps it can. If knowledge is a proposal, then what I'm proposing is another knowledge.

WEBER: This would indicate that mysticism may be dynamic and even world-historical—subject to time and change. But Lao-tze said, "He who knows does not speak; he who speaks does not know." For him, there was no third possibility.

BOHM: Well, that was Lao-tze's proposal; how far he wanted to carry it I couldn't say. But I want to propose something else: the need for a new modality which can comprehend the totality, the unlimited. What we call metaphysics confronts an inherent difficulty in attempting to think about the totality, because the whole can neither be asserted nor denied in a consistent way. We often say that thought is both limited and unlimited, for in one sense, thought is boundless and can go on forever, while in another sense, thought establishes limitation. But to say that it is both limited and unlimited only serves to identify the opposites. Therefore, what I am saying is that it is neither limited nor unlimited. In other words, we have been looking at thought in the wrong way. Thought does not merely reflect things; it is something in and of itself. It is a real factor in the world.

WEBER: What follows from that?

BOHM: Ordinarily, thought reflects a reality other than itself, but we are fast approaching a state where thought reflects a reality that *is* itself. This calls for a new approach. In a way, thought has become like a work of art: it can be a message about something else, but in addition it is a reality which displays itself, that is, it is a display of some inner idea, intent or perception. And the thought of totality displays itself.

WEBER: Can you give an example? The idea that the thought of totality displays itself is not entirely clear to me.

BOHM: Every thought forms a display in what I call the imaginal world, in terms of the feeling, the image, the idea, the excitement, the muscular tension, which are associated with the thought. For example, I may have a thought of a chair. If I close my eyes, I display the chair to the imagination. That display is a reflection of an actual chair, but I can also invent something like a unicorn which has no correspondence in the actual, although there *might* be or have been such a thing. And then we can go further and discover displays that are entirely the product of thought and do not reflect anything other than themselves. The thought of totality is such a display.

WEBER: What puzzles me is that your entire cosmology is characterized by ideas of the whole and of wholeness. How does that differ from the idea of totality?

BOHM: We do not grasp totality when we think of it, but what I mean by wholeness is undivided flowing movement, unbroken, all-encompassing. The word "totality" seems to have a certain finality about it—a completeness which is inherently static, whereas insofar as wholeness is dynamic and has room for flow, it is inherently incomplete.

WEBER: It is incomplete because it doesn't mortgage away the future—the "not yet."

BOHM: That's right. Whatever we display is incomplete, and that leaves room for movement. So we say that wholeness is the undivided flow of movement which is displayed in this or in that—in other words, in every finite aspect which is abstracted from it.

WEBER: Yet under this movement, this flux, there are characteristics of order and clarity.

BOHM: I would say that order is a proposal that can account for our experience, whereas disorder cannot; therefore no person could possibly do other than tacitly accept the proposal of order.

WEBER: There are many people in the scientific community, however, such as Jacques Monod, who talk about "chance and necessity." Similarly, to B.F. Skinner, everything is just the result of the mechanical motion of blind and inert matter.

BOHM: Physics has shown that the mechanistic order doesn't fit experience, and if it were going to work any place at all, it should be physics. Still less does it work in the field of mind. Actually, in this field it works mainly in certain rather limited areas such as teaching pigeons to peck in a certain sequence.

WEBER: You have characterized a certain kind of order as intelligence.

BOHM: There is no proof of this, you understand. We can merely say that this assertion offers a better order to explore than the limited kind that Skinner or Monod propose. It is better not only because it can explain things more clearly, but because it will lead to more harmonious results.

WEBER: Can you expand on this? Can we, for example, have a direct experience of such intelligent order?

BOHM: I have said that when the content of thought is totality, it is carrying out a dance: making a display which is fundamentally its own deep inner nature, the whole of itself. In that process it becomes totally involved, and therefore it becomes in a way a work of art which is displaying its inner principle rather than anything superficial. But in so doing it becomes typical. If there were such a thing as a true totality, all it could display would be itself. So in a way, thought becomes a symbol or metaphor—an activity which is a living example of what infinite means, for when a thing truly displays its own inner nature, it is a microcosm of infinity. And isn't that what a good work of art is? Therefore, in some poetic sense, it becomes relevant to art. So you can come to the experience of wholeness, through the experience of nature as well as of art, and perhaps in other ways as well. I certainly believe that thought itself can bring you to this experience of wholeness insofar as it is able consistently to cease to reflect anything other than itself. At that moment, there is an *enactment of wholeness*.

WEBER: When it does that, you say thought is creative. Is it also revelatory of the inner recess of the implicate order?

BOHM: Yes, if it is a living enactment of the wholeness.

WEBER: In the Eastern traditions, that thought or mind has two kinds of functions: one which is associative, reactive, logical or analytic; the other, synthetic, intuitive, perceptive of wholes. Do you subscribe to this idea?

BOHM: Within the realm in which thought reflects something else, it may be analytic, or it may perceive wholes. But I'm trying to go beyond both of these approaches, to the thought which is not attempting to reflect anything other than itself.

WEBER: When the kind of thought that went into Einstein's work was articulated, didn't it also enact and reflect something of the order of the universe?

BOHM: Yes, but Einstein considered himself to be thinking about the universe. He didn't think that his thought was enacting itself.

WEBER: What is the difference?

BOHM: There is no completely consistent way of making the universe the content of metaphysical thought, because the latter has already questioned what lies beyond. Metaphysical thought has a drive inherent in it to go further, to the point of being without an external content.

WEBER: You are saying that we should be paying attention to the phenomenology of thought—how it operates, what it is in itself, rather than just what it is about.

BOHM: Yes, that's right. Mind has thought, feeling, desire, will, attention—all this and more. On the one hand, thought emphasizes the perception of categories, such as the universal and the particular, but on the other hand, every phase of thought is naturally expressed through feeling as well. All these aspects flow into each other; they are all implicating each other. And I'm saying that when we come to the thought of wholeness, it too will flow into the feeling of wholeness. Anybody who attempts to think seriously of the whole experiences a vastness as well as an intensity of feeling.

WEBER: And this, according to what you are saying, is dangerous?

BOHM: It's both dangerous and necessary, because it cannot be avoided. It is a danger we must face if the system—that is, the whole world of knowledge, everybody's thought—is to come to any real order.

WEBER: All right, it's dangerous. But why is it necessary?

BOHM: You cannot stop thought from moving on beyond limits. Thought is already implicitly beyond any limit that it sets up; that's the way it's built. Given that, what can we do to bring about order?

WEBER: In other words, *we* have to ride *it*, not the other way around.

BOHM: Otherwise it will take hold of us. The first thing is to understand it, to work together with it. It's no use saying to this tremendous energy, which overpasses any limit it sets up, "Keep away from the totality question, ignore it, pretend it isn't there!" Human thought is a tremendous instrument which has not been used properly, and thus its destructive effects have predominated. It has the potential for constructive effects, but I think it is extremely dangerous to pretend to know what we don't know.

WEBER: You have said that what interests you especially is the flow between the implicate and the explicate—between matter and the spiritual—which creates balance and sanity. Could you go into this a bit more?

BOHM: Again that is a proposal, although it seems a reasonable one to me. I've tried to indicate that the opposites, like the limited and the unlimited or the absolute and the relative, are actually categories of thought. They don't stand up in the end. Therefore, these opposites are displays which have limited utility. It is the same with spirit and matter; they are opposites which thought itself has produced, based on perceived differences which also don't stand up. They are useful, perhaps necessary, but the attempt to regard them as fixed and final is artificial.

WEBER: You're proposing that the movement between this unseen world and the tangible, empirical world is what human life is basically about, and that when life is anchored in both there is sanity and balance.

BOHM: I would like to say how I think these opposites are related. When you trace a particular absolute notion to what appears to be its logical conclusion, you find it to be identical with its opposite, and therefore the whole dualism collapses, as Hegel found. Reason first shows you that opposites pass into each other, then you discover that one opposite reflects the other, and finally you find that they are identical to each other—not really different at all. The two opposites may be first treated as independent, but you will find that each is the principle of movement of the other.

I would like to look at spirit and matter in that way. If we look at matter, it appears inert because although it is moving, that movement is mechanical. Then suddenly something creative presents itself, and we attribute that to spirit. I call that a matter of form in thought: a form which thought sets up whenever it sees something it can't explain. Therefore spirit becomes a principle of movement of matter (and vice versa, since the condition of matter is the principle whereby spirit can act). So we can see the movement of matter as occasioned by spirit. Therefore, if you were to look at the total movement, you could say the matter and spirit were identical.

WEBER: Matter is saturated with spirit, and spirit embeds itself within matter. These two are not separate in reality.

BOHM: They are completely interpenetrating.

WEBER: Did I understand you to say that when you push matter to its furthest extent, when you really understand it in depth, then you get cosmic consciousness, cosmic mind?

BOHM: Some kind of cosmic order that will eventually be seen as implicate consciousness.

WEBER: Matter and spirit are really one and the same, but they also represent two different languages. The mystic has been working on the premise that consciousness is one; the physicist, that matter is one. What you are saying is that the novelty, at this juncture in our history, lies in the fact that the physicist is now willing and *able* to see this wholeness, and this development can help open a dialogue.

BOHM: Quantum mechanics and relativity have shown the failure of the mechanistic order and the need for another order, which I call the implicate. This is parallel to the order which we have observed in mind, so it becomes possible to have a relationship between those two realms. The mystic may either experience the immanence or the transcendence of wholeness, as we mentioned before, both of which he finds very difficult to talk about, except in poetic or symbolic terms. One approach for him is to say nothing, but that does little for mankind's need for a new perception. So if we can find a language in which mind and matter are seen to be of the same order, then it might be possible to discuss this experience intelligibly.

Some mystics have indeed indicated that the implicate order is actually relevant to their experiences and insights. Of these, the one who comes closest to the definite suggestion of such an order is Nicholas of Cusa, with his use of the terms *implicatio, explicatio* and *complicatio,* and even more with his statement, "Eternity both enfoldeth and unfoldeth succession." In a similar vein, Krishnamurti has said (though he does not like to be called a mystic) that a human being has to flower on goodness, and this means, of course, to unfold. More generally, words suggesting unfoldment from the mysterious ground of all that is an enfoldment back onto the ground are not at all uncommon in the language used by those who (whether they call themselves mystics or not) feel that they are in direct contact with this ground.

WEBER: All this suggests not only that we transform as eternity unfolds in us, but also that eternity may transform, as it returns to itself in a richer way; through our participation. This fundamentally changes the impossible question as to the "why" of creation and of mankind's long history and shows us to be part of the whole enterprise.

BOHM: Yes. We have at least the potential to participate. However, with respect to time and eternity, I would say further that each is the moving principle of the other.

WEBER: That proposal challenges the image the existentialists and the positivists have made of man and gives him great dignity, in that his life transforms the whole process or parts of it.

BOHM: Yes, we may participate in the whole and thus help to give it meaning. This is a position more favored in the West than in the East, which is inclined to make the human being rather a small thing in the cosmos. But we are nevertheless an intrinsic feature of the universe, which would be incomplete without us in some fundamental sense.

WEBER: Our finiteness is somehow indispensible to the infinite?

BOHM: Again, the important thing is the flow between these two opposites, the infinite and the finite. Hegel said that the infinite contains the finite, and in some sense that is true. But I would rather say that both the infinite and the finite have a role to play. You could say that there is an infinite which contains all of the finite, but also that the infinite has to be seen in all these finite ways. So I look at metaphysical thought as a series of movements in a dance— movements that we make in which we are able to see our errors and so move on. In carrying out this dance, we bring order into the whole universe, not only to ourselves. It is through the errors we make that we are able to learn, to change ourselves and to change everything.

WEBER: This brings to mind your earlier objection. With respect to the introduction of consciousness into quantum mechanics, you said that your objection was founded on the fact that it was inconsistent. But if one were to conceive of *both* quantum mechanics and thought as in the implicate order, then there would be a natural place for their interconnection.

BOHM: Which can now be explored.

WEBER: You also said earlier that if one understands matter profoundly enough it may turn out that experience of the normal, the paranormal and the mystical all have one and the same root in the implicate order. What makes you feel that as a possibility?

BOHM: I have said that in music, and in visual and other sensory experience, the implicate order is primary in that the sense of flowing movement is experienced *before* we analyze it into the elements which express that movement or display it. You may listen to music and later break it down into notes which you can display either in imagination or on a piece of paper. Ultimately, the same thing is true in vision, but we have become so used to fixing our attention on objects that we don't perceive this. We tend to see each object as fixed and separate, because we return to the same object (this tree, this rock) again and again. Therefore the flowing movement regenerates the same thing over and over, causing us to lose sight of the movement itself, except perhaps in rare instances when we look at a stream or the sky, where there are no fixed objects which can be focused on. But all our experience, including thought, begins in immediate awareness of this flowing movement. When we carry metaphysical thought to the point where it reflects only itself, it too turns into a flowing movement between opposites, such as the finite and the infinite. And if we experience thought and feeling, instead of naming and fixing them, feelings will flow into thoughts, thoughts into feelings.

WEBER: How do you relate this to the idea of the normal, the paranormal and the mystical?

BOHM: I say that all of this is normal experience, which is misunderstood because we emphasize the description of objects, thoughts and feelings, instead of the flowing movement between them. Carrying this farther, we could say that in the relationship between two people, each is the moving principle of the other. We ordinarily don't experience that moving relationship, and so we see each as a separate and independent being, which is in fact not true.

WEBER: They are not really separate beings.

BOHM: No. Let's say a person is thinking or feeling something. If he were by himself he would move in a certain way. Presented with another person, he starts to move differently, in response to the other.

WEBER: Some people interpret this in another way, saying that I'm still a separate globule, even if your responses force me to modify mine.

BOHM: But how do they force you? If you watch, you'll see that there is no choice, no compulsion; it happens, and then you justify it.

WEBER: You're saying, therefore, that we're linked to one in the implicate domain, and this is what we respond to.

BOHM: That's right. Mankind is one implicate domain, both physically and mentally, which we distort by saying that it is only "the many." The proposal that mankind is "the many" is valid up to a point, but beyond that point it fails.

WEBER: Would it be fair to say that in the implicate domain mankind is one, but in its explicate expression we each seem to be little points of entry.

BOHM: The whole function of the explicate order is to display things as separate. In fact, this display becomes a guide to further activity. The activity is always one, but the display may be misleading. For example, a pair of opposites consists of something and something else; as Plato said, "From the one and the other, everything was made." When we say that there is one, we think of it as complete, whole, and when we say there is the other, that too is a "one," complete, whole. But later we find that this separateness is not final, for the moment you think of another, the thought of the other *is* you.

WEBER: In other words, that thought is part of your reality at that moment.

BOHM: It's just as powerful a guide to your energy as is a thought about yourself. Therefore we say that the other becomes the moving principle of what we call you, just as you are the moving principle of what we call the other.

WEBER: Is the reasoning analogous when we say that the normal, the paranormal and the mystical are at root one?

BOHM: That's right. The question is what do we mean by "other." Matter may be the other for us; we move it and it moves us. So isn't it possible that there is a kind of intelligence in matter that is immanent, which makes it possible for matter to respond? We are the other for matter, and therefore when it is confronted by us it will do something different. We know this happens through physical contact, but it may happen mentally as well.

WEBER: You're making it sound as if matter were alive!

BOHM: That is what I have proposed: that inanimate matter is an abstraction which we get when we leave out the potential of life. But there may be more than a potential: there may be a sort of living energy in all matter that manifests in us in certain ways which it doesn't do in the rock. If that were the case, if a sort of intelligence were generalized throughout nature, then the speculative proposal that inanimate matter might respond to our thought is not so illogical. This would be the domain of the paranormal. When we come to so-called mystical experience, we could again say that this oneness is carried to the *n*th degree.

WEBER: In other words, you're saying we are not only ignorant about ourselves but also about matter.

BOHM: Yes, we are fundamentally ignorant about matter. And we *are* matter after all.

WEBER: And the difference between, say, the rock and ourselves might be that it knows less about us than we know about it, but it may "know" as much about the cosmic dimension in its own way.

BOHM: It may. And if paranormal experience is real (which I can't be sure of), then perhaps those who have it are able to let the rock know about us, and that's why it would move if asked to. That is my proposal.

WEBER: In holistic medicine, it has been found that the very thought of oneself as being physically well affects the nervous system profoundly. I've heard people who work in cancer therapy (i.e., Simonton, Achterberg, Lawlis) speak of the fact that the nervous system cannot distinguish between a visualized response and an actual one.

BOHM: That's the point I've been making: the display in consciousness is the guide to the whole response of the body and the mind, whether for good or ill. If the display is confused, the results will be bad; if the display is orderly, it will work harmoniously.

WEBER: So the power of thought can be so great that one can think oneself into illness and into health. Specifically how do illness and health fit into the implicate order?

BOHM: This is a question of the harmony of the organism. One does not find perfect order or harmony, for whatever exists is bound to change or die. I would like to propose, with respect to evolution, that natural selection is not the whole story, but rather that evolution is a sign of the creative intelligence of matter exploring different structures which go far beyond what is needed for survival. Although survival in the environment determines which of these will go on and which won't, it cannot be the only factor in evolution. If it were, there would be no reason for the development of human beings with such a complex brain. Indeed, rats are far better at survival than we could ever hope to be. It is thus hard to see survival as the whole explanation. One could say, rather, that evolution results from the creative movement of matter, which is infused with intelligence. None of these developments is perfect, and therefore there is a degree of malfunction, of ill health, in nature. But when man came on the scene, mind began to play a role in perpetuating and aggravating this illness—but also in discovering its cures.

WEBER: I suppose the rock cannot misuse its capacity in the same way that man can misuse his mind.

BOHM: Well, the rock is going to be itself, a rock. But through the kind of thought which grasps the universal, not just the particular, the mind can see possibilities which don't yet exist, and bring them into realization through their display.

WEBER: Then possibility is a living reality for man, but not for the rock?

BOHM: Genuine possibility is, yes.

WEBER: To revert to the mystic and the physicist, it might be fair to say that the mystic may experience nature as a whole in its "suchness," without knowing anything of the exquisite details of its organization? Perhaps it is only the scientist who can speak of nature's plan in all its complexity.

BOHM: Not merely the details—the universal principles as well. The scientist also attempts to find proposals for universal laws. Therefore he sees nature globally as well as in detail; in this lies his creativity—his enactment of wholeness. The mystic has a different domain: in himself he enacts the immanence and the transcendence of the whole universe. The artist and the musician enact the whole they see creatively, and the mystic is not too different from them, in that he too is a creative artist in his own way.

WEBER: Expressing what—wholeness?

BOHM: The wholeness within his own experience, in his very being. The same thing is true of metaphysical thought.

WEBER: How does the mystic's expression differ, then?

BOHM: It may not. Hegel claimed that his logic was another expression of his mysticism.

WEBER: Are you saying that the work of the mystic, the scientist, the artist and the philosopher are all different expressions of the same reality?

BOHM: Yes. And together they may do something that they could never achieve separately. If they could engage in a dialogue, they could really produce something that could be called "higher" thought.

WEBER: Because it would embrace all of these modalities.

BOHM: And something new which lies beyond any or all of them.

WEBER: Somehow this evocation of vastness evokes for me the vastness of space which science is exploring today, and which has some parallel to the vastness of space experienced in meditation. Can we discuss meditation?

BOHM: There is some parallel in the sense that both thought and matter are in the implicate order. We go from the explicate to the implicate, then to a deeper multidimensional level, thence to some vast ocean outside of space as we ordinarily experience it. Perhaps meditation will lead you deep into this ocean of physical and mental energy, which is universal.

WEBER: By mental you don't mean thought?

BOHM: No, beyond thought, although it doesn't exclude thought.

WEBER: Could you enlarge on that? This is one of Lama Govinda's central ideas.

BOHM: It is hard to enlarge it. Space is a certain order, whose simplest form is the three dimensions or coordinates of Descartes. But if you follow this idea into quantum mechanics, you see a much more subtle multidimensional order, which eventually dissolves into a vast ocean of energy. The order of space is therefore the ground on which anything can exist or take place in the material world, and it is also the ground on which anything can be experienced or known in the mind.

WEBER: But the space in quantum mechanics is not capable of being experienced, whereas the space in meditation can be.

BOHM: Nevertheless, the ground in both is ultimately the same. We don't directly experienced the space that quantum mechanics talks about, but we may experience something which has a parallel, and that parallel may have an origin in the deeper ground common to both.

WEBER: Govinda says, in his *Foundations of Tibetan Mysticism*, that the way we experience space is an indicator of the state of our consciousness, and that our concept of space changes as our consciousness changes. Do you have any view on that?

BOHM: If you are primarily focused in the explicate order, your sense of space will be confined to the spaces between a lot of separate objects. As you go further into the explicate order, you begin to see that these objects contain each other and fall into each other. Eventually you will see them as forms within a much vaster space, and finally, a space in which no forms are created. I think this corresponds to different stages of consciousness.

WEBER: If one had an experience of the limitless infinitude of space, one would have an infinitude of consciousness?

BOHM: It would be consciousness which was infinite not in terms of extension, but in its self-determined character. There is a sort of analogy to be found within the system of real numbers, where it is shown than an infinity can map onto itself. In this sense, you could say that the infinity of being can map onto knowing, and thus knowing and being are ultimately identical in the infinity—in that infinity which is not extensive but *intensive*.

The point I want to make, however, is that the display of what that kind of being is requires a space which is entirely different from that in which we display mechanical objects. Therefore, we could say that consciousness has to become commensurate with that different space in order to discover it. Consciousness, in fact, has to change its very state.

9
THE TAO OF PHYSICS
REVISITED

A Conversation with Fritjof Capra
Conducted by Renée Weber

WEBER: You've written *The Tao of Physics*, which has been out for five years, and I gather there are about a quarter of a million copies in print. So lots of people have been influenced by the book. How do you feel now about the claims of the book and about some of the reaction the book has generated?

CAPRA: The book was published five years ago, but, of course, I began this exploration much earlier, and I think it's been just about a decade since I discovered these parallels between modern physics and Eastern mysticism. Now I should add right away that I wasn't the only one who discovered these parallels. Other people have hinted at the parallels, but I was the only physicist who explored them in detail. And I began the first steps of this exploration in 1970; I finished the book in 1974.

WEBER: Are there other books that take the same position, and do you think they reinforce the view that you take in *The Tao of Physics*?

CAPRA: Yes, they do. There has been a book published roughly at the same time with mine, by Lawrence LeShan called *The Medium, the Mystic and Physicist*. There have been books in England also and there was a book recently called *The Dancing Wu Li Masters* by Gary Zukav. All these books strengthen the case in the sense that they make the parallels known to a wider public, and they stimulate discussions. Actually, the Zukav book, which is very often mentioned in connection with mine, does not add anything to the debate. Zukav reiterates the idea that I expressed several years earlier, which, of course, he knew very well because he had read my book. But it helps because the more these parallels are discussed by

215

the public, and also by various professional groups, the more interesting they become, I believe.

WEBER: You made mention of the fact that you are really the only
working physicist who has taken on this task of making the
connection.

CAPRA: You see I know several physicists who have thought about
the parallels to mysticism but who somehow did not feel it was
worthwhile or didn't feel like going into this and really exploring it.
It was a big decision for me, too, because I had to take time off from
physics and dedicate my whole time and energy to this task.

WEBER: Do you think, Fritjof, that some of these physicists feared
that their professional reputations would be impaired?

CAPRA: That was probably very much a part of the question, and
it *did* impair *my* reputation, although I wasn't that well known to
begin with.

WEBER: You were very young when you wrote this book.

CAPRA: I was young, and I was not that well known, but it did
effect me very strongly professionally because I practically had to
drop out of physics for about three years.

WEBER: You mean to write the book.

CAPRA: Yes. We do research in physics by writing papers and
then getting grants. But the kind of research I was doing in Buddhism and Taoism didn't get me any physics grants. Although I
kept up with physics during all that time, I wasn't active in research.
So I didn't have any financial support until, eventually, I found a
publisher. By the way, 12 publishers turned it down. Finally Wild-
wood House in England took it and gave me an advance. In this
country Shambhala published it. They were my second publisher.

WEBER: Other than sacrificing the time to do research, do you think
the claim of the book itself somehow jeopardized your reputation (among
or in) the community of physicists?

CAPRA: I think it definitely did. However, when the book came
out and physicists read it, those who read it recognized right away
that I knew what I was talking about when I talked about physics.
To the best of my knowledge, there are no errors in the book, and
what is more, physicists recognized that I did a fairly good job in
presenting those complex concepts to a lay audience. Most physicists teach undergraduates and nonphysics students, and they know

that this is very difficult. So I was happy to see that this was acknowledged right away. I was taken seriously with half of the book. I was not taken seriously with the other half, but they came around to it slowly, and I think there's a definite change of opinion now in physics circles about the book. I know that. I know several physicists who were very much against the connection with mysticism in the beginning, but who are now buying *The Tao of Physics* for their friends and recommending it. So I'm very happy, generally, with the development in the physics community.

WEBER: You know in Princeton I had a short interview with Eugene Wigner in his office.

CAPRA: Oh yes?

WEBER: Yes. And we talked a little bit about any possible connection between Eastern mysticism and physics. In my purse I was carrying *The Tao of Physics,* but I decided to withhold it until the perfect moment in the conversation. At one point I felt we had just about reached the proper moment and was about to tell him this book might interest him when he jumped up, went to a desk which was piled with papers and books, pulled out *The Tao of Physics,* brought it over to me and said, "I think this would interest you."

CAPRA: You know many physicists were very threatened by the book.

WEBER: Why is that?

CAPRA: I think because mysticism is thought of in the scientific community as something very vague, describing something fuzzy, nebulous and highly unscientific. Now to see one's cherished theories compared with this highly unscientific activity is threatening to physicists. I've heard that from many of them. On the other hand, I also know that some of the great physicists of our century were immensely enriched by the recognition that the basic concepts of their theories were similar to those in mystical traditions. Some of them found this difficult in the beginning. But ultimately they regarded it as a great intellectual and cultural enrichment of their lives. First and foremost was Heisenberg. I had several discussions with him. I lived in England then, and I visited him several times in Munich and showed him the whole manuscript chapter by chapter. He was very interested and very open, and he told me something that I think is not known publicly because he never published it. He said that he was well aware of these parallels. While he was working on quantum theory, he went to India to lecture and he was a guest of Tagore. He talked a lot with Tagore about Indian philosophy. Heisenberg told me that these talks had helped him a lot with his work in physics, because they showed him that all these new ideas in quantum theory were in fact not all that crazy. He realized there was, in fact, a whole culture that subscribed to very similar ideas. Heisenberg said that this was a great help for him. Niels Bohr had a similar experience when he went to China. Various other physicists either have told me or have written to me that they have seen these parallels as a great enrichment. But of course it needs some breadth of mind and some intellectual maturity to recognize that.

WEBER: Fritjof, now I want to ask you something that really strikes me as proper at this moment. You've said that some physicists felt threatened by the notion that what for them had always been a synonym for unclear thinking—mysticism—suddenly was offering a cosmology that not only was taken seriously but that really looked, on the surface at least, as if it paralleled their own cosmology. Now what would you say to the criticism that what may *look* like similarities on the surface and in language need not be similar at all underneath. I think that a number of critics have made that point.

CAPRA: First of all, we should clarify this view of mysticism as being vague and nebulous. It is an erroneous view. People who really study mysticism, who experience it, who practice it and also who write about it know very well that mystical experience has nothing to do with nebulous and unclear thinking. Unscientific, yes. It's a very different approach.

WEBER: Nonscientific, shall we say?

CAPRA: Right. Nonscientific is a better term. But it's not unclear and nebulous and vague. It can be very clear, very precise and very reliable. Now when you talk about the parallels, the question of whether they are superficial, just a similarity of words, will always occur since we have a limited number of words. You could find parallels to all kinds of philosophical traditions.

WEBER: The claim is that the language is accidentally similar but not in a central way. Therefore this doesn't warrant the claim that there is a similar reality imbedded in each of these terms.

CAPRA: Well, to tell you the truth, this is what I thought myself. This is how I began.

WEBER: So you were skeptical yourself, in other words.

CAPRA: Yes, I was. My first article in *Main Currents in Modern Thought* 1972, starts with that argument. And I said that it may seem that these parallels are superficial, and, as far as I remember, I said that one could draw parallels to Marxist philosophy or to any kind of philosophy on the basis of a similarity of words. Some of my recent critics have also made that remark, and it amuses me that I started off with the same kind of doubt. What convinced me of the substance of these parallels were two developments. First was the increasing consistency of the parallels. The more I studied them, the more areas I explored, the more consistently the parallels appeared. Let me give you an example.

In relativity theory, one of the most important developments has been the unification of space and time. Einstein recognized that space and time are not separate, that they are connected intimately and inseparably to form a four-dimensional continuum: space/time. A direct consequence of this recognition is the equivalence of mass and energy and the intrinsically dynamic nature of all subatomic phenomena. The fact that space and time are related so intimately implies that subatomic particles are dynamic patterns, that they are events rather than objects. So the role of space and time and the dynamic nature of the object studied are very closely related.

In Buddhism, you discover exactly the same thing. In the Mahayana school, they have a notion of interpenetration of space and time, and they also say that objects are really events. I have a quote in the book by D. T. Suzuki which says that the fact that objects are events can only be understood when it is realized that space and time are interpenetrating. This kind of consistency really struck me. And it goes throughout the whole exploration. The more you see this consistency, the more you realize that the parallels are not accidental. There's no single proof, of course, and in the epilogue I say that you can never prove that these similarities are relevant or fundamental. But you come to realize it more and more as you study the realm of similarities.

Now that was one development. The other one is connected with the fact that you cannot learn mysticism by reading books. You have to practice it, at least to some extent, to have an idea of what the mystics are talking about.

WEBER: You mean you have to experience it. You really have to plunge into it.

CAPRA: You have to follow some discipline or some form of meditation or some way to get into these other states of consciousness that the mystics talk about.

WEBER: Would you say that meditation is the analog of the verification in physics?

CAPRA: Yes, and that's how I set up the comparisons in the book. I compare the scientific experiment with the meditative observation and the scientific theories with the various images and doctrines and metaphors of the mystics. Now I have not gone very far in the practice of a spiritual tradition. I am most attracted by Taoism, as you might guess from the title of the book. I have a Chinese teacher; I practice Taoist meditation, T'ai Chi, and so on. Through this practice, I began to understand these parallels, not only intellectually, but somehow with my whole being.

WEBER: Can you explain that?

CAPRA: Well, it is something that is not easy to explain. But I can assert very sincerely that I have experienced all the similarities between physics and mysticism that I talk about in the book, at a level that is much deeper than an intellectual level. And the two developments—the consistency of the parallels and the intuitive experience—went hand-in-hand.

WEBER: In your own mind, this rules out that there's a superficial or glib or accidental mapping of these two things.

CAPRA: Yes, because I know more about them than I can say in words. This may sound like an unusual argument coming from a scientist, but it is not. You see in our culture these intuitive aspects of scientific discovery or any other kind of discovery are just not emphasized. But physicists know them very well. For instance, Einstein experienced relativity theory before he formulated it. Bohr experienced quantum mechanics before he formulated them. Feynman experienced quantum field theory and Chew experienced S-matrix theory before their formulation.

For example, when you read Feynman's account of quantum field theory in his Nobel prize speech, you can *feel* that the way he talks about electrons and electromagnetic waves and quantum fields comes really from a deep experience. Feynman is an extremely gifted teacher because of that fact, you see? Because he has his physics in his bones.

WEBER: He speaks from within and puts it in concepts.

CAPRA: Right. Geoffrey Chew, the physicist I work with at Berkeley, the originator of the bootstrap and of S-matrix theory, has that theory in his bones. I can see him struggling for words, but I know very well by observing him that he really knows what he means without being able to say it. Eventually, of course, he also finds the words, the mathematics, and all that.

With Bohr it was the same thing. I talked with David Bohm about Niels Bohr. Bohm knew him, and he told me that nobody really understood Bohr. Bohr was not very good with words, and you can see that when you read him. He couldn't express himself too well, but he had an incredible power of persuasion. And that power of persuasion was like the power of the guru. And, by the way, here is another interesting point: when you listen to physicists talk about various theories and various people, then Bohr is maybe the only physicist who's treated like a guru. It's very interesting. People would never say "Einstein said this or that." People outside of physics would say that. But within physics we would never say "Einstein said so and so," we would say "Relativity shows" or the "Lorentz transformation shows," because we know the theory, we can derive it ourselves. We don't need Einstein today. But when it comes to quantum theory and its interpretation, people always refer back to Bohr.

WEBER: You're saying he experienced his concepts on many levels of his being. They were not just in his head, but he somehow lived them and knew them in a deeper way. But now here is a problem that seems to me to need further clarification. What would you say about two physicists who hold competing theories, rival theories, like bootstrap and quark theory, and each of them gives the feeling that he lived and has known it from within?

CAPRA: Well, I would say in that case, that the aspects of the theories that they experience intuitively are likely to be the aspects that survive. Those are what you could call the flavor of the theory, the quantum reality or the relativistic reality.

WEBER: But to them it's so clear it is part of them, you're saying.

CAPRA: Yes. The part that is contradictory has to do with the mathematical framework. Should we use waves or matrices? Should we use quarks or should we use topology? These questions, eventually, are resolved and what is valid in the two theories will survive.

WEBER: So, the point that you're establishing is that in writing *The Tao of Physics*, though at first you were as skeptical as physicists in general would have been, two factors have convinced you: the increasing consistency; and this extra-logical factor, a kind of intuitive conviction coming from your own experience. You're saying, really, that you began to take seriously, along with your training and knowledge as a physicist, other models of approaching experience. And the two began to harmoize and intertwine.

CAPRA: And I learned how to use them, when to use one and when to use the other. I developed a technique to use them both and not let them interfere with each other.

WEBER: You didn't worry unduly that these wider avenues to inquiry would somehow influence your work in physics?

CAPRA: Let me think about that. I did worry about it, yes. I wasn't worried about my work in physics at the mundane level, whether I would get a grant or not, whether I'd be able to do research. I was worried about it at a quite deep intellectual level. And now that you mention it, I remember asking Krishnamurti about this problem. I met Krishnamurit in 1968 or 1969 at the University of California at Santa Cruz. He gave three lectures on three consecutive days, and they really stirred me up. It was one of the strongest influences I had in those early days. He talked about freedom from the known and stopping thinking and all that, and I sensed the power of his presence and of his words and it worried me. I remember my wife and I went home afterwards, and we sat down by the fireplace and talked about it, and I was really worried.

WEBER: Because he was commending the very thing that as a physicist you had been trained to fear and to avoid.

CAPRA: Yes. He was commending abandoning what I had studied and in which I had a lot of emotional investment. I actually was in the same situation that most physicists find themselves in when confronted with the ideas of mystical traditions. Only for me it came at a very early stage. It was long before I started writing. Anyway, I had an audience with Krishnamurti, and I asked him my burning question: "How can I be a scientist and follow your advice—not to think; freedom from the known; living in the moment; and all of that?" He answered the question in two minutes, and it solved all my problems. He said, first you are a human being; then you are a scientist. And he said, at an existential level, at a spiritual level, you realize what goes beyond thought and you realize the larger reality. He didn't use these terms; I don't remember what exactly he said, but it was something like that. Then, he said, you could specialize and do all your science, and it's marvelous to do, science. That's what he said, and I was never threatened afterwards.

Later on, much later, I found a very beautiful quote from a Tibetan Buddhist monk which said something like "once you realize the approximate nature of all concepts, then you can really love them, because you love them without attachment."

WEBER: Very good.

CAPRA: That really has been my leitmotif in all my subsequent work.

WEBER: Do you think some of the people who became nervous about the parallels, either on behalf of mysticism or on behalf of science, hadn't grasped what you've just been talking about?

CAPRA: Well, I think maybe that's true for some of them.

WEBER: You must have had quite a bit of criticism over these years.

CAPRA: Oh yes. In the last five years I gave a lot of lectures to general audiences, but also to physicists, psychologists, physicians and many other professional groups, who picked up *The Tao of Physics* and invited me to lecture. So, I've had a very rich exchange of ideas, and in this rich exchange I have also encountered quite a few critics.

WEBER: What were their main arguments?

CAPRA: Well, I would like to mention three recently published articles that express the principal arguments that I have heard many times. They are serious and thoughtful arguments. The authors are Jeremy Bernstein, Ravi Ravindra and Ken Wilber. Bernstein is a physicist and a journalist, and Ravindra has a dual appointment in the departments of physics and religion at Dalhousie University in Canada.

WEBER: Ken Wilber, of course, is well known to the readers of *ReVision* as its editor-in-chief and as an author. So, you said that these three critiques contain similar arguments.

CAPRA: Yes, but it is intertaining to compare their styles. Whereas the critiques of Wilber and Ravindra are philosophical and rather detached, that of Bernstein operates at a totally different level.

When you read his review, you notice immediately that his reaction to my book is very emotional, and parts of the review are very aggressive.

I mention this because it's interesting for the things we just said about physicists being threatened. He is quite a typical example. Now I don't know Bernstein personally. I've never met him, but the review is full of snide remarks and rather insulting comments. I cannot help but think that Bernstein is very threatened and feels very insecure.

WEBER: Can we get into some of the specifics of his criticism?

CAPRA: I would say that the most important argument, which he shares with the other two critiques and which is an argument I've heard often, is that today's scientific facts will be invalidated by tomorrow's research. How, these critics ask, can something so transient as a model or theory in modern physics be said to corroborate mystical experience, which is supposed to be timeless and eternal? Does this not mean that the truth of mysticism will stand or fall with the theories of modern physics? This argument sounds very convincing, but I believe that it is based on a thorough misunderstanding of the nature of science. This misunderstanding of science is unfortunately very widespread and is something that I talk about in all my lectures. Now I cannot fault Ken Wilber for this misunderstanding because he's not a physicist, but I am surprised about Bernstein and Ravindara who are both scientists and who really should know better. They assert correctly that there's no absolute truth in science. But they totally misrepresent the nature of scientific research.

WEBER: How is that?

CAPRA: Well, let me quote Ravindra who says, "Every age has thought as we do now that we have the right answers." Now this is quite wrong when you speak about modern science. In modern science we do not think any longer that we have the right answers. We have come to realize that whatever we say is an approximation; it's a limited model.

WEBER: It's tentative.

CAPRA: Well, it will be tentative at the beginning. But even complete theories, like quantum mechanics, special relativity, Newtonian mechanics, Maxwell's electrodynamics, etc., which are no longer tentative, are nevertheless approximate and limited. They do not tell you the truth. They give you approximate descriptions of reality, which are improved in subsequent development in successive steps. This is how we do research. We improve our theories in successive steps. Now I think that this is fairly well known within science, but not so much outside of science. Physicists have this reputation in our society of knowing the truth. Now, the point that is relevant here is that when you improve theories in successive steps with new models, the knowledge does not change in an arbitrary way. It's not that today this is a fact and tomorrow something else will be.

WEBER: According to Thomas Kuhn, when a theory is really overthrown, you have a whole new paradigm, and that happens rarely, isn't that right?

CAPRA: Right. But even when it happens, the new theory is still related to the old one in a well-defined way, although in a scientific revolution, you don't know that until afterwards. And the new theory does not invalidate the old one in an absolute way. It merely improves the approximation. Newtonian physics is the standard example. Quantum theory did not show that Newtonian physics was wrong. It showed that it was limited. In the realm of macroscopic physical phenomena, in everything connected with machines and so on, Newtonian physics is still the best model. It is still used. Whenever you build a car, you implicitly use Newtonian physics.

WEBER: So you're saying quantum theory neither displaced nor replaced Newtonian physics, but supplemented it.

CAPRA: It supplemented it, and it displaced it in a different realm of phenomena. When you go beyond the range of validity of the theory, then it is replaced. Now when you have a new theory, you don't know the range of validity. It's only when you discover things that don't work, that you come to the scientific revolutions. And that's a very difficult process.

WEBER: And science is conservative. It doesn't easily allow a whole theory to be overthrown. It's the last thing it wants to have happen and it will make other adjustments, if possible.

CAPRA: Heisenberg's account of the 1920s is the most vivid account that I know of the struggle of replacing a theory. Now, it is important to notice that when this extension occurs, not all the concepts of the old theory are modified. I believe now it is precisely those views and concepts that are not modified or invalidated, but remain, which are the ones that show the parallels to the mystical tradition. Now this is a difficult question, because obviously you will ask what kind of concepts they are. What types? I think this a very interesting and extremely difficult question which should be explored.

WEBER: Could we go into some aspect of it?

CAPRA: I can't give you a general criterion, but I'll give you an example. Let me again talk about Newtonian physics. One of the key discoveries of Newton, maybe *the* key discovery, and certainly one of his most famous, was the discovery that there is a uniform order in the universe. As the legend goes, Newton discovered this when an apple fell down from a tree, and he realized in a sudden flash of intuition that the force that pulls the apple from the tree is the same force that pulls the planets toward the sun. That was the starting point of Newton's theory of gravity, and that led to everything else. Now the point that I want to make is that the insight that there is uniform order in the universe is implicit in Newtonian physics, and is not invalidated by quantum mechanics or relativity theory. On the contrary! It is confirmed and enhanced by these theories. In the same way, I believe, the fundamental unity and interrelatedness of the universe and the intrinsically dynamic nature of its phenomena—the two basic themes of modern physics—will not be invalidated by future research.

WEBER: You feel that they can't be.

CAPRA: I feel it very strongly. It's not something that I can prove, but I feel very strongly that they will be affirmed even more. Since these are also the two basic themes in mystical traditions, the world view of science will come ever closer to the views of the mystics, as we go along refining our theories. So it is true that the concepts of today will be replaced by the concepts of tomorrow, but they will be replaced in an orderly way. And the basic themes that I use in my comparison to the mystical traditions will be enforced, I believe, rather than invalidated.

WEBER: Is this a hunch, or is it that, over the last three centuries, you see that physics has been flourishing with a direction that, by extrapolation, we feel isn't going to be capriciously reversed?

CAPRA: You're talking about the notions of intuition and consistency we mentioned before. I have observed the consistency of these two themes emerging in physics and mystical traditions.

WEBER: So on the basis of that, you are saying that any changes that come about—and there will be many; it is the nature of physics to change—will be in the direction of further refinement of these two themes.

CAPRA: I should also say that in the last five years this intuition has been confirmed by the new biology and the new psychology that are now emerging. So now I feel on much firmer ground. It's not just physics; it's science as a whole that goes in this direction. I believe that at the present level of science it is already apparent that mysticism, or the perennial philosophy, provides the most consistent philosophical background to all scientific theories. And I challenge anyone to show me a different philosophical tradition that is more consistent with modern physics, biology and psychology.

WEBER: What comes to mind is a criticism in quite the opposite direction that Ravindra made in his *ReVision* article. He says that the belief that science is reaching mystical truth is based on what he called naive and arrogant assumptions.

CAPRA: This statement again is based on a total misunderstanding of science. I should say in fairness, that Ravindra in this article, does not explicitly refer to my work or to my book. And this statement and others make me believe that he has either not read it at all or has not read it carefully. Because this is a point I hammer home again and again in the book. Almost in every chapter, I emphasize the necessity of recognizing the approximate nature of science and that we will never reach the mystical truth. That is a very different framework.

WEBER: You feel that there will always be a gap because scientists are mapmakers and the mystical experience is part of the territory. Would that be a fair way to put it?

CAPRA: Yes, that would be a good way to put it, and you would say that as you go on refining your maps, eventually, maybe not in practice but in principle, you will get to a point where you will have to give up speaking or writing or thinking rationally if you want to go any further. This is the point that mystics always make. Lao Tzu, for instance says in the *Tao Te Ching*, "Those who speak do not know, and those who know do not speak."

WEBER: Were physicists in this quandry when they were first fully confronted with facts that they couldn't symbolize adequately in quantum mechanics?

CAPRA: Well, you see for them this event was so earthshaking that they didn't really know what was going on. Heisenberg told me that

Bohr thought they would not be able to describe the atomic phenomena rationally.

WEBER: In a way the common denominator, I suppose, of the state of affairs is that common-sense language, ordinary language to philosophers or Wittgenstein's terms, simply cannot contain either of these insights, the mystics' or the quantum physicists', isn't that so?

CAPRA: That's right, that was the great discovery of Heisenberg. He showed precisely that our common concepts do not describe the atomic reality completely. And that, of course, is one of the very bases of my comparison with mysticism.

WEBER: Fritjof, one of the critiques is that books like yours do a disservice to physics, to science, in linking it to a cosmology espoused by mysticism. What is your position on that?

CAPRA: I have very strong feelings about that; I'm glad that you're bringing it up. I think it is a very serious matter. We know now in physics, since Heisenberg, that the classical ideal of scientific objectivity can no longer be maintained. Scientific research involves the observer as a participator and this involves the consciousness of the human observer. Hence, there are no objective properties of nature, independent of the human observer. Now this insight, which is, by the way, one of the main parallels to mystical knowledge, implies that science can never be value free. The detailed research, for instance knowing the mass of the proton or the interaction between particles or the structure of the crystal, will not depend on my values, my political belief and so on. However, this research is pursued within the context of a certain paradigm, a broader vision of reality, which involves not only concepts but also values. And therefore science is always implicitly subscribing to a set of values, and scientists are not only intellectually responsible for their research but also morally responsible. There's no way of escaping this responsibility. Since Heisenberg, this has become abundantly clear, or should have become abundantly clear.

WEBER: I think you and David Bohm agree on that. He has said the same thing many times. He feels strongly about it. Also, Bohm has said that when physics pretends to itself and to the community-at-large that it is value free, the ideal of being value free is *itself* a value. Therefore it is not value free.

CAPRA: Definitely. Furthermore, you can say that what happens is that a so-called value-free science just espouses the prevailing values of society. That is very clear in economics, for instance. Economists who were influenced by the Cartesian world view tried to build mathematical models that didn't contain values. And of course what they did was espouse the values of the Cartesian paradigm and of our society.

WEBER: And you feel this is one of many such values. They could have espoused alternative paradigms.

CAPRA: Of course, I show in my new book, *The Turning Point*, how the new values will affect these various sciences and lead to new paradigms.

WEBER: The so-called purest of sciences, physics, cannot escape the presence of values.

CAPRA: Right. Now from this point of view, you see, the connection between physics and mysticism is not only very interesting but also extremely important. Because we have to put it into the present cultural perspective, into the perspective of the values of the current culture. Now what are the values of our culture? Well, look at what scientists are doing. Half of our scientists and engineers today work for the military. In my lectures I often say that modern physics can lead us to the Buddha or to the bomb. It's up to us to choose one of these paths. And it seems to me that at a time when so much scientific work is wasted by using an enormous potential of human ingenuity and creativity to develop even more sophisticated means of total destruction, that the paradigm of the Buddha cannot be overemphasized. This seems to me to be very crucial. Therefore, to link science to mysticism does not take away anything from its grandeur. On the contrary, it ennobles science, and in our present situation, because of the nuclear threat, it may well be crucial to the survival of humanity. So I take this argument very seriously, and I fight it with all my enthusiasm and with whatever power of persuasion I have.

WEBER: When you say, physics can lead us to the Buddha or the bomb, the question arises: how close is the connection?

CAPRA: Well, I think what physics can do is help to generate ecological awareness. You see, in my view now the Western version of mystical awareness, our version of Buddhism or Taoism, will be ecological awareness.

WEBER: Because of this interconnection of being that they all assert?

CAPRA: Yes, the fundamental interconnectedness, and interdependence, the role of mind in human beings, societies and eco-systems, all this shows you quite clearly that we depend on our natural environment, and if we destroy it, we destroy ourselves. So as a scientist, to work for the military or even to advocate nuclear power which many scientists do, is for me, the height of folly.

WEBER: You think it's a contradiction in a way.

CAPRA: Of course it is. The Newtonian behavior of a non-Newtonian scientist. That's what's so remarkable about science. There are many, many physicists who work on these beautiful theories. Maybe they don't care about the implications, but they work on theories that have profound philosophical implications that go way beyond Descartes and Newton. Then those same scientists go home and act in a very Newtonian way.

WEBER: Would you say that it's because they have not understood the implications of the theory integrally?

CAPRA: That's right. That's the very crux of the matter, because the rational mind can detach itself from the human being and not feel things intuitively. It is no accident that those physicists who are the most intuitive, the Einsteins, the Bohrs, the Bohms, all have been active politically or socially, because they feel it in their bones, and they know about the implications.

WEBER: You were saying that if scientists understood the content of their own theories not only intellectually but also integrally, with all the levels of their being, they would see the inevitable social, interpersonal implications.

CAPRA: And this is where books like mine may help. I speak their language, and I think I can pave the way to such an understanding.

WEBER: One of the criticisms made of your book and this whole way of looking at things is that you are confusing two domains and two approaches, two realities, and two ways of understanding. The fundamental issue, it's been said, is that the physicists and mystics aren't even talking about the same world, and that you are assuming invalidly that they are. What is your reply?

CAPRA: This is an argument that has come up several times in the past. The argument usually goes that physicists talk about a quantum reality that is, however, almost totally irrelevant to ordinary macroscopic phenomena, while mystics deal precisely with those phenomena and see the things in that ordinary world which have almost nothing to do with the quantum world. So are they not talking about two different worlds? Now, first of all, I think it's important to realize that the quantum realities are not irrelevant to macroscopic phenomena. This is generally not appreciated. For example, the solidity of matter, the fact that you cannot walk through doors or walls, is a direct consequence of the quantum reality. It is something that comes from a certain resistance of atoms against compression which cannot be explained in terms of classical physics. I don't want to go into the details here, but in *The Tao of Physics*, I explain how quantum physics explains this phenomenon. This is one of the most important physical phenomena in the ordinary world—that matter is solid. And there are several others that can't be explained in terms of classical physics. So maybe we should rephrase the argument and say that mystics do not deal explicitly with quantum reality, whereas physicists do. Now as far as the idea of two different worlds is concerned, I believe that there is only one world, and Ken Wilber who makes this argument of two worlds, I think, will agree with me. I think if we just got together and talked about it, I cannot believe that he would disagree. There is one world, this awesome and mysterious world, as Castaneda called it—a term which I really love. There's one reality but this reality has multiple dimensions, multiple levels and multiple aspects. Physicists and mystics deal with different aspects of reality, and, of course, I emphasize this in *The Tao of Physics*.

WEBER: They deal with different *aspects* of one and the same reality. That's the point you're making.

CAPRA: Exactly. Physicists explore levels of matter; mystics explore levels of mind. And what they have in common in their explorations is that these levels in both cases, lie beyond ordinary sensory perception. So when Wilber says that mystics see interconnectedness and interpenetration in the ordinary realm, that is not correct because their mode of perception is not ordinary.

WEBER: But he would say that although their mode of perception is not ordinary, that which they perceive is what we call the ordinary world, the ordinary tree, the rock and the river.

CAPRA: But you see we have said before that you can no longer separate the mode of perception from the thing which is perceived.

They form a unity. So if the perception is nonordinary, then the reality is not ordinary. There's no way to separate those two.

WEBER: And this is exactly what the new physics is trying to get across.

CAPRA: This holds also for physicists. Quantum physics also is a nonordinary mode of perception through very sophisticated instruments. So, on the one hand, you have scientists probing into matter with the help of very sophisticated instruments, and, on the other hand, you have mystics probing into consciousness with very sophisticated techniques of meditation. Both reach nonordinary levels of perception, and at these nonordinary levels, it seems that the patterns, and principles of organization that they observe are very similar. Now the elements they observe are not the same. Mystics do not talk about subatomic particles. They don't talk about atoms, molecules or anything like that. But the way in which subatomic patterns are interrelated for physicists mirrors the way in which macroscopic objects are interrelated for the mystics.

WEBER: You are claiming, then, that analogous to the sophisticated machinery that allows quantum physicists to see the world in its way is the mystical view. That the mystic's eyes are unitary eyes, which unify the ordinary Newtonian world in ways analogous to the subatomic world.

CAPRA: That's right. You see the universe is one interconnected whole, and this whole, this process forms patterns. We discern these patterns and in everyday life we separate them and regard them as isolated objects; and then we say there's no connection between these objects. But in doing so, we have already made an approximation and we have left out the connection which was initially there. And there are many traditional nonliterate cultures that, as a matter of course, would regard things as interconnected and would not separate out the patterns as we do.

WEBER: Those cultures haven't been conditioned out of it? They haven't been taught *not to see it* in that way?

CAPRA: I suppose so.

WEBER: Somebody could make the criticism that what physics does at the subatomic level and the patterns of interconnection it sees are quantitative and neutral in a sense. It doesn't perceive that interconnectedness as a spiritual quality that mystics hold, for example: that everything is love; everything is peace.

CAPRA: Certainly physics and mysticism are by no means the same endeavor. There's much more to mysticism than just a certain view of the material world. There's also much more to physics. There's the mathematics, the engineering aspects, the technology, the experimentation and so on. These two endeavors of looking at the world and trying to understand the world overlap, and I'm studying the overlap. But there's much more to both sides.

WEBER: You know it's been said that the subatomic realm is a realm the mystic has never seen and doesn't claim to have seen.

CAPRA: Well, nobody has seen the subatomic realm. It's a realm that is far too small to be seen.

WEBER: With machines even?

CAPRA: That's why I say that the perception of physicists is nonordinary because the machines are an extension of the senses. We do experiments so that an electron will cause a certain event which will cause another event which will cause another event and so on, and eventually it will end up in the click in the Geiger counter or in the dark spot on a photographic plate or something like that. That we can observe. So we observe only the end of a long chain of events.

WEBER: In this unitive mystical vision, what is it that the mystic sees?

CAPRA: It is an experience of reality that goes beyond our own sensory experiences, which includes sensory experiences but goes beyond it.

WEBER: But what about the object? We've said that what the physicist sees is the end result of a long chain of events and experiences that he then reads back inferentially via his own machines. Can you detail the analogous process for the mystic? When he looks with mystical vision at the world, what is he seeing?

CAPRA: I think you would have to ask a mystic. I'm a physicist. I know what we do, I don't know what they do.

WEBER: The whole argument turns on this point; namely, are there or are there not analogies, similarities between the mystical view and that of the modern physicist? We more or less understand what the physicist is seeing, but if the mystic is not looking at that very deep realm of the inner structure of matter, then is he looking at something yet deeper than that?

CAPRA: I think the mystic is looking at something deeper in a different direction or in a different dimension. Something like that. So it's a different aspect of the same reality. As I said before, physicists go into matter, mystics go into consciousness. That's the main difference in the dimension.

WEBER: I'm wondering what metaphors or symbol systems one can bring in to clarify what the mystic is doing, since that, in a way, is the heart of the controversy.

CAPRA: The mystic is looking at the ordinary, everyday reality in a nonordinary mode of perception. And perceives this reality somehow in its very essence or in a more fundamental way, in a deeper way. The patterns and principles of organization that emerge from that experience are very similar to the patterns and principles of organization we observe in physics when we go to very small dimensions. Mystical perception goes beyond intellectual distinctions, and so it goes beyond space and time, beyond subject and object, inner and outer worlds. It transcends these categories.

WEBER: Is the mystic describing a world that also transcends the hierarchical structures referred to in the perennial philosophy?

CAPRA: Well, the concept of hierarchy is the central part in Ken Wilber's argument, and it is to me the most interesting part. According to Wilber, the most striking feature of the perennial philosophy is the fact that it presents being and consciousness as a hierarchy of levels, moving from the lowest, densest and most fragmentary, to the highest, subtlest and most unitary. Wilber says that in most of these traditions, there are six major levels: the physical, the biological, the mental, the subtle, the causal and the ultimate. And in his review he gives a very beautiful summary, as he does also in his books, of these levels of consciousness or levels of being. He calls them ontological levels. And he says that any account of the mystics' world view that leaves out this type of hierarchy is bound to be superficial. Now I think there are a number of things that I can say about this. Physics certainly does not contain the notion of these levels, but science does. I mean other sciences, like biology, psychology and so on. But before I talk about this, I have to talk about terminology, about the term hierarchy. I don't think hierarchy is a good term to use for these levels we observe.

WEBER: Now why is that?

CAPRA: Well, what we observe in nature is what I like to call a stratified order. We observe levels of differing complexities which are highly stable. I'll give you an example. Let's start again with Newtonian physics, as we did before, and talk about the motion of two bodies, for example the planetary motion of the earth around the sun. This is quite easy to deal with mathematically, in terms of Newtonian science. If you have three bodies, it gets much more complicated. If you get 100, it's impossible, because, mathematically, it's too complex.

WEBER: You have too many variables by that time.

CAPRA: Yes, but if you get 1,000,000 it becomes very easy again, because then you do statistics and then you have thermodynamics, so you reach a level of complexity at which you can use a different language and it becomes easy. Similarly with a few atoms you do quantum mechanics. If you take many atoms, you can still do it, because we have various techniques of approximation which allow us to deal with many atoms. But if there are too many, it gets too complex. However, with many, many more atoms it becomes easy again. You do chemistry. See? Then you let the atoms or molecules become larger and interact and the chemistry becomes exceedingly complex until, at a certain level, you realize, my God, they're forming cells. Then you can do cellular biology. Then the cells become very complex, impossible to handle, until suddenly you realize that it's a tissue. And then the tissues become complex and you realize that's an organ, and then the organ becomes very complex; let's say you are dealing with the brain, the most complex organ, and then suddenly you can switch to a totally different level and you do psychology instead of neurophysiology. So there are these levels of complexity which are extremely striking.

WEBER: Just to clarify: when you say that at a certain point the topic becomes exceedingly difficult to handle, you mean, if one were to stay with that viewpoint, that the subject itself requires a new *focus* and that's what we call a new field, so to speak. When you move from physics to chemistry to biology, you say the complexity of the material itself demands a new organization, or new way of looking at it.

CAPRA: Yes. Now these various levels that we observe are not separate but are all mutually interconnected and are all interdependent. Although we have systems within systems, as we would say in modern language, this is not a hierarchy. It's often called a hierarchy, but this is really not a good term to use because hierarchies exist only in the social realm, for instance the hierarchies of the church; that's actually where the term came from.

WEBER: Could you explain the origin of this?

CAPRA: Well, the Greek word means "the sacred rule." It was originally the rule of the pope over the archbishops and the bishops and the prists and, I guess, it probably was the rule of God over the archangels and the angels and so on. That was the original hierarchy. And now we have the hierarchy of various human organizations; the hierarchy of a university for instance with the president, the deans, and so on. Those are hierarchical structures. The important point is that in human hierarchies, the higher levels dominate the lower ones. They are hierarchies of power and control. Although there is relative autonomy and freedom at various levels, the power flows from the top to the bottom. This is not the case with these natural levels where all levels are interrelated and interdependent and influence one another. That's why I prefer to use the term "stratified order," rather than "hierarchy."*

WEBER: Ken Wilber's claim is that the higher influences the lower, but the lower levels do not in the same way include and influence the higher. You're saying that is not so?

CAPRA: Let me first talk about what we observe in the natural world, then we'll go back to his argument. In the human organism, for example, we have organs and the organs consist of tissues and the tissues of cells, but each of these levels interacts directly with its total environment and influences every other level. In my new book, I have taken the symbol of the pyramid, which is the classical symbol of a hierarchy and I have turned it around. I have made it into a tree. Now the tree contains exactly the same information about the relation between the levels: there's one stem, there are several branches; there are more twigs; and there are even more leaves. So you also have systems within systems but the tree, of course, is an ecological symbol. In the tree you see very clearly that the nourishment comes both from the roots and from the leaves. The sun nourishes the leaves and the roots bring nourishment out of

*Editor's Note: In developmental psychology, hierarchy is a technical term for increasing complexity, differentiation and integration as explained, for example, by Werner, "Wherever development occurs it proceeds from a state of relative globality and lack of differentiation to a state of increasing differentiation, articulation, and hierarchical integration." That specific concept is central to the modern schools of developmentalism.

the earth. So it comes from the heavens and from the earth, if you want to be poetic. Both are needed, and none is primary, and all the levels are always interacting with one another in the environment. So this is a much better image for the multileveled structure that we observe in nature. Now it's also interesting historically and culturally that hierarchical systems are characteristic of patriarchal cultures. A hierarchy is something associated with male consciousness.

WEBER: Can you go into that?

CAPRA: Sure! Look at the original hierarchies! The popes are men, the bishops are men, God is a man and so on.

WEBER: What about Mary?

CAPRA: Oh, that's interesting. Mary comes from the prepatriarchical religion. Mary is the ancient Goddess, because God was female before he became male.

WEBER: Even in the West?

CAPRA: Yes, even in the West. Especially in the West, in what they call the old Europe, around the Mediterranean.

WEBER: I don't know if that's generally known.

CAPRA: It's not known because we're in a patriarchical culture, in which this kind of knowledge is not supported, but it is coming out now. There are now several books on this subject. Now I bring this up because when Wilber says that all perennial philosophies emphasize hierarchies, that is not quite true. Hierarchies are emphasized mainly by those which are patriarchical traditions. Taoism for instance which I believe has its roots in a matriarchical culture, and which always emphasizes the feminine element, does not have hierarchies. Hinduism does, Buddhism does, and Islam and Christianity do. But there are other traditions which do not have hierarchies. So I think it's important to realize that hierarchical structures are not a law of nature, but are human constructs.

WEBER: I would like to come back to Wilber's argument that the higher incorporates, includes, embraces, contains the lower in a way that the lower cannot contain the higher. It is a nonsymmetrical relationship. What would you say about that?

CAPRA: That is correct, but you don't have to call it higher and lower. Think of the tree again; I just want to clarify the terminology.

WEBER: Do you think that the terminology misleads because it emphasizes the governing principle more than you feel is justifiable?

CAPRA: Yes. Power and domination rather than complexity. For me these are levels of complexity. Now the structure of these levels ultimately depends on how we look at them. Again, as we have said before, patterns of matter reflect patterns of mind, and whatever we look at depends on our concepts. I feel that Ken Wilber takes these levels a little too seriously. When he says "there are six major levels" that is true, but ontological levels, like all other concepts, ultimately are *maya*. The way in which we divide reality is illusory and relative, and, as we would say in science, approximate.

WEBER: A working definition. Not a hard and fast structure in nature.

CAPRA: Right. Wilber says, for example, "Physics and mysticism are not two different approaches to the same reality, they are different approaches to two quite different levels of reality." Now that is true, but ultimately these two levels, too, are the same; they're different aspects of the same awesome and mysterious worlds in which form is emptiness, and emptiness is form.

WEBER: And yet you wouldn't deny the usefulness of making the distinction?

CAPRA: Oh no, of course not. It is extremely useful. What I'm saying is that as we go up and down the tree, so to speak, our attention focuses on levels where we recognize stable patterns. But these levels are as much levels of our attention as a level of reality out there.

WEBER: Also, I think one of Ken's concerns was that at different levels, the organism can more clearly, more comprehensively reflect the universal consciousness, and a higher organism can do this far more richly than can, say, a rock. Now, would you agree with that?

CAPRA: Of course. I would say that a rock doesn't reflect it at all, in the sense of thinking about it, experiencing it, being aware of the universe. I think the awareness starts with living organisms, biological organisms. At a very high level of complexity, we have self-awareness, we have consciousness, organisms being aware of themselves as thinking, feeling, beings.

WEBER: What about this notion of the comprehensiveness of levels?

CAPRA: Let's talk about the different levels. One of the arguments of Wilber's is that the notion of interpenetration, for example, is perceived by physicists at the material level. That's the only level physicists deal with. And he recognizes and appreciates the parallel to mysticism. When I say, in *The Tao of Physics*, that the notion of interpenetration which is characteristic of Mahayana Buddhism, has a strong parallel in the bootstrap theory in particle physics, Wilber agrees very much with that. Bernstein, by the way, seems to think that the bootstrap is something that is quite outdated, but he is not quite up to date with what has been going on in physics. There has been a tremendous breakthrough in the last five years in bootstrap physics, to the extent that we are no longer talking about a bootstrap model but a bootstrap theory. Which is sort of a measure of the progress we have made.

Anyway, the interpenetration level that physicists and mystics perceive, Ken Wilber calls a one-dimensional interpenetration. Then he says that according to the mystics, there's interpenetration in many dimensions; the different levels also interpenetrate, and physics does not have anything to say about that.

WEBER: They interpenetrate vertically, not just horizontally?

CAPRA: Right. I agree that physics has nothing to say about this, but science does. I have spent the last five years studying the relationships between physics and the other sciences and have found that there is a natural extension of the concepts of modern physics to other fields. The natural extension is the framework of systems theory. The systems approach deals very much with these levels in biology, in psychology, in the study of social systems and so on. The exploration of systems concepts in these areas, and of the implications for our society and culture, is the subject of my forthcoming book, *The Turning Point*. I have found that this systems approach confirms the parallels between physics and mysticism and adds other similarities: the concept of free will, the concept of life and death, the nature of mind, the nature of consciousness and so on. There is a profound harmony between these concepts, as expressed in the systems view, and the corresponding concepts in mystical traditions. I can't go into the details here because this is a very complex subject, but I discuss it very extensively in my new book.

WEBER: Could you give us just a rough working definition of systems theory?

CAPRA: Sure. First, the term is a misnomer because it is not a theory, in the sense of relativity theory or quantum theory. It is more a point of view, a framework, a language.

WEBER: A conceptual framework to bring things together?

CAPRA: Right. It is a framework that studies systems, which are integrated wholes that derive their essential properties from their interrelations, rather than from the properties of their parts. So, the systems approach is complementary to the reductionist approach. It concentrates on the interrelations, the interconnections and interdependence. It is also a thoroughly dynamic approach. It studies principles of organization, and it considers processes as more fundamental than structure. You can see already, because of these two aspects—the interdependence and interrelatedness and the dynamic nature, which I regard as the two basic themes of modern physics—that this is a natural extension of modern physics.

WEBER: I think that gives us an idea of the essence of the systems approach.

CAPRA: Let me also give you some examples of systems. There are living and nonliving systems. I'm particularly interested in living systems, living organisms. You can use these terms interchangeably. So a cell is a living system, a tissue is a living system and so is an organ; all the levels that we talked about just before are all living systems. A person, a family, a culture are social systems. Ecosystems also are living systems. You see, the systems view is a unified view because the various criteria and regularities that it explores are applied to all these levels. So you can make the same statements for a cell that you can make for a family or an equal system. Of course, the elements are very different, but the principles of organization are similar.

WEBER: How does this systems view of life resolve the question that we've been exploring between the heirarchy and the stratified way in which things are organized?

CAPRA: When science is expressed in the systems language, it can deal with these various levels of complexity in a unified way. I see this as the future of science. But the systems view, like the bootstrap view, is still a minority view. The majority of biologists would not follow the systems approach at this moment.

WEBER: They look at individual parts.

CAPRA: Yes, they would look at genetics, individual parts and so on.

WEBER: They have the Cartesian view, whereas you're saying that this is the new vision, emphasizing interdependence, interconnectedness, the dynamics of the whole.

CAPRA: But I should say that both reductionism and holism are necessary.

WEBER: I understand. You are not suggesting that we abolish the other. You are saying we should supplement one with the other.

CAPRA: If you want to get the full story, then you need both views. Because either one gives you only half of the story. This is what I see as the future of science, and I see a future science as no longer distinguishing between disciplines.

WEBER: That's a very radical view.

CAPRA: Yes, and by the way Heinsenberg already said that years ago. In one of his books, *The Part and the Whole,* he ends with his view of future science, and I agree very much with that. I have come to believe that in the future we will apply a network of models, and we will use different languages to describe different phenomena at different levels. We will not worry any longer whether we are doing biology or psychology or physics or anthropology or whatever; we won't be worried about these classifications.

WEBER: What you're suggesting is revolutionary. But what would you say to the following objection? In urging this as desirable, aren't you reverting back to ancient modes that hampered the rise of science at one time? Let's remember that before the Renaissance, everything was studied as a whole, and precisely in this way, science dragged its feet. It was specialization that finally gave science its strength. Now when people hear what you're suggesting, won't they be immediately worried that we will lose the gains due to specialization made since the seventeenth century?

CAPRA: No, we won't. It's a question of balance. In those old days they were too holistic. Then the pendulum swung in the other direction, and we were too reductionistic. And now there's a long way to go back before we start worrying about being too holistic.

WEBER: I have argued this myself, so I fully agree. And you might even say that what was avant-garde and visionary in those days is now outdated and reactionary. It would seem perfectly logical that with the increasing knowledge explosion, synthesis is again the avant-garde mode, isn't it? It's a kind of dialectic.

CAPRA: Right. Also from the point of view of evolution there's an interesting point. It is often said that reductionism, the analytic mind and so on, was the way of the organisms to survive, because it's very important when you gather your food that you can distinguish between things. Well, now it's just the opposite. With the nuclear holocaust threatening us, what we need now for survival is synthesis, the ecological perspective, the holistic view.

WEBER: So at different times, different emphases are appropriate.

CAPRA: Absolutely.

WEBER: I understand. And you're arguing for balance not for exclusivity.

CAPRA: That's right. We should have integrative views but should not throw out what we have gained. For instance, let's take the theory of evolution. The Darwinian theory gives us only half of the story. Genetics, the mutations, natural selection and adaptation are an important part but will never explain the phenomena of evolution.

WEBER: What do you think is lacking, then?

CAPRA: The systems view. Again I have it all in the new book. So what we need is the systems view of evolution which contains the notion of self-transcendence, of living organisms reaching out creatively into new territory to create new structures and new modes of organization. Only the integration of these two views, which is still very far from being done, will give us the whole story.

WEBER: So you're saying that human beings who don't define themselves in a way that includes others and the animals and the whole complex ecological system aren't going to survive.

CAPRA: That's right. Now, for the first time, what is at stake is not the survival of the individual or the survival of the species, but the survival of the planet, the survival of life on the planet. So it's a really new dimension, a turning point.

WEBER: And you are tying that directly to epistemology: the way we perceive and define.

CAPRA: That's right. I believe that the current multifaceted crisis is primarily a crisis of perception.

WEBER: You sound like Krishnamurti.

CAPRA: Well, then I'm in good company.

WEBER: Both he and David Bohm keep stressing this point. In your book, the specific arguments that would get the reader to assent to that are worked out, right?

CAPRA: Right. What I have explored is the crisis of perception. I'm saying that we are in the midst of a paradigm shift; the old paradigm is the Cartesian, Newtonian world view, the mechanistic world view. The new paradigm is the wholistic, ecological world view. And we need this shift of perception. Our society, our universities, our corporations, our economy, our technology, our politics are all structured according to the old Cartesian paradigm. We need the shift.

WEBER: Let's bring all these points together. How does the mystical vision fit into all this?

CAPRA: What we have then in the new paradigm is a science that deals with these levels, a multidisciplinary approach to the multileveled reality that we observe. And at all these levels the concepts of science show strong similarities to the concepts of the mystics. I feel on much firmer ground with this assertion than I did ten years ago. It's not just physics that has parallels to mysticism, it's also biology, psychology and various other sciences. And it's interesting that in mapping out this new systems approach, I am basing what I say very much on the work of Ken Wilber. He precisely advocates this approach in the field of psychology. And he has come up with this concept of spectrum psychology, which allows one to unify the various schools of psychology and psychotherapy into a coherent framework, which is exactly the bootstrap approach that I am advocating. And as I said before, the philosophy of mystical traditions, the perennial philosophy, is the most consistent philosophical background to modern science at all these levels.

WEBER: You are saying that the underpinning for what you argue has got to be done if we're going to survive. It also coheres with modern science. Now I want to pick up something you said a few minutes ago: Would you say that in the last five years since you've been researching the material for your new book you've also had to bring in *values* in a way that the book on physics did not have to bring in?

CAPRA: Yes of course. Especially in dealing with economics. Economics is the science that is concerned most centrally with values because it is the science that deals with production, distribution and consumption of goods. Now the kind of goods you buy and the way you spend your money depend very much on your value system. Economists, in the name of being objective, have embraced the values of the Cartesian paradigm without saying so explicity.

WEBER: Are they aware of it?

CAPRA: Well, many of them are not. And I show that in great detail in my book. I have a whole chapter on the history of economics.

WEBER: Do values shape the way we perceive, or does the way we perceive shape our values? Or is it both simultaneously?

CAPRA: Let me think about that. I think values and modes of perception are so closely connected that it's difficult if not impossible to separate them. Let me give you an example. Let us talk about analysis versus synthesis or self-assertion versus integration, competition versus cooperation. These are two groups of values. There has been recent research that one of the differences between men and women is that women find it on the whole easier to perceive in an integrated way rather than in an analytic way. They are better in dealing with people, for instance, whereas men are better in dealing with the perception of objects in space, you know, rotating objects mentally in space and so on. Of course there are men and women who can do either one, but on the average there is a difference between men and women in that respect. This now becomes closely intermixed with values because as men dominate in the society, they would say that the analytic mode is better than the integrative mode. They would then say that science is more valuable than philosophy, or poetry. So it's difficult to say what came first, the mode of perception or the value. The two are really very closely interrelated, I feel. It is also important to note that it is the Cartesian view that values competition more than cooperation and therefore sees only the competition in nature and not the cooperation. And with that, sees the separation, the separate objects, rather than the interconnected patterns.

WEBER: In its epistemology, it pounces on that mode of perception that confirms its inclinations, its prejudices and its social values.

CAPRA: That's right. Now there's another point in connection with multileveled structures, and that is the argument that physics and mysticism are not complementary, because they are not mutually exclusive. According to Ken Wilber, the latter transcends and includes the former, not excludes it.

WEBER: You don't agree with that?

CAPRA: I don't agree with that because I simply think there's a confusion here. There's a confusion between the phenomena that are observed and the methods which are employed. The two approaches, I believe, are complementary because of the basic complementarity of the rational and the intuitive mind or the rational and intuitive modes of consciousness. Which I think is a very basic complementarity in human nature. And, by the way, this is a complementarity which also becomes clearer from the systems point of view. So the approaches of physicists and mystics are complementary. But the areas of study are not complementary. They are neither mutually exclusive nor does one include the other, but they overlap.

WEBER: Fritjof, to tie together what we've been talking about, I want to propose considering a hypothetical example, let's call it science fiction or philosophy fiction. Let's postulate that there is a physicist who is so good at his work that he is Nobel caliber; he's a Nobel prize winning particle physicist who later in his life also explores consciousness to such a depth that he becomes the equivalent of a Buddha figure. In my mind, this person has to be both a Nobel quality physicist and a "Nobel quality" spiritual person. He's absolutely adept at both. What, if anything, can he tell us that an ordinary physicist, an ordinary mystic, could not tell us. In particular, I guess, I'm asking, would he know more? Is his advantage only that he would be better able to relate one pardigm to the other? Or could he propose, for example, by virtue of his also being an enlightened consciousness, more perceptive, crucial experiments in physics that would somehow bear on inner states of consciousness? I'm curious as to whether you have any views on this.

CAPRA: Well, it's, of course, very difficult to imagine such a person because of the complementary nature of the two approaches. You would have a hard time becoming a Buddha figure after being a Nobel caliber physicist. But anyway, let us talk about a first rate Einstein, or any of the great physicists. Now such a person has already a high degree of intuition. And this intuition will be sharpened through the mystical training. And then once he went through this mystical training and became enlightened, he would be sublime in his intuition; he would also, by some miracle, not have forgotten his mathematics. He will be able to get back and resume where he left off and do the physics.

WEBER: Would he have an advantage over other physicists in doing pure physics?

CAPRA: He would have the advantage of being able to work much better. Because somebody who goes very far into meditation can marshall his or her energies in a much better way. I know this from experience because I know physicists who are involved in mystical traditions, who are Zen Buddhists or Vendantists; they do the same work in six hours that other people would do in ten hours. That would be one advantage.

WEBER: My next question is: could he forge a bridge between the language of physics and the language of mysticism, or the models thereof? Could he better interpret the one world for those in the other world?

CAPRA: Well, one would think so, but it depends on what kind of physicist we are talking about. If we are talking about a Neils Bohr figure, then he would have difficulty with language, as Bohr had. If we talk about a Feynman, but that's almost a contradiction in terms because Feynman is so against this whole mysticism.

WEBER: I know that, but remember this is my science fiction example, and we're allowed to speculate wildly.

CAPRA: O.K., we'll do some genetic engineering combining Feynman and the Buddha into one person. So then he would have an advantage, and he would be able to interpret mystical experience in terms which make contact with the scientific terms. As far as coming up with mathematical models is concerned, I think he would do it just on the basis of being a good physicist.

WEBER: I suppose that is a more conservative interpretation of what I have in mind. I mean something much wilder. Could he as a scientist formulate experiments that no one now has the imagination to propose?

CAPRA: No, I don't think so.

WEBER: Why is that?

CAPRA: Because this requires a totally different mind frame. You see, not even the theorists are often very good at proposing experiments. It's the experimental physicists who are good at this, because they know the machines. They have this direct contact with the apparatus, and they are good at proposing experiments. In the good physics institutions and research centers, there's always a close collaboration and a close contact between the theorists and the experimenters. But I don't think that any mystical insights would help with those details.

WEBER: But you feel the *theoretical* component would be affected.

CAPRA Yes, because theories are always based on a certain philosophy, or predilection.

WEBER: And an intuition. This person would be more deeply in touch with alternative modes of space and time and consciousness and interconnectedness, not just intellectually but literally. He would have lived in and experienced those modes.

CAPRA: Yes, but you know, as I said before, physicists also have that without being mystics.

WEBER: But to a lesser degree, you were saying. Now this is a full blown version of it, isn't it?

CAPRA: Well, I don't know whether he could be any more full blown than Bohr was. I really don't know.

WEBER: Do you think Bohr felt himself indissolubly one with the universe?

CAPRA: Definitely, definitely.

WEBER: There is evidence?

CAPRA: Oh yes, definitely.

WEBER: But that is the description you've attached to the mystic?

CAPRA: Yes.

WEBER: So you're saying Bohr was a mystic.

CAPRA: Yes, oh yes.

WEBER: Earlier in the interview you said he was a highly intuitive person, but now you are going further.

CAPRA: Well, I now take mystic in a broader sense. Bohr did not have any mystical training, and I don't think he meditated on a regular basis. But his work was his meditation.

WEBER: I understand. He got a personal conviction of the unity of things in a way that didn't necessarily involve sitting down cross-legged in a room.

CAPRA: Right. Bohr's science was his mysticism. And you know, I would almost suspect that this hypothetical person, if he really wanted to do physics and were a mystic, would just do physics. You see, in the Eastern traditions, the most enlightened becomes the most ordinary. And so these great sages just went around cutting firewood and drawing water.

WEBER: After you're enlightened, the mountain is once again a mountain.

CAPRA: Yes, and the proton would become a proton, the electron an electron, and our Buddha would just be a physicist.

WEBER: Thank you very much.

10

REFLECTIONS ON THE NEW-AGE PARADIGM

A Conversation with Ken Wilber

RV: Of various authorities in the transpersonal field, you seem to be one of a very few who have expressed strong reservations about the so-called holographic theories. I wonder if you could tell us why.

WILBER: Well, it's very difficult in a short discussion to explain the various lines of critique. The holographic paradigm is immensely exciting at first glance, I think, but the more you go into it, the more it begins to lose its appeal. You simply have to take all sorts of strands—epistemological, methodological, ontological—and follow them up.

RV: Then you agree with certain theorists, such as Peter Swartz of The Stanford Research Institute, that the holographic paradigm is a nice metaphor but a bad model of reality.

WILBER: It is a bad model, but I'm not sure it's even a good metaphor. The holographic paradigm is a good metaphor for pantheism (or panentheism), but not for the reality described by the perennial philosophy.

RV: How do you mean that?

WILBER: Well, the perennial philosophy—the term was made famous by Huxley but coined by Leibniz—the transcendental essence of the great religions—has as its core the notion of advaita or advaya—"nonduality," which means that reality is neither one nor many, neither permanent nor dynamic, neither separate nor unified, neither pluralistic nor holistic. It is entirely and radically above and prior to *any* form of conceptual elaboration. It is strictly unqualifiable. If it is to be discussed at all, then, as Stace so carefully pointed out, it must involve paradoxical statements. So, it is true that reality is one, but equally true that it is many; it is transcendent, but also immanent; it is prior to this world, but it is not other to this world—and so on. Sri Ramana Maharshi had a perfect summary of the paradox of the ultimate: "The world is illusory; Brahman alone is real; Brahman is the world."

RV: So if you leave out any of those paradoxical aspects, you end up advocating one side of a subtle dualism?

WILBER: Yes. The transcendentalists, and also the monists, agree that "the world is illusory and Brahman alone is real," but they overlook the equally true but paradoxical fact "Brahman is the world." On the other hand, pantheism is the reverse, and perhaps worse—it agrees that "Brahman is the world," or the sum total of the universe, but it overlooks the equally important fact that Brahman is radically prior to the universe.

RV: Why is that "worse"?

WILBER: Because pantheism is a way to think about "godhead" without having to actually transform yourself. If god is merely the sum total of the empirical universe, you don't need to fundamentally enlighten yourself to see that god, because *that* god is already clunking around in your visual field. Pantheism is the favorite god of the empiricists—the "nothing morists," as Plato would say—those who believe in "nothing more" than can be grasped with the hands.

RV: And the perennial philosophy maintains that the absolute is immanent in the world but also is completely transcendent to it?

WILBER: Yes. Plato's cave is still an excellent analogy, as long as we remember its paradoxical nature. There are the manifest shadows in the cave; there is an absolute Light of reality beyond the cave; and ultimately they are not-two. . . .

RV: The shadows and the Light. . . .

WILBER: Yes. But none of those three points can be overlooked, as Ramana said. Now the problem with pantheism is that it mistakes the totality of the universe with that which is radically prior to or beyond the universe. That is, pantheism confuses the sum total of all the shadows *in* the cave with the Light beyond the cave. And the danger of that philosophy is that, if one thinks Godhead is merely the sum of things and events in the universe, the sum of shadows in the cave, then one ceases to try to get *out* of the cave. One merely contemplates one's own level of adaptation, and tries to add up the parts.

RV: What's the danger with its opposite world view, that of extreme transcendentalism?

WILBER: A hatred of the shadows. It shows up in violent asceticism, in antimaterialism, and especially in antisexual ethic and life repression. The idea is that the world itself is somehow evil, whereas all that is evil is the world perceived apart from, or other to, God. When God is seen to be in the world, as the world, the world is radically divine. Grace, as St. Thomas said, is supposed to perfect nature, not obliterate it.

RV: So you were saying the hologram is a good metaphor for pantheism.

WILBER: Yes, in my opinion, because it basically deals only with the totality of parts, the holographic blur, and its relation to individual parts. In the hologram, the sum total of the parts is contained in each part, and that sum-of-the-parts-being-in-each-part is supposed to reflect the transcendental oneness underlying the manifold separateness. But the only way you can say that the hologram is a metaphor for Brahman or Tao is by reducing Brahman to that sum of the parts, which is then present in each part. But that by itself is exactly pantheism.

RV: You mean the whole is not the same as Brahman, or the absolute?

WILBER: No, of course not. Brahman is *in* the world *as the whole world,* it is true, but the whole world in and by itself is not exclusively Brahman, because you could theoretically destroy the whole world but that wouldn't destroy Brahman or Buddha Nature or Tao. Besides, Brahman itself destroys the whole world at the end of the four yugas, or at the end of every kalpa. Anyway, pantheism makes the mistake of confusing the whole world with Brahman, and the hologram is a good metaphor for the whole/part relation.

RV: And you're not saying that is totally wrong, just partial.

WILBER: Yes, it covers the immanent but not the transcendent aspects of the absolute.

RV: What about the notion that the holographic paradigm posits a frequency realm or implicate order under the explicate order of events. Isn't that analogous to the unmanifest, or the Light beyond the cave?

WILBER: Well, again, I think that is initially the obvious thing to say, and a lot of people have agreed with it. I'm not sure it holds up, however. To begin with, Bohm's implicate order is directly related to something like a vast sea of quantum potential energy, out of which there crystalizes, so to speak, concrete matter events. These events are related not by field forces, Einsteinian or Newtonian, but by their degree of implication, or how far out of the matter-energy sea they have emerged.

RV: That implicate sea has been compared by many to the unmanifest and infinite source of the mystics.

WILBER: Yes, I know, but the problem is that the quantum potential is merely tremendously huge in size or dimensions; it is not radically dimensionless, or infinite in the metaphysical sense. And you simply cannot equate huge in size, potential or actual, with that which is without size, or prior to any dimensions, high or low, subtle or gross, implicate or explicate.

RV: So the implicate sea, potential or actual, is really quite different from the infinite ground of mysticism.

WILBER: In my opinion, that's exactly right. They merely sound similar if described in superficial language, but the actual difference is profound. But see, David Bohm is perfectly aware of that. That's why he speaks of the "source" as being beyond both the explicate and implicate spheres. Somehow, people seem to ignore that part of what he says.

RV: OK; and Pribram's holographic brain?

WILBER: If you take a tape recorder and record various sounds, the tape will store those sounds or "memorize" them. So will storage systems based on optical holography. The noises come in all dynamic and flowing—or temporal—but they get translated into a "frozen" or "timeless" state in the tape. But just because the information is stored in a "timeless" fashion doesn't mean that the tape recorder is in a transcendental or eternal state. The human brain also stores information, perhaps holographically; in the process it naturally translates it from a dynamic or moving state into a "timeless" or stored condition, and when you call up that information you read it out from this frozen state. But this "timeless" or frozen condition has little to do with a metaphysical or mystical eternity. For one thing, break the tape recorder—destroy it—and there goes your eternity. An eternity dependent for its existence on a temporal structure, tape or brain, is a strange eternity.

RV: But what about the frequency realm?

WILBER: Yes, the brain is said to read out information by analyzing frequencies, or by plugging into a realm where "there is no space, no time, only events (or frequencies)." Now I am not questioning that theory; I'm sure the brain does analyze spatial and/or temporal frequencies. I just don't see that that has anything to do with a transcendental ground which is eternal and infinite. First of all, frequency means cycles per second or space per time. The same is true of "event densities." The fact is, the so-called frequency realm is simply a realm with space-time structures different from those of the linear or historical mind, and the mind has to impose its structures upon the less structured frequency realm. But in any event, or in any way you wish to interpret it, the frequency realm still has *some sort of structure*, whether that structure be blurred, vibratory, frozen or whatever. And structure cannot be confused with that which is radically without structure, or perfectly dimensionless, transcendent and infinite. If you do mistake that frequency realm for some sort of eternal ground, instead of seeing that it is simply less structured noise, then it appears that you're dealing with some sort of mystical theory, whereas you're actually dealing with the simple mechanics of sensorimotor perception.

RV: But that theory is frequently coupled with Bohm's ideas.

WILBER: Yes, that is initially the obvious thing to do. If you equate the frequency realm with the implicate order, and then equate the unfolded or read-out information with the explicate realm, it naturally appears that you have a paradigm which covers the emergence of manifest thought and things from an unmanifest and timeless ground.

RV: But since both the implicate order and the frequency realm have some sort of form . . .

WILBER: Yes, it's not a good metaphor for the perennial philosophy. At best, it's a decent metaphor for pantheism.

RV: In your original critique of the holographic theories, you used the concept of hierarchy quite often. Do you still feel it is important?

WILBER: Yes, absolutely. If we return to Plato's analogy, there are the objects in the cave and there is the Light beyond—but the point is that some objects are closer to the opening of the cave. That is, there is a gradation in ontology—as Huston Smith summarized the essence of the world's great mystical traditions, "Existence is graded, and with it, cognition." That is, there are levels of being and levels of knowing, leading, as it were, from the very back of the cave up to and through the opening.

RV: And the absolute is the highest level of this gradation?

WILBER: Not exactly, because that would be dualistic. It is paradoxical, again. The absolute is both the highest level of reality *and* the condition or real nature of every level of reality. It is the highest rung on the ladder, *and* it is the wood out of which the ladder is made. The rungs in that ladder are both the stages of evolution at large and the stages of human growth and development. That was Hegel's and Aurobindo's and Teilhard de Chardin's message; evolution is moving through the links in the Great Chain of Being— starting with the lowest, or matter, and moving to biological structures, then to mind, then to subtle and causal realms, and finally to supermind or omega point. It's not that the absolute or supermind only comes into existence at that last stage—it existed all along, but could only be *realized* when consciousness itself evolved to its highest estate. Once we get out of the cave we see there is and always has been *only* light. Prior to that final and highest stage, there seems to be nothing but shadows, but we don't realize they are shadows, having no point of comparison. So anyway, the absolute is both the highest stage or goal of evolution and the everpresent ground of evolution; your real and present condition and your future potential or realization. Anything less than that paradox is dualistic.

RV: Where does hierarchy fit in?

WILBER: Well, the stage-levels of evolution and ontology *are* the hierarchy. But hierarchy only covers one-half of the paradox—it covers the fact that certain levels are closer to the Light than others. The other half of the paradox is, of course, that all things are already and fully Buddha, just as they are. All things are already One, or always already One, and all things are trying to evolve toward the One, or omega point.

RV: That's why you are Buddha but still have to practice.

WILBER: Yes, if Buddha were not omnipresent, it would not be Buddha, but if it were only omnipresent, you would be enlightened right now. Dogen Zenji has made all that very clear. But if you leave out any side of that you get into theoretical trouble. You could paraphrase Orwell: "All things are God, but some things are more God than others." The first part of that is God's omnipresence; the second part is God's hierarchy. The stage-levels of evolution show increasing structural organization, increasing complexity and integration and unity, increasing awareness and consciousness. There is even a sense in saying, as Smith and Schuon and the traditionalists do, that each higher level is more real, or has more reality, because it is more saturated with Being. In any event, evolution is hierarchical—rocks are at one end of that scale, God the Omega is at the other, and plants, reptiles, mammals, humans and bodhisattvas fill up the middle, in that order. *And,* God is the very stuff, the actual essence, of *each and every* stage-level—God is not the highest level, nor a different level itself, but the reality of all levels.

RV: I think you are right that most or all of that has been overlooked by the holographic theories, but is all of that really necessary for a basic paradigm? Aren't you being picky?

WILBER: I know what you mean—why not take the paradigm and run? Don't spoil a good thing; physicists are talking mysticism! [Laughing] I can see the headlines now: "Scientists at M.I.T. today announced they discovered God. That's right, God. Asked whether God was compassionate, merciful, all-pervading, radiant, all-powerful and divine, a senior researcher was heard to say, 'Gee, we're not sure; we think it's a photon.' "

Look, it was some of the proponents of the holographic theories that claimed they had a paradigm that could explain the fundamentals of mystical religion. So we go to the authorities on mystical religion, or the perennial philosophy in general, and see what they say. According to Huston Smith, for example, four levels of being are the absolute minimum you can use to explain the world's great mystical religions. Those are physical body, symbol-mind, subtle-soul and causal-spirit. No major religion recognizes less than that. Many, however, give a more detailed cartography, frequently involving seven levels—the seven chakras, for instance, of kundalini yoga, which is probably the most archetypal paradigm of existence ever devised. The seven generally are: 1) physical or material, 2) emotional-sexual (prana or bioenergy), 3) mental, 4) higher mental or psychic, 5) subtle or archetypal, 6) causal or unmanifest, and 7) ultimate or unqualified.

Finally, you can, if you are very careful, group these levels into three broad categories, for convenience, say. Since most people have evolved to the mental level(s), it's useful to speak of those levels below the mind—the material and biosensory realms—as premental or submental, and those above it—soul and spirit—as transmental. That gives us three general realms, known variously as matter, mind and spirit, or subconscious, selfconscious and superconscious, or instinct, reason and intuition and so on. Those three realms, for instance, have been explicitly mentioned by Hegel, Berdyaev and Aurobindo.

RV: All of which has been overlooked. . . .

WILBER: All of which has been overlooked. The problem with the popular holographic theories, as well as the general "new physics and Eastern mysticism" stuff, is that they collapse the hierarchy. They go from saying "all shadows are ultimately illusory" to saying "all shadows are equally illusory." That is, they latch on to such phrases as "All things are One" or "Separate entities don't exist" or "Isolated things are merely shadows" and then overlook the distinctions between the shadows themselves. They collapse the shadows; they collapse the hierarchy.

RV: Now you said "popular" theories. Do the more academic versions escape this problem?

WILBER: The theories don't, but I think many of the theorists do. Most of the people who either introduced the physics/mysticism thing or at least used it for effect have increasingly refined and sophisticated their views. David Bohm has clearly moved toward a more articulated and hierarchical view, even if he objects to the word hierarchy. And Fritjof Capra never said that physics and mysticism were the same, although he did try to draw so many parallels that the public thinks he did. Anyway, he has moved quite beyond his introductory statements in *The Tao of Physics*. I'm just afraid the public never will. They have latched onto physics equals mysticism with such passion that Capra's new and more sophisticated—and necessarily complicated—ideas will never reverse the tide. Anyway, it's not so much those scholars, or ones like Marilyn Ferguson or Renée Weber who are trying to interpret their findings for us, that I have in mind when I criticize the pop mysticism and the new physics or holographic craze. But definitely the holographic paradigm, in and by itself, falls into that pop mysticism, and I simply think that is a real problem.

RV: Now that hierarchy collapse which occurs in the holographic paradigm—that's related to the error of pantheism, correct?

WILBER: Yes. Almost identical. It mistakes the sum of illusions for reality. You take the phenomena, the shadows, claim they are "all one," and then confuse that sum total of shadows with the Light beyond. As Schuon put it in a blistering attack, pantheism denies distinctions on precisely the plane that they are real. It confuses an essential with a substantial identity. That's also exactly what the holographic paradigm does.

RV: The implications of that collapse would be what? Or, well, what does a theory lose when it loses those various dimensions?

WILBER: It loses all the differences in methodologies, epistemologies and cognitive interests. All of those crumble.

RV: Could you back up?

WILBER: First off, each higher level cannot be fully explained in terms of a lower level. Each higher level has capacities and characteristics not found in lower levels. This fact appears in evolution as the phenomena of creative emergence. It's also behind synergy. But failing to recognize that elemental fact—that the higher cannot be derived from the lower—results in the fallacy of reductionism. Biology cannot be explained only in terms of physics, psychology cannot be explained only in terms of biology and so on. Each senior stage includes its junior stages as components but also transcends them by adding its own defining attributes.

RV: Which generates hierarchy. . . .

WILBER: Yes. All of the lower is in the higher but not all the higher is in the lower. A three-dimensional cube contains two-dimensional squares, but not vice versa. And it is that "not vice versa" that creates hierarchy. Plants include minerals but not vice versa; the human neocortex has a reptile stem but not vice versa, and so on. Every stage of evolution transcends but includes its predecessor—as Hegel said, to supersede is at once to negate and to preserve.

RV: But that doesn't apply to godhead or the absolute, does it?

WILBER: It applies to the paradoxical aspect of God that is the highest of all levels of being. God contains all things, but all things do not exclusively contain God—that would be pantheism.

RV: The other side of the paradox is that what every person or thing is, whether enlightened or not, is still only God.

WILBER: Yes. Anyway, each stage-level of the hierarchy is, as Huston Smith pointed out, a more-or-less unified totality that can stand on its own, so to speak. Likewise, all of the elements of each level are said to be mutually interdependent and interrelated. Each level of hierarchy, in other words, is a type of holoarchy.

RV: So the elements of *a given level* are mutually interacting. But what about elements from *different* levels? How do they interact, or do they?

WILBER: They interact, but *not* in a mutual or absolutely equivalent fashion, and for the simple reason that they aren't equivalent. If the higher levels contain attributes not found on the lower levels, you simply can't have bilateral equivalence between them. My dog and I can interact on the level of sensorimotor perception, but not on the level of symbolic mind—I mean, we don't discuss Shakespeare.

RV: But don't the Eastern traditions say that *all* things are perfectly, mutually interpenetrating?

WILBER: No, that's pure pop mysticism. The actual traditions are much more sophisticated than that. But I suppose you are referring to Hua Yen Buddhism, or Kegon—the school associated with the *Avatamsaka Sutra.*

RV: That seems to be the most often quoted or referred to.

WILBER: According to Hua Yen, there are four fundamental principles of existence, none of which can be dismissed. One is *shih,* which means separate thing or event. Two is called *li,* which means transcending principle or pattern. Three is called *shih li wu ai,* which means "between principle and thing there is no obstruction," or perhaps "between noumenon and phenomena there is no boundary." And four is called *shih shih wu ai,* which means "between phenomenon and phenomenon there is no obstruction." Now the last item has been seized, isolated from its context, and made the basis of pop holistic philosophy. It's very misleading.

Anyway, the point is that the world is indeed an interrelated and interpenetrating series of thing-events, but not in the merely one-dimensional fashion of pop mysticism. All things interact through karmic association and karmic inheritance, but those of greater structural organization do not act absolutely equivalently with their junior dimensions, nor can junior dimensions embrace senior ones.

RV: OK, but now we come to the crux of the matter. What about the absolute? Isn't it equally at every point?

WILBER: It is, as I said, paradoxical. All of the absolute is equally at every point, *and* some points are closer to the absolute than others. The hierarchy deals with the manifest universe, where there are levels of increasing reality (or decreasing illusion) leading up to the absolutely real. And those levels are not one-dimensionally and equivalently interacting. I don't know of a single authority on the perennial philosophy—Smith, Schuon, Guénon, Coomaraswamy, Pallis—that would make that type of statement, or that would deny relative hierarchy.

RV: But couldn't physics have discovered the other side of the paradox—the absolute oneness or infinite whole underlying the manifest world?

WILBER: Follow it through. We already saw that what physics *has* found is actually a unified interaction of material shadows; it discovered that various physical particulars are interrelated processes—but interrelated shadows aren't the Light. As for the implicate order, we saw it was actually a huge energy dimension; it wasn't radically dimensionless or metaphysically infinite. And if you mean that physics could actually have evidence, concrete evidence, for the absolute. . . . Well, the absolute itself, being all-pervading and all-inclusive, is not other to any phenomenon and therefore could not be detected by any sort of instrument or show up in any sort of equation. That which can be functionally useful in an equation must be a variable *different* from other variables, but the absolute is different from, or set apart from absolutely nothing.

RV: I see; so there is no way it could even enter an equation or make any difference in terms of theoretical information?

WILBER: None whatsoever, or else it would be itself merely more information, which would make it perfectly relative, or nonabsolute.

RV: Then what is it that the new physics *has* discovered? I mean, if it's not the Tao, what is it?

WILBER: In my opinion, it is simply the holoarchy of level one, or the fact of material or physical energy interrelation. The biologists discovered the holoarchy of their level—level two—about thirty years ago; it's called ecology. Every living thing influences, however indirectly, every other living thing. The socio-psychologists discovered the holoarchy of the mental level—the fact that the mind is actually an intersubjective process of communicative exchange, and no such thing as a separate or radically isolated mind exists. Modern physics—

well, it's what, almost a century old now?—simply discovered the analogous holoarchy on its own level, that of physical-energetic processes. I don't see any other way to read the actual data.

RV: OK, but now why couldn't that physical holoarchy actually be the *same* oneness underlying the biological and psychological and other levels? Why couldn't all of these approaches—physics, biology, psychology and so on—simply be approaching the same underlying holistic reality from different angles?

WILBER: Start by explaining what you mean by "different angles," and you will find you are necessarily reintroducing the very differences you wished to overcome by saying "one reality." That is, you have merely moved the problem back one step. *If* there are these fundamentally different approaches to one reality, then tell me first *why* the approaches *are* different. Tell me why the study of physics is different from the study of literature, for instance. As you pursue that question very carefully, you will find that those differences are not merely arbitrary. They are not simply interchangeable or equivalent approaches, because they take as their subject matter various classes of events that *are* different because they display different dimensions of structural organization and evolutionary advance and developmental logic. The approach to studying hydrogen is fundamentally different from the approach to studying, say, the meaning of *Hamlet*, if for no other reason than that the one is submental and the other is mental. Now those are *not* two different approaches to the same reality, they involve two different levels of reality. Further, that reality—the absolute as absolute—is disclosed in its entirety or essence only on the highest or ultimate level of being. And then only to the soul that has itself evolved perfectly to that state.

RV: I understand. So there's only one more possibility—can't you say that since all things are ultimately made of subatomic particles, physics *has* shown us an ultimate oneness?

WILBER: All things are not ultimately made of subatomic particles; all things, including subatomic particles, are ultimately made of God. But you mention the most popular position, which is really an extreme form of reductionism. It's popular, I guess, because it fits the hierarchy collapse.

RV: Reduce all things to material particles, then discover the particles are holoarchic, then claim that that holoarchy is the Tao.

WILBER: Yes, that's right. There's a strange appeal in the simplicity of the reductionism. Part of the problem is simply that the physicists are so used to working with the material world, they tend to call it "*the* world" or "*the* universe," and so they say things like "Physics has proven all things in the world are one," when of course it has done no such thing. It has not explained or even touched bio-ecological unity, let alone socio-psychological community and so on. Physics deals with four major forces—strong and weak nuclear, electromagnetic and gravitational. But it can't tell you anything about the force of emotional-sexuality, which comes into existence on level two. It can't tell you about what constitutes good literature, or how economics works, or why children have Oedipal complexes, or the meaning of a dream, or why people commit suicide and so on. All of those are mental symbolic events that begin on level 3. Physics doesn't deal with "*the*" world, you see? As I say, the whole thing has been very misleading.

RV: But there are important parallels, is that right?

WILBER: You mean parallels between the various levels, laws of the various levels?

RV: Yes. I mean, can't the laws of physics tell us something, anything, about the higher levels?

WILBER: Yes, I think they can, but we have to be very careful here. The lower will display its version of an analog law first—the lower emerges first in any developmental sequence, and so it is extremely tempting to say that the lower stands in a causal relation to the higher analog law. That's why I went to such pains in *Up from Eden* to point out that the higher comes *through* the lower, then *rests on* the lower, but doesn't come *from* the lower.

RV: It comes from, or gains its reality from, its senior dimension, not its junior dimension, correct?

WILBER: Yes, via the process of involution.

RV: Maybe we can come back to that point. For now, what is an "analog law"?

WILBER: The idea is simply that every event and principle on a lower level is merely a reduced version or a reflection downward or a lesser degree of those events and principles found on higher levels.

RV: Could you give some examples?

WILBER: This is not a novel idea; it's extremely well developed in the traditional philosophies. According to Hinduism, for example, the absolute bliss of Brahman goes through a series of stepped-down versions, or dilutions, until it appears as the sexual thrill of orgasm. In Christian mysticism, you find such ideas as that natural law is simply a partial version of mental rationality, which itself is merely a reduced reflection of the Divine Logos. The Buddhist vijnana psychology holds that there are four classes of consciousness, each being a stepped-down version of Universal Mind. This is correlated with the idea of the four bodies of Buddha; which is almost identical to the Vedanta notion of four bodies and four major states of awareness—gross, subtle, causal and ultimate or *turiya*. The point, with reference to bodies, is that the body or substance of a physical entity, such as a simple rock, is actually a reflection downward of the freedom and vitality of the subtle body associated with mind, and the subtle body itself is merely a trickle of the causal body—and *that* is just a contraction in the face of eternity or turiya.

RV: The idea also exists in the West?

WILBER: Oh yes; I assure you you can give just as many examples, from the neo-Platonists to the Victorine mystics. Interestingly, it forms the crux of perhaps the most influential of modern Western philosophers—Whitehead.

RV: Was he influenced by the traditionalists?

WILBER: He must have been aware of them, but I think he came to the notion more or less on his own. You know, the truth will out and all. I'd like to think the obviousness of the truth simply couldn't escape one such as Whitehead. Anyway, he took the notion of junior dimensions being essentially reduced versions of senior ones, and completely turned the typical approach to reality on its head. He said that if you want to know the general principles of existence, you must start at the top and use the highest occasions to illumine the lowest, not the other way around, which of course is the common reductionist reflex. So he said you could learn more about the world from biology than you could from physics; and so he introduced the organismic viewpoint which has revolutionized philosophy. And he said you could learn more from social psychology than from biology, and then introduced the notion of things being a society of occasions so that individuals were societies of societies— the notion of compound individuality. Naturally, he held that the apex of exemplary pattern was God, and it was in God, the ultimate compound individual or the greatest society of all societies, that you would ground any laws or patterns found reflected in reduced versions in the lower dimensions of psychology, then biology, then physics. The idea, which was brilliant in its statement, was that you first look to the higher levels for the general principles of existence, and then, *by subtraction*, you see how far down the hierarchy they extend. You don't start at the bottom and try to move up by addition of the lower parts, because some of the higher parts simply don't show up very well, or at all, on the lower rungs. Perhaps his favorite examples were creativity and love—God, for Whitehead, was especially love and creativity. But in the lower dimensions, the creativity gets reduced, appearing in humans as a modicum of free will but being almost entirely lost by the time you get to atomic particles. Maybe we could say that the Heisenberg uncertainty principle represents all that is left of God's radical freedom on the physical plane. But the point is that if you try to understand the cosmos in the reverse direction, from atoms up, you are stuck trying to account for free will, for creativity, for choice, for anything other than a largely deterministic cosmos. The fact is, even with its little bit of Heisenberg indeterminancy, the physical universe is much more deterministic than even level two, biological beings. Any good physicist can tell you where Jupiter will be located a decade from now, barring disaster, but no biologist can tell you where a dog will move two minutes from now. So Whitehead, by looking to illuminate the lower by the higher, and not vice versa, could make creativity the general principle, and then understand determinism as a partial restriction or reduction of primary creativity. If, on the other hand, you start at the bottom, then you have to figure out a way to get free will and creativity out of rocks, and it just won't work. That it is reductionistic is the nicest thing you can say about such approaches.

RV: That's extraordinary, because I've seen so many attempts by new-age thinkers to derive human free will from electron indeterminancy, or to say that human volition is free *because of* the indeterminant wave nature of its subcellular components, or some such.

WILBER: Yes, it appears the thing to do. It's a reflex thing to do—finally, after decades of saying the physical universe is deterministic and therefore human choice is an illusion, you find a little indeterminancy in the physical realm and you go nuts. It's only natural you then try to explain human freedom and even God's freedom as a blow-up of the lowest level. You get so excited you forget you have just pulled the reductionist feat of the century; God is that big electron in the sky. The intentions are so good, but the philosophy is so detrimental. And imagine this: there are plenty of physicists who feel that the physical realm really is purely deterministic—Einstein, for one—and that future research may disclose subatomic variables that *are* purely causal. I'm not saying that will or will not happen, but theoretically, what if it does? Does poor God then lose Its creative power? The day the determinant variables are found, does human will evaporate? You see the problem?

RV: Yet so many new-age thinkers are using physics and neurophysiology to establish their claims of higher transcendence or mysticism or just human free will.

WILBER: Yes, and in a way that even orthodox philosophers find horrifyingly reductionistic. Let me read you a quote from a recent president of the American Philosophical Association: "The body can be free, no matter what may be true according to quantum laws; and moreover, it could not be free by virtue of the latter alone. For if its freedom is merely that of electrons, then, as has been well said it is freedom of the electrons but not of the body. This objection to some recent attempts to treat human freedom as simply derivative from quantum mechanics and nerve structure is, I believe, quite valid." The point, of course, applies even more so to the Tao, and yet new-agers seem to be applying it even less.

RV: I think all that is very clear. But now on a popular level, a general level, is there anything wrong with such books as *The Dancing Wu Li Masters* or any of the other new-age, new paradigm books?

WILBER: No, not at all, I don't think so at all. That's not really what I'm talking about. I'm simply saying that you have to be very careful about the statements you make if you want to extend them from popular hyperbole into a real and enduring paradigm. Statements like "The universe is a harmonious, interrelated whole" or "All things are One" or "The universe is dynamic and patterned, not static and fixed" are superb introductory material; we've all used them to get our points across in a general way. But beyond that, they are very misleading.

RV: How, specifically?

WILBER: Well, if you take two columns and in column A you write words like fixed, static, isolated, manyness, discrete, and in column B you write fluid, dynamic, pattern, holistic, oneness; then I would guess the vast majority of new-age thinkers imagine that the mystical view is in column B. But in fact mysticism is concerned with transcending *both* column A and B. Column B is just as dualistic as column A, for the simple reason that the two columns are opposites or mirror images and thus both are partial. Reality is *not* holistic; it is not dynamic, not interrelated, not one and not unified—*all* of those are mere concepts about reality. As Chuang Tzu said in "Three in the Morning," to say all things are one is just as dualistic as to say all things are many. That's why Zen says reality is "Not two! Not one!" That is not some sort of very subtle or terribly sophisticated mystical doctrine. It is the simplest and most fundamental of all mystical doctrines. Murti's classic *The Central Philosophy of Buddhism* has made that very clear, certainly for Mahayana, as have writers from Schuon to Guénon to Coomaraswamy for the other traditions. That is simple, bottom-line mysticism.

Rv: The absolute cannot be qualified in any sense?

WILBER: Correct, including the sense you just gave it. The absolute—and here we have to speak somewhat poetically—cannot be characterized or qualified because it is not set apart or different from any thing and therefore could not be described as one thing or event among others. It is *nirguna,* or without attributes, or *shunya,* void of characterization. Since there is no place outside the absolute, there is no place you could take up a stance so as to describe it. If you could get outside it, it would cease to be the absolute.

Rv: And so . . .

WILBER: Well, here's a crude analogy. Say the entire universe consists of only three objects—a square one, a round one and a triangular one. God is not the sum of those objects, whether they are considered things or events. . . .

Rv: As pantheism maintains. . . .

WILBER: Yes; God is not the sum of those objects because you could destroy those objects and God would still exist. Therefore neither can you describe God as being any of the attributes of each thing—God is not a circular square triangle. And most important, God is not another object in addition to the three objects. God is not One Thing set apart from the many. God is not a dynamic thing, a holistic thing or a patterned thing.

RV: Staying with your analogy, can you say anything about what God would be?

WILBER: As long as you remember it is a metaphoric and not descriptive statement. God is not one thing among many things, or the sum of many things or the dynamic interaction of many things— God is the condition, the nature, the suchness or the reality *of* each thing or event or process. It is not set apart *from* any of them, yet neither is it in any way confined *to* them. It is identical *with* the world, but not identical *to* it.

RV: Is that why you earlier said the absolute is prior to the world but not other to the world?

WILBER: Yes. That is the doctrine of *tathata,* or suchness—Eckhart called it the *isness* of each thing-event; the Taoists call it *tzu jan,* the so-ness of every object; it is also very close to the meaning of both *dharma,* for Buddhism, and *sahaj,* for Vedanta. Anyway, the doctrine of suchness, combined with the doctrines of advaita or nonduality and *shunyata* or unqualifiability, form the most fundamental and elemental starting point for all mystical traditions, although the terminology is, of course, different.

RV: And it's those basics that seem to get left out of so many new-age accounts of science and mysticism?

WILBER: I think so, yes. Apparently the author wants to say that modern science has discovered that certain objects are actually processes and not static things, or triangles and not circles, and so the Tao is triangular, just as good ole physics says. The Tao contains things and it contains events, but it can be characterized by neither. It is not different from them, but neither is it defined by them.

RV: And you could also say that because the frequency realm is actually a different realm from the readout realm, these are merely *two different* realms, and so the one could not be the mystical suchness of the other?

WILBER: Yes, that would be another important point. The frequency realm is simply one realm among others, not one without a second. I hadn't thought of it that way before, but that's true. Please let me say again that I think the frequency realm does exist, but that I honestly think it just doesn't have anything to do with mystical events or with a truly transcendent-immanent ground, and you've simply given another and very fundamental reason why.

RV: I wonder if we could now move on to the notion of episte-mology, because you said earlier that the evolutionary hierarchy is also a hierarchy of knowledge. Could you elaborate?

WILBER: Each level of the Great Chain is a level of prehension, as Whitehead might say. Each level prehends, or somehow touches or cognizes, its environment. As we said earlier, each level is a stepped-down version of absolute consciousness. Anyway, if we use our simple three-level hierarchy of body, mind and spirit, then the three corresponding modes of knowing are sensory, symbolic and intu-itive. The Christian mystics refer to them as the eye of flesh, the eye of reason and the eye of contemplation. Even Aristotle was pefectly aware of these realms—he referred to them as techne, praxis (or phronesis) and theoria.

RV: And they are hierarchic?

WILBER: Yes. Just as the eye of reason transcends but includes the eye of flesh, the eye of contemplation transcends but includes the eye of reason.

RV: Can science as we know it be extended to cover all three realms? Can we have a higher science of being? The new paradigm seems to say we can.

WILBER: Depends, I guess, on what you mean by science. Look at it this way; we have at least these three modes of knowing—sensory, symbolic and contemplative. These modes correspond to the physical body, the mind and the spirit. That is simple enough, but it becomes a little more complicated when you realize that the mind, for in-stance, can look not only at its own level but at the other two levels as well, and in each case you would get a fundamentally different type of knowledge. Here, I could draw it like this:

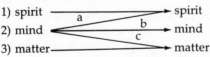

RV: So we have three basic modes and realms of knowledge: the physical-sensory, the mental and the spiritual. (These are numbered 1, 2 and 3.) And then, within the mental mode itself, we have, what, three subsets?

WILBER: Subsets is fine. . . . (These are lettered a, b and c.)

RV: Depending upon which of the three realms the mental mode takes as its object?

WILBER: Yes. Following my favorite orthodox philosopher, Jürgen Habermas, we can characterize the three mental subsets like this. When the mind confines itself to sensory knowledge, the mode is called empirical-analytic, and its interest is technical. When the mind works with other minds, the mode is hermeneutic, phenomenological, rational or historic, and its interest is practical or moral. We now add the mystic view, which Habermas doesn't directly cover, and we say that when the mind attempts to cognize the spiritual realm, its mode is paradoxical or radically dialectical, and its interest is soteriological. Here, I'll put it on the diagram:

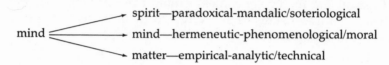

RV: What exactly is hermeneutics?

WILBER: The study of interpretation and symbolic meaning. In the hands of such sophisticated philosophers as Gadamer or Ricoeur, it really comes to mean mentality in general, or symbolic intentionality and meaning and value. See, the reason that empirical-analytic studies are so limited—limited, in fact, to the sensory realm—is that they can't even disclose the nature or meaning of mental productions. There is no empirical test, for instance, which will disclose the meaning of *Macbeth,* or the meaning of value, the meaning of your life and so on. Meaning is a mental production and can be determined only by interpretation, or what Heidegger called the hermeneutic circle.

RV: Most people understand what you mean by empirical-analytic. Could you comment on the third subset, the paradoxical?

WILBER: The idea is simply that when the mind attempts to reason about the absolute, it will necessarily generate paradoxes, for exactly the reasons we have been discussing. When reason operates in this mode, we call it paradoxical. I have also heard the word "mandalic reason" used, and I like that. Either one is fine.

RV: Now you are saying that paradoxical reason is not contemplation, but it does have its uses, correct?

WILBER: Yes, exactly. Both of those points should be emphasized. The first is that paradoxical or mandalic reason—which is what results when you try to think or write about the Tao or Spirit or Buddha

Nature—is not itself spirit, nor does it disclose spirit per se. Here, let me just number all five modes like this:

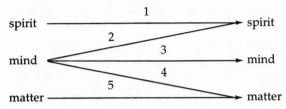

Number 5 is simple sensory-material perception. Number 4 is empirical-analytic mental knowledge, or mind's ideas about the sensory-material world. Number 3 is hermeneutic and introspective and phenomenological knowledge, or mind's knowledge about mind. Number 2 is paradoxical or mandalic reason, or mind's attempt to think about spirit. Number 1 is spirit's direct knowledge *of* spirit, which is nonmediated or nonsymbolic knowledge, intuitive and contemplative.

RV: And your first point is that number 2 should not be confused with number 1.

WILBER: Yes, and that is an extremely elemental point. There is no way to directly understand spirit except by radical spiritual transformation, or the direct opening of the eye of contemplation in your own case. You can read, think and write about the Tao all day, and none of that is the Tao. No mental theory is even close to Brahman.

RV: And since, if you do reason about Tao, you will only generate paradoxes, there is no way to state one position over another. I mean, you can't say the Tao is dynamic flux, because that's half of a dualism in the paradox.

WILBER: That's true. You can't say it without contradicting yourself, as both Nagarjuna and Kant clearly pointed out.

RV: I'm not sure I follow that point.

WILBER: Well, say you say the Tao is constantly changing, that nothing is permanent, everything changes. That's a self-contradiction, because you are claiming everything changes except, apparently, the fact that everything changes, which must therefore be a *permanent* fact. Contradiction. It won't work. Same thing happens if you claim reality is relative, dynamic, one, etc.

RV: So the Tao is permanent and impermanent?

WILBER: Or neither, or even neither-neither, as Nagarjuna would have it. But you see the point—reason generates paradoxical statements when it tries to grasp the absolute.

RV: But your second point was that that type of reason has certain uses?

WILBER: Definitely so, as long as we don't confuse mandalic reason with actual intuition-contemplation. One of its uses is to try to hint to other minds what God might be like. Hegel used such dialectical reason with great force, although he always came too close to confusing it with spiritual intuition. Another purpose, which was used with extraordinary skill by Nagarjuna, is to use the dialectic to demolish reason itself and thus pave the way for actual contemplation, or *prajna*.

RV: How, exactly?

WILBER: Nagarjuna would be faced by an opponent who wished to characterize the absolute—the brahmins claimed god was absolute being, certain nihilist Buddhists claimed it was extinction, others claimed it was pattern, others said it was monistic or unitary and so on.

RV: All of which are partial and dualistic?

WILBER: Yes, and Nagarjuna would demonstrate that point by turning the opponent's logic back on itself, at which point it would contradict itself. See, if you try to make a statement about reality as a whole, then your statement is part of that reality, at which point it becomes like a hand trying to grasp itself or a tongue trying to taste itself. You end up either in an infinite regress or in a blatant contradiction. Nagarjuna would use this inherent limitation in reason to exhaust reason's attempts to grasp spirit, at which point, if the thing is done carefully, you become more open to actual contemplative insight—the mind just shuts up, and in the gap between those thoughts, *prajna* is born, or at least can be. But as far as reality goes, it is neither being nor nonbeing, nor both nor neither—those were Nagarjuna's four categories, and they were based on the Buddha's original "inexpressibles." Whatever reality is, it can only, *only* be "seen" upon *satori*, or via actual contemplative insight.

RV: And if you try to state what is "seen" you will only generate paradox. . . .

WILBER: Yes, but those paradoxes, used skillfully, as *upaya*, constitute mandalic reason—and that is one of its uses.

Rv: We were talking about science, about a higher science.

WILBER: Well, as I said, it depends upon what you mean by science. If by science you mean careful knowledge, then *all* realms can be scientific. But science really means, or at least we certainly associate it with, forming some sort of theory and then checking the theory against evidence. I really don't think we can define science without that.

Rv: And a theory is a mental production?

WILBER: Yes. The sensory mode—number 5—does not itself form theories because it is presymbolic. And the spiritual mode—number 1—does not itself form theories because it is trans-symbolic; its actual operation is immediate and nonconceptual insight.

Rv: So that limits theoretic activity to the three mental subsets.

WILBER: The activity itself, yes. It is only the mental modes that form theories, although the theories themselves can try to take account of the other realms, realms which themselves do not directly form theories. Of course, science as we know it is theory directed toward the physical realm. That is, it is empirical-analytic theory, or mode number 4. The mind creates a theory-map of the objective biomaterial world, looks carefully at that world, usually by altering that world in controlled ways, and then fits the map to it. A good map becomes a model, and a model that is never disproven becomes a law.

Rv: The question is whether science can rise to mode number 3 or even number 2.

WILBER: Yes. So start with number 3, or phenomenological psychology and historic-hermeneutic inquiry. I would immediately point out that if science—using that word for the moment in a broad sense—can rise to mode number 3, the empirical-analytic methodology *cannot* rise to that level, and that is the great problem. If we correctly leave the exclusively empirical-analytic mode behind, then the so-called "new science" of the mental sphere, or mode number 3, has been around a very long time under the name of phenomenology, and I think it great arrogance for the "new and higher" scientists to just barge in on the field and claim they're going to get it right. On the other hand, if they bring their empirical-analytic methods with them, then they are simply disguised reductionists.

Rv: In neither case, then, is there such a thing as a higher science?

WILBER: I don't see how, unless—and you are perfectly free to do this—you stretch the word terribly. What you have to look out for then is making the word "science" worthless. See, if you start applying it to all realms—"We're going to have a science of phenomenology, a science of hermeneutics, an empirical science and a science of contemplation or religion"—well, the term loses all meaning. The word science becomes a constant and thus drops out of all the equations, and then we're right back where we started, which is trying to figure out the various epistemologies.

RV: So modes number 1 and number 5 are not themselves theoretic modes. . . .

WILBER: They can be the subject matter of theoretic modes,but are not themselves theoretic modes. The one is transmental, the other, submental.

RV: Mode number 4 is definitely theoretical, or can be, and it is checked by empirical-analytic means. . . .

WILBER: Yes, and that is orthodox science.

RV: What about theory in mode number 3?

WILBER: That is phenomenological philosophy, introspective psychology, intersubjective communication, interpretation, value systems and so on. This mode does form theories or maps of what the subjective and intersubjective world is like.

RV: But those theories are not checked by empirical-analytic means, because they aren't sensory referents?

WILBER: That's right; they are checked by hermeneutical procedures, by interpretation, by communities of like-minded interpretors, by direct phenomenological apprehension and so on.

RV: Could you give an example?

WILBER: What you and I are doing right now. We are exchanging meaning, symbolic meaning, and arriving at interpretive understanding. "What do you *mean* by that?"—meaning, you know. That is not an empirically reducible event, and it cannot be explained by physics, chemistry or biology. *Hamlet* is not made of electrons; it is constructed of symbolic units of meaning which, if reduced to the paper on which they are written, are simply destroyed. But I suppose a classic example is Freud. Despite his rampant attempts at socio-biological reductionism—and it was absolutely rampant—his methodology was almost entirely hermeneutic and phenomenological, which is why I think he still has much to tell us, and why so many structuralists are returning to him for insight. Lacan is now said to be the foremost psychological thinker in Europe, and Lacan is two things: a structuralist in the line of Levi-Strauss and a brilliant Freudian. Anyway, Freud's methodology was basically to watch the client's production of words and symbols and then try to figure out what those symbols might really mean. His assumption was that a dream, for instance, must occur on two levels, because the client is actually the author of the dream—it's his or her dream—but the client either professes not to understand its meaning or suffers the dream as a passive witness. The dream, in other words, is composed of two texts, a manifest text and a latent or hidden text. And it's the hidden text that is causing the problems. So part of the analyst's job is to find this hidden text, decipher it and interpret it to the client. It's like finding an Egyptian hieroglyphic, and no merely sensory evidence will help here, because what you are dealing with is how trains of subjective symbols slide over each other to create a world of meaning, intention, value, desire and so on. It's exactly like a Rorschach blot—the empirical blot is fixed and given; it's composed of so much ink arranged in just one way. But the symbolic meanings that can ride on that blot are numerous, and they can't be determined by empiricism at all. So Freud's technique was to use linguistic dialogue in order to disclose hidden texts, then translate or interpret those texts so as to make the meaning of hidden symptoms more transparent to the client. It was that transparency, where before there had been opaqueness, that helped effect the cure. The interpretation, in other words, leads to insight or understanding. Through repeated observations and interpretations, Freud was able to create various maps or theories of the psychological sphere, theories that could not be tested empirically, like mere behaviorism, but which *could* be tested by those who were willing to take up the discipline of introspective interpretation. That Freud's reductionism crippled many of his maps and theories is sad, but that is not the fault of his methodology. It was a pure case of in garbage, out garbage.

RV: So mode number 3 can be theoretic in that it also forms and uses maps and models of its own level.

WILBER: Yes, but its verification test is hermeneutic, not empiric. Or rational-phenomenological, not sensory. Or linguistic, not physical. Call that science if you wish; I just think those who do are terribly unclear about why and what they're doing.

RV: And mode number 2. That's paradoxical—can that be theoretic?

WILBER: I think so but theory in a looser sense. As I said, paradoxical reason has its uses, as long as we are careful. Theory in this sense would involve creating maps or cartographies of the higher and transcendental spheres, for the aid of those who have not yet seen them, and also for general knowledge purposes. Mandalic maps, as it were.

RV: Could you check those maps?

WILBER: Yes, but only by actually transforming to the spiritual realm, or by awakening mode number 1. You absolutely could not verify them using empiric or hermeneutic procedures.

RV: But would those maps also be paradoxical?

WILBER: Yes, definitely. It sometimes doesn't appear that way because each system, merely for consistency, usually works with only one side of the paradox. Thus the Buddhists will call the highest level Void, Hindus will call it Being, the Taoists will claim it is ever-changing, and the Christians will say it is everlasting. All are right—or wrong; it makes no difference. It's paradoxical. You see, paradox is simply the way nonduality looks to the mental level. Spirit itself is not paradoxical; it is not characterizable at all. But when the mind tries to think about it, then nonduality shows up as two contradictory opposites, both of which can be shown to be equally plausible because neither is complete by itself. The best you can do therefore is affirm *both* sides of the duality, or deny them both. The former gives you paradox; the latter, double negative. I use mandalic reason to cover both, although it applies better to paradox. But my point is that neither of them should be confused with mode number 1 or actual contemplation.

RV: I want to make sure I've got this straight. There are five modes of knowing. . . .

WILBER: At least five; remember we are working only with the simplified three-level hierarchy.

RV: OK, at least five. Of those five, only three—the three mental subsets—are involved in theoretic knowledge.

WILBER: Yes.

RV: Of those three, one is empiric, one is phenomenological and one is mandalic.

WILBER: Yes.

RV: And science, the scientific method, is basically concerned with theory in the empirical-analytic mode.

WILBER: In my opinion, yes. You can expand science if you want, but you merely run into other already fully established disciplines and procedures. People talk about expanding physics; but if you expand physics, all you will get is biology, and beyond that, phenomenological psychology and conceptual philosophy and so on. But then it's no longer physics at all, is it?—except in an empty sense. But I really want to emphasize that I honestly don't care how you use the word "science." I am concerned only with the actual structures of knowledge, such as sensorimotor, empirical-analytic, hermeneutic-historic, contemplative and so on. These structures are most definitely different; they cannot usurp the roles of others— each has its own place and function. Where you hang the word "science" on that list will not change that list at all, and it's the list that interests me. My only worry has been that advocates of a "new and higher" science all too often have in mind *one* of these modes, usually the empiric, and they want to expand that mode over all the others. That results in reductionism, which leads to hierarchy collapse, which involves the fallacy of equivalent shadows, which gives pantheism. . . . So use science any way you wish, but first please say what you mean by the term, give its methodology, distinguish it from other modes and disciplines, and then we'll see what you've got. I think Willis Harman is a good example of what to do: every time he speaks of a higher science, he explains its proposed methods and aims, and he clearly points out that it's really just basic psychological phenomenology anyway.

RV: On the notion of the applicability—or inapplicability—of empirical science to higher realms, such as the mental-subjective or the transcendental-spiritual, doesn't research in brain physiology—which is empirical—tell us something about mind and its operations?

WILBER: Yes, of course. Brain research is extremely exciting and important, but I think it is also extremely limited.

RV: In what sense?

WILBER: Well, take Freud's thoughts on the matter. In his last book he stated pretty clearly that even *if* we could figure out every connection between the brain and consciousness, then—and these are his own words—"it would at most afford an exact localization of the processes of consciousness and would give us no help toward understanding them." As I said—and as almost everybody has recently discovered—Freud was primarily interested in hermeneutics—in interpretation and meaning and symbolic discourse.

RV: His first major book was *The Interpretation of Dreams*.

WILBER: Yes. Even if we can localize the dream—say in the right hemisphere—and even if we can describe its chemical components, we still don't know its *meaning*. That meaning is discoverable only in the hermeneutic circle, only in my life's history and its intentions.

RV: Mode number 3 and not number 4.

WILBER: Yes. And this insight is now producing an entire renaissance in nonempirical, nonreductionistic, nonbiological psychology. You have the interpersonal or object-relations theorists—Sullivan, Guntrip, Fairbairn, Jacobson, Erik Erikson. You have the linguists and structuralists—Lacan, Roy Schafer, Ricoeur. The information theorists—Bateson being the most famous. All of these are related to symbolic transfer or hermeneutics, and it's revolutionizing psychology.

RV: Can you give a short example, say in terms of pathology?

WILBER: Sure. Originally symptoms were conceived in energetic or biophysical terms. The id pushes here, the ego pushes back, the compromise is a substitute gratification in the form of a symptom. The shadow, or personal unconscious, was a product of forces. Very thermodynamic. Now without denying that bioenergetics are also involved, the new understanding simply points out that the self is not so much a present biophysical event as it is a story or a history. The self, the mental self anyway, is a linguistic structure, a creation of history and a creator of history. It lives via communication or dialogue, it is constructed of units of meaning, or symbols, and it lives out a course in time, or history. It is a story; it is a *text*. And the only way you understand a text is by good interpretation, just as the only way you understand *War and Peace*, for instance, is by good interpretation. What does it really *mean*, see? What does my life mean? Where is it going? Why am I doing this? What value does this have for me? And that's hermeneutics.

RV: And pathology?

WILBER: Pathology is related to bad interpretation, or maybe misinterpretation. And the shadow is no longer the seat of unconscious forces, it's the seat of misinterpretation. In a sense, the shadow is a hidden text or subtext, and so it produces scripts whose *meanings* baffle you—bad hermeneutics, or poor hermeneutics, as when the person says, "I don't know why I did that, wonder what it means?" The shadow is a text you secretly write, a text whose authorship you refuse to admit.

RV: And so therapy?

WILBER: Is a process of assuming or reassuming the authorship or responsibility for your own life text, your own self.

RV: And none of that can be easily explained in empirical or physiological terms?

WILBER: The hermeneutics? No. But I would like to add that the system I'm working with utilizes both the bioenergetics of the body's prana, or emotional-sexual distributions, and the mental units of meaning that transcend but include the simpler bioenergetic feelings. Both are important, but the hermeneutics more so. In the seven-layer scheme I gave earlier, diet and exercise deals basically with level 1; bioenergetics and emotional-sexual cathexis deals with level 2; and hermeneutics and symbolic interpretation deals with level 3 and part of 4. None of those can be tossed out. The problem with pure hermeneutics is that it tries to say the id is just language, which is silly. A dog has sexual impulses and no language. Humans have both. Trying to reduce one to the other is just not useful. They both slot in the hierarchy.

RV: And so, is empirical physiology without any fundamental use for the understanding of mental hermeneutics?

WILBER: No, no, that's reverse reductionism; I didn't say that. Hermeneutics transcends but includes the effects of physiology, as I have said for each level of the hierarchy. So the effects of physiology can be best understood in terms of degeneracy theory, I think.

RV: Which is?

WILBER: If you look at every stage in evolution, what you find is that—this has been pointed out often—each higher stage is synergistic to its junior components; it includes them but is more than them.

RV: That's "transcends but includes."

WILBER: Yes, same idea; synergy is the same idea. Bring lifeless matter together in certain complex ways, and you generate something that is more than the sum of its parts. You generate life or prana. Life is synergistic in reference to matter and cannot be reduced to, or fully explained by, matter. Likewise, bring prana together in certain complex ways, and symbols begin to emerge. But symbols—or psychology—cannot be explained by life—or biology—just as biology cannot be explained by rocks. Each is synergistic in reference to its predecessors. Now the opposite of synergy is degeneracy. If A is degenerate to B, then two or more states of B can be sustained on top of a single state of A. For example, if you make a telephone call, then a certain amount of electrical energy is passing along the lines. But information is also passing along the lines, and you cannot tell how much information, what type of information or the quality of information that is being transmitted on the mere basis of the amount of energy supporting it. For example, with the same amount of energy—say, 100 kilowatts or whatever—you could say "Hello, how are you" or "zizzy lollop thud." The former carries information; the latter, mere noise. Several different states of information transfer can be sustained on the same state of energy exchange. In this case, energy is degenerate with regard to information.

RV: And that occurs at all stages of evolution?

WILBER: Yes, at every level of the hierarchy. Really it's a simple notion; it's just the opposite of synergy.

RV: And you see that relationship in the brain and mind?

WILBER: I think that is certainly a possible explanation. The brain is basically the biophysical substrate for the mental processes. We would also expect spiritual processes to leave their footprints in the biophysical substrate, either directly or via the mind. But in no case could mind or spirit be reduced to brain or explained entirely or merely by brain physiology. The Rorschach blot is still a good analogy: there is one physical substrate, the actual ink blot, but it supports several different mental interpretations, and you can't say the interpretations are just ink. I think it's the same with brain and mind.

RV: The brain is degenerate with regard to mind?

WILBER: Yes. That would mean that the changes in brain physiology would not be correspondingly as significant as the changes in mind values. For instance, I can be in the beta brain-wave state, and have two successive thoughts of wildly different truth-value, say, "$2+2=4$" and "$2+2=5$." The difference in EEG between those thoughts is extremely small, but the difference in truth-value is tremendous. So there *are* physiological correlates, but they are degenerate with regard to mind. The differences in physiology are not as significant as the differences in the truth values of the propositions. Incidentally, notice that you cannot establish the truth or falsity of the propositions by any amount of physiological studies. You have to go outside the brain's physiology, into the intersubjective circle of logic and communication, in order to verify mental truths, because, as we've said, mind transcends but includes physiology, and the truths of the former cannot be entirely contained in the truths of the latter. No amount of EEG sophistication could help you prove or disprove Keynes' theory of macroeconomics, for instance.

RV: But that would still give brain physiology an important effect on mind, but not a causal effect, correct?

WILBER: Yes. This theory still gives us a definite brain-mind connection and interaction, but it doesn't postulate wild dualism on the one hand or simple monism or identity on the other. Further, it suggests that the brain is as complex as it is because nothing less complicated could serve as the biophysical substrate for logical and symbolic processes, but it avoids the reductionism of saying, for example, that literature is fancy electrons.

RV: So theoretically, if we understood brain physiology in depth, we could produce general states and moods and improve the substrate, like memory capacity and so on, but we could not produce specific thoughts or ideas in the mind.

WILBER: Yes. Changing physiological states would be like changing Rorschach blots. You would get a whole new series of moods and responses, but you couldn't control all the specific mental interpretations or actual contents. So brain would still have a significant effect on mind but not a determinant or causal effect on mind. This also fits very well, I think, with such researchers as Elmer and Alyce Green, who maintain that "all of brain is in the mind but not all of the mind is in the brain."

RV: That's hierarchy and degeneracy.

WILBER: Absolutely. But this still leaves us with the important tasks of mapping out the degenerate relationships between mind and brain, and also between spirit and brain. Correlations of brain waves with dreaming, for example.

RV: And because of degeneracy, you can tell from physiological changes *that* a person is dreaming but not exactly *what* he or she is dreaming?

WILBER: Yes, that's exactly degeneracy.

RV: This is slightly off the topic, but what *would* determine the dream content?

WILBER: Well, a quick answer would be that the past history of the text-self is now getting a reading, especially its hidden subtexts. The shadow is on stage. And the content of the shadow is not determined by present physiology as much as it is by past history, the actual past events that constitute the story and the history that this person recognizes as a self. That's why Habermas calls this mode the hermeneutic-*historic*. And finally, that's why Freud was drawn to the idea of trying to trace the *historical* genesis of symptoms. He wanted to use a historical reconstruction method to help the person see when he or she began to write hidden or secret or guilty texts and stories, to see how the person repressed the shadow by creating a secret author. The secret author shows up in dreams and symptoms, and the job of the therapist is to help the person *interpret* the meaning of the symptoms—you know, "your anxiety is really masked or hidden rage"—until the person can reown them, reauthorize them, reauthor them. So even if physiology can't tell us what the shadow says or means, it can tell us when it is on stage—and that's tremendously important. I think the same thing will hold true of any psychospiritual correlates we can find in the biophysical substrate. So these correlations, even though they are degenerate, are very important.

RV: And this theory allows us to look for correlations of the higher in the lower without having to reduce the higher to the lower?

WILBER: That's my opinion, yes.

RV: In a related vein, what do you think of Prigogine's work. Doesn't it offer an empirical basis of higher transformations?

WILBER: In my opinion, it doesn't because I agree literally with Marilyn Ferguson that Prigogine's work—I'll read this—"bridges the critical gap between living systems and the apparently lifeless universe in which they arose."

RV: In other words, it applies basically to the gap between level 1 and level 2 in the 7-level hierarchy?

WILBER: I think so. It describes the complexities of material perturbations that allow life or prana to emerge through—but not from—matter. They are really exciting equations, but they don't easily or clearly cover the higher levels, levels 3 through 7.

Rv: Why not? Surely it has some general applicability?

WILBER: Well, it is definitely true that there are analog laws on all levels of the hierarchy, as we said earlier. The question is, not whether transformation occurs on all levels, because it does; the question is, which level of structural organization do these equations actually describe? I think it is fairly well agreed that these equations deal primarily with thermodynamic energies and entropy, not with symbolic information and not with transphysical and transmental insight. Dissipative thermodynamic structures seem best representative if biomaterial transforms, or levels 1 and 2. They are *examples* of general transformations, therefore, but not paradigmatic among them. They are a subset of evolutionary transformations, and not the sole or exemplary type. As we earlier put it, they are downward reflections, or reduced versions, of the transformations that occur on the higher levels, and so naturally they all have certain similarities, just as the electron and human will are "indeterminant." But trying to use the lower-level manifestation of the general principle to explain the higher-level prototype of that very principle is what we want to try to avoid. So I think Prigogine's work is very important, not because I can then say he has proven the laws of psychological or spiritual transformation, but because he has demonstrated that the transformation process itself extends all the way down the hierarchy to the lowest levels. It shows up in an extremely reduced form, as we would expect, but there it is.

Rv: So thermodynamic dissipative structures would be degenerate with regard to higher transformations?

WILBER: Yes. With respect to the brain-mind interface, if dissipative structures apply to levels 1 and 2, it follows they would apply to the brain or biophysical substrate of the mind, and thus assume the importance, limited but definite, that we discussed earlier.

Rv: But are there ways to explore and verify any of the higher modes themselves, since they aren't scientific or at least empiric?

WILBER: Yes, of course. There is phenomenological investigation and its verification in a community of intersubjective interpretors—just as you and I are doing now. There is contemplative practice and its verification by a community of trans-subjective meditators—as happens, say, between Zen master and student.

RV: But using phenomenology and hermeneutics as an example, wouldn't mere interpretation make truth a wildly subjective affair?

WILBER: It depends upon the caliber of the community of interpretors. Look, empiric science rests upon a community of facts—if you get bad facts, you get bad science or at least partial science. Just so, real philosophy, psychology and phenomenology—not behaviorism and not positivism, those are empiric and not rational affairs—depend in large measure upon the quality of the community of interpretors. Good interpretors, good thinkers, ground good phenomenology. They discover those truths that apply to the subjective realm, and in that sense the truths are subjective truths. But that doesn't mean mere individual whim. First of all, a bad interpretation will simply not mesh with general subjective consensus. It is rebuffed by a reality that is subjective but very real and very lawful, just as a bad scientific fact is rebuffed by other facts. Second, a phenomenological truth, in order to be recognized as truth, must be *tested* in a community of like-minded interpretors, just as a scientific fact, to be so, must be tested against the community of other facts. It's no mere wishful thinking and subjective license. The hermeneutic test is just as stringent and demanding as the empiric test, but of course the empiric test is easier because it is performed by a subject on an object, whereas phenomenology is performed by a subject on or with other subjects. Much more difficult.

RV: Isn't that what has helped reductionism so much? Everybody wants the methodological elegance of physics?

WILBER: I think so. We are lured into thinking physics has *the* method, instead of seeing that physics is working with the simplest level of structural organization and thus produces relatively simple and easily reproducible truths.

RV: But aren't you pulling a type of reverse reductionism yourself? I mean, when we look into the subatomic world it's every bit as complex as the biological world or the human symbolic world.

WILBER: Well, it's complex, but not as complex as higher levels, for the simple reason that a human being, say, contains electrons but electrons don't contain human beings. Thus all the complexities of the electron are contained in humans, but humans also contain other complexities found only in humans—guilt, anxiety, despair, desire.

Rv: Yes, I see. So we should give equal or greater emphasis to rational-phenomenology and hermeneutics and so on?

WILBER: Yes, certainly, but hermeneutics alone is not the ultimate answer. See, just as empiricism wants to reduce symbol to sensation, hermeneutics wants to reduce spirit to symbol. It wants to claim God is a mere idea, or only an idea, in the community of intersubjective interpretors. It refuses to include in its methodology the practice of contemplation—mode number 1—and thus it fails to see that God can be verified as a transcendental reality by a community of trans-subjective meditators.

Rv: Even though, on the mental plane, various communities of meditators would interpret spirit differently.

WILBER: Exactly. When the mind speaks of spirit, it generates paradox or contradictory interpretations. That's as it should be. But what is verified in meditation itself is not a particular interpretation of spirit, but a direct and immediate identity with and as spirit, and that occasion is not subject to interpretation because it is not a symbolic or mediated event. On the mental level, however, there are *only* interpretations of the event, most paradoxical, and that is inescapable. "They call Him many who is really one."

Rv: Aren't there a lot of paradoxes in modern physics—what have been called quantum koans—and couldn't that suggest that physics is somehow involved in fundamental reality, in mandalic logic?

WILBER: Yes, that point has been raised a lot. But first off, just because the absolute always generates paradox doesn't mean that paradox always indicates the absolute, OK? But beyond that, I personally think there are very few genuine paradoxes in any branch of science. A real paradox, remember, means that two mutually contradictory occasions are known to occur simultaneously and equally. For instance, if at this very moment it is raining and not raining on my house, that would be a real paradox.

Rv: What about wavicles—a particle acting as a wave in one situation and a particle in another?

WILBER: Well, that's the point; it is a wave in one situation and a particle in another. In any given experiment, it never acts equally and absolutely as a perfect wave and a perfect particle simultaneously. It oscillates, or alternates, its mutually exclusive truths, and that is a complementarity, not a real paradox.

RV: Are there no genuine paradoxes in science or philosophy?

WILBER: I wouldn't put it that strongly, but I think it is safe to say that most apparent paradoxes turn out to be ordinary contradictions, which simply means you have made a confused step somewhere. In empiric research, contradictions usually indicate that a series of experiments have been run incorrectly. It is usually cleared up by more refined research. In rational-conceptual inquiry, what seems to be a paradox usually results, as Russell and Whitehead demonstated in *Principia Mathematica*, from violating the theory of logical types. Even though Spencer Brown has suggested ways to reformulate the types theory, it is still extremely useful. Bateson almost made an entire career out of it.

RV: To put it bluntly, what is it?

WILBER: It simply states that a class cannot be a member of itself. It came up in trying to define number as the class of all classes similar to a given class. But the idea is very simple: the class of all chairs is not itself a chair, the class of all apples is not itself an apple, the alphabet is not itself a letter and so on. Anyway, if you violate the logical typing of your symbols, then you generate a pseudo-paradox. It's not a real paradox because it's just based on bad semantics. For instance, if you take one word-symbol, say "chair," and then give it two meanings, each of a different logical type, then create a sentence using that word, you can generate a pseudo-paradox. You might say, "That chair is not a chair." It is a particular chair but is not a universal chair, not the class of all chairs. When semanticists say—Korzybski's famous utterance—"Whatever you say a thing is, it isn't!"—that's not a real paradox. What they mean is that "whatever you say a thing is"—that is, the name you give it, the symbol you use to describe it—is not to be confused with the particular thing itself. The former is the class; the latter, the member, and the class is not a member of itself—that is a direct application of logical typing, and it is behind much of modern semantics and the map/territory theories. And it says that wherever you generate what looks like paradox, you've confused your logical types.

RV: I remember that theory now. Isn't it the way Russell solved the famous paradox about the Cretan who said, "Everything a Cretan says is a lie." Since a Cretan said it, was he telling the truth or lying?

WILBER: Yes, the idea was that the Cretan was making a statement about statements, and that is of a logical type different from statements in general, and so he wasn't contradicting himself. You judge the statement and the meta-statement on their own terms, decide in each case whether it is true or false and there goes the paradox. See, the theory of logical types is really just a way to group classes and sets into a hierarchy of increasing comprehensiveness. Each level in the Great Chain, for example, is of a higher logical type, even though not all of the levels themselves are actually made of logic. And in that larger sense, the theory of logical types—which says don't confuse types—says "don't collapse the hierarchy."

RV: Didn't the types theory also lead to the double-bind theory of schizophrenia?

WILBER: It really was the heart of most of Bateson's work. What happens in schizophrenia, according to Bateson, is that two messages of different logical types contradict each other, and the person, who takes both to be equally true, oscillates between them, until he shakes himself to pieces, so to speak. Because he cannot easily differentiate logical types, he takes both messages, which are merely contradictory, as being equally true or paradoxical. Then he can neither reach a compromise with them nor throw one of them out, because they are now equal but opposite.

RV: He's in a double bind.

WILBER: He's in a double bind. He violated logical typing, which generated a pseudo-paradox which shakes him apart. It happens in any sort of information feedback system. If you take a machine that is supposed to turn itself "on" at a given lower limit and "off" at a given upper limit, and then you start moving those limits together, the machine will turn off and on in increasingly shorter intervals. If you then collapse the difference between the limits, the machine will tell itself to turn off at the same time it tells itself to turn on. It's caught in a "paradox" and right there in front of your eyes it will shake wildly until it breaks down. Anyway, I am saying that just as in such schizophrenic thinking, and unless you are explicitly using mandalic reason, then paradox usually means there is actually just a contradiction somewhere—it indicates sloppy thinking, not transcendental reason. In empirical-analytic theory and research as well as in phenomenological-rational theory and research, what appears to be

a paradox is usually an indication of pathology in your system—
something went wrong somewhere. Instead of saying I'm working
with the Tao, I'd go back and retrace my tracks.

RV: You earlier mentioned Whitehead and how, in your opinion,
he didn't exactly agree with the holographic theories. I think what
you said then was clear enough, but the more I think about it the
more confusing it is.

WILBER: How so?

RV: It is generally thought that Whitehead's philosophy fits the
holographic theories in at least two ways. One, he said everything
in the cosmos interacts with everything else. And two, doesn't his
philosophy fit with the notion, made famous by the Heisenberg
uncertainty principle, that the subject affects the object when it
perceives it? Or do you disagree with Whitehead there?

WILBER: Well, no, I generally agree with Whitehead, but Whitehead
disagreed with both those ideas.

RV: Didn't Whitehead say that everything prehends everything
else in the cosmos?

WILBER: What he said was that a thing prehends everything in its
actual universe, and its actual universe consists only of its ancestors,
not its contemporaries and not its descendents.

RV: I don't follow.

WILBER: Whitehead maintained that the universe consists of a
series of occasions which come into existence for a few seconds or so
and which then fade into cosmic memory, so to speak—very like the
Hinayana Buddhist notion of momentary dharma-events. Anyway,
each entity or occasion, as it comes into existence, is regarded as a
subject, and this subject prehends, or is somehow aware of, its
immediate predecessors or those occasions that helped to form it. So
those predecessors, or ancestors, are objects to the present event,
the subject. As that subject passes, it becomes object for its descendents and so on. So each subject prehends all of its ancestors, to some
degree, however minimal—but notice that no event can prehend its
descendents, and no event can prehend its contemporaries.

RV: Why not?

WILBER: Because events just coming into existence don't have
time, so to speak, to get to know each other. Two truly simulta-

neous events are without mutual influence at the precise time of their simultaneity. They haven't had the chance to enter the causal or karmic stream. The influence they do have will be on the occasion that immediately succeeds it—that influence is causality in Whitehead's system. If two subjects are in the same vicinity, the odds are high that they both may become object for the same eventual subject. But otherwise, no interaction. And an entity cannot prehend its descendents anymore than Christopher Columbus could be aware of you or me.

RV: So an entity prehends all its ancestors, but not its contemporaries and not its descendents?

WILBER: That is Whitehead's view, yes.

RV: And you agree with that?

WILBER: Yes.

RV: But what about precognition. Isn't that an example of a present occasion prehending a future one, or a descendent?

WILBER: Look, if precognition is absolutely real and absolutely possible, then all events are already absolutely determined for all time. There is then no such thing as free will, no such thing as actual creativity or true free emergence, there isn't even such a thing as Heisenberg's uncertainty principle. The universe is, through all times and on all levels, absolutely a deterministic machine. I don't buy it, myself.

RV: OK, what about the second point, the idea that physics has supposedly proven that the subject in many ways creates its object.

WILBER: Are you asking whether I agree or whether Whitehead does?

RV: Start with Whitehead.

WILBER: He disagrees absolutely. And remember Whitehead was perfectly aware of modern quantum mechanics.

RV: He denied quantum mechanics?

WILBER: No, he denied, or at least refused to embrace, some of the terribly unsophisticated philosophical interpretations of QM, such as that the object is created or even altered when prehended by a subject.

RV: What was his idea?

WILBER: As each occasion comes to be, as it becomes subject, it prehends its ancestors or causal objects and is thus changed by the objects, or formed by its immediate past. But the object is not changed, and indeed could not be changed, by its subject or by being prehended, because the object now only exists in or as the past, and you can't alter the past by merely thinking about it or prehending it. Again, it's like saying that what Columbus did could affect you, but what you do now does not affect Columbus. White-head's point was that, since all events are coming to be and ceasing to be in a stream of flux, change or time, then essentially the same thing applies during the milliseconds involved.

RV: You agree?

WILBER: Yes, definitely. That is simply another way of saying that the subject contains the object but the object doesn't contain the subject, and *that* is simply another way to say that there are indeed nonmutual or nonequivalent relationships. Hierarchy is, of course, the strong version of that fact.

RV: So you don't agree with the new-age theories that say the human brain as subject creates the objective world it perceives?

WILBER: It might indeed create order in its world of perception, or in the material world of noises, but it doesn't create that world itself.

RV: If it did there would be an infinite regress?

WILBER: Yes. But the point can be established more easily—the human brain didn't evolve until 6 million years ago, but the cosmos is 13 billion years old. There were lots of things around before brains existed. As for the so-called participant-observer in physics, or the necessity for the object to be perceived by mind in order to collapse its state vector, the vast majority of physicists—including David Bohm's classic 1975 paper that perfectly shredded Jack Sarfatti's wild claims on the subject—find the idea either unnecessary or down-right ridiculous. But many new-age theorists think they must believe in the idea because they confuse the events occurring on the merely physical level with the entire Tao; they think that because Buddha Nature or God is one with all things in the act of perceiving-creating them, that the human mind itself must try to do the same thing for electrons.

RV: What about such related topics as the Whorf-Sapir hypothesis, the idea that language, or the mind, creates the world, and that different languages in fact create different worlds. There seems to be a lot of support for that notion.

WILBER: There is a partial truth there, but it is very confused, because again we have failed to say what we mean by the phrase, "the world." Do we mean the physical world, the biological world, the sociological world, what? Because, you see, I believe that the Whorf-Sapir hyopthesis is perfectly wrong in reference to the physical, biological and submental spheres in general. I do not believe that the linguistic mind creates rocks and trees, although obviously it creates the words with which we represent those entities. A diamond will cut a piece of glass no matter what words we use for "diamond," "cut" and "glass."

RV: So if there were no human minds, there would still be physical and biological entities in existence.

WILBER: Yes. Again I remind you of the obvious fact that those levels antedated the human brain or mind by billions of years.

RV: So where is the Whorf-Sapir hypothesis correct?

WILBER: Symbols do not create the material or biological spheres— levels 1 and 2—but they do create, literally, the mental spheres— level 3 and parts of 4. But it's not just that there are these higher mental levels and that symbols reflect them. The higher mental levels *are* symbols. They are *made* of symbols the way a tree is made of wood. So notice we have these two general realms under discussion—the mental and the submental—and that symbols play a different role with regard to each. They basically *reflect* the submental world but they help to *create* the mental world. In the first case they basically *represent;* in the second, they also *present.* For example, the symbol "rock" represents an independently existing rock. Take away the symbol, and the rock, or whatever it is, is still there. Language does not create that world. But entities such as envy, pride, poetry, justice, compassion, goals, values, virtues exist only in and as a stream of symbols. Take away the symbols and those entities are gone. Alter the symbols, and you shift the sense of those entities. Different languages do exactly that, and that is where the Whorfian concepts find some applicability.

RV: Now isn't the difference between the symbols that *represent* the submental realms and the symbols that *create* the mental realms the same as the difference between empirical-analytic modes and hermeneutic-historic modes?

WILBER: Definitely—same thing. And that's why the methodologies, the interests, the structures and the verification processes are so different in the two modes. See, if you are working with the empirical-analytic mode, then you are basically working with the "mirror" model of truth—the model made famous by the positivists, such as Wittgenstein's early work. Propositions are true if they reflect the facts correctly—that type of thing. An empiric proposition is true if it more or less accurately mirrors or pictures or represents the sensory world. That is all as it should be. That model is just right for empirical truth. But when it comes to the purely mental or phenomenological world, the simple mirror or only reflective model no longer works. In a sense you are still doing reflective work—you know, you are still proposing theoretic maps and models, as we earlier discussed; but you are no longer using symbols to represent non-symbolic occasions. You are using symbols to look at other symbols, a process which *creates* new worlds with new possibilities and new truths, and those truths are not empirical or merely sensory, and so a simple mirror model no longer works. Or we could put the analogy like this: with empiric propositions you are trying to mirror the lower realms in symbols so as to better comprehend them. But in the mental world, where symbols look at symbols, it's like using one mirror to reflect another mirror which reflects the reflection, and so on in a circle of meaning that you and I co-create whenever we talk. That is the hermeneutic circle. The self is aware of itself only by taking the role of other—but the same is equally true of the other. So here we are, two mirrors in discourse co-creating each other in communicative exchange. And the way you find your way around in that world, that hermeneutic circle, is radically different from dropping rocks and seeing if they fall at the same speed in a vacuum, right? In empiricism, the symbols you use to represent the world simply represent the world, more or less. But in the mental and linguistic world, the symbols you use to represent that world are also involved in creating that world, and there is the great difference.

RV: What happens if you ignore that difference?

WILBER: The phenomenologists try to make all empirical truths into mere subjective co-creations. You know, the human mind helps co-create dirt, etc. Similar to the over-extended version of the Whorf-Sapir hypothesis. The empiricists, on the other hand, try to reduce the hermeneutic circle to mere sensory transactions. Since they can't find any sensory referents, however, they proclaim mind to be a black box. They refuse to try to map out the hermeneutic circle and instead content themselves with monitoring muscle twitches, as Tolman put it. Philosophy degenerates into only positivism, and psychology degenerates into only behaviorism.

RV: So an overall paradigm. . . .

WILBER: An overall paradigm, in my opinion, would have to include all of the modes of knowing we have discussed, and all the correlative methodologies. It would include sensory investigations and empirical-analytic hypotheses and tests. It would include hermeneutic-historic investigations and interpretations, conceptual analyses and syntheses. It would include mandalic cartographies of the higher realms, however paradoxical at spots, and it would include an actual summons to contemplative practice. Further, the overall paradigm, its simple existence, would demand a social evolutionary stance, a social policy geared to help human beings evolve through the stage-levels of existence. This would involve both attempts to help vertical transformation to higher levels and also attempts to clear up the distortions and oppressions that have occurred horizontally on the levels already in existence. The vertical is connected with soteriological interests; the horizontal is the normative or emancipatory interests, as Habermas uses the term.

RV: Couldn't that lead to "we-know-best-for-you" social engineering?

WILBER: No, because in this paradigm transcendence cannot be forced. There are only *participants* in emancipation. You can only force slavery; you can't force a person to be free.

RV: It seems to me that your major concern over the holographic or new-age paradigms in general is that most of these issues in methodology and epistemology are overlooked or ignored. The hierarchy, as you say, has collapsed.

WILBER: What happens is that when the hierarchy is collapsed, you lose all these relative distinctions. The different methodologies—sensory, empirical-analytic, mental and so on—collapse. And the different interests of human inquirers—technological, moral, emancipatory, soteriological—all collapse. And all sorts of other problems start up. That was the problem with the original holographic paradigm. Since they had only two levels, then the frequency realm had to be the same as the implicate realm, and the read-out information had to be the explicate realm. And dissipative structures had to be the link between the frequency realm and the fold-out information—and so on. But then Bohm stated that the implicate level wasn't ultimate; there was a realm "beyond both." That gives three realms. Recently, he has spoken of several levels of the implicate realm. That gives us maybe six levels in all. Now that's much closer to the perennial philosophy. My own feeling is that as soon as he starts describing these realms in a little more detail, he's going to end up describing the traditional Great Chain. He's already speaking of "relatively independent subtotalities"—pretty much Huston Smith's definition of realm or level for the perennial philosophy.

RV: In the last interview in *ReVision*, he tended to include matter and thought as one realm.

WILBER: Well, I think that is part of the problem he might have inherited from Krishnamurti. Krishnamurti is so interested in the Light that he almost refuses to even discuss the shadows. Hence, he tends to commit hierarchy collapse and lump things like matter and symbol together.

RV: Because all shadows are ultimately illusory he thinks they are equally illusory.

WILBER: Yes, that's hierarchy collapse. I think Bohm stepped into this rather loose philosophy, and so he intended to include matter, prana and mind as more or less equivalent parts of the explicate sphere. He then had to look at the implicate sphere as something that existed more or less equally alongside or under material things and mental thoughts. He thus veered off from the traditional view, which would say that what is implicate to matter is simply élan vital, prana, the life force.

RV: So prana is the implicate order in which matter is embedded?

WILBER: I think that would be correct, traditionally. But that doesn't preclude the possibility that matter rises from a physical energy-sea. This seems to me the original meaning of Bohm's physical implicateness or, at least, quantum potential. My point is that both matter and the physical energy sea crystallize out of prana. In that sense, prana is implicate to matter.

RV: And prana is what? Or mind relates to prana how?

WILBER: Prana is implicate to matter but explicate to mind; mind is implicate to prana but explicate to soul, soul is implicate to mind but explicate to spirit; and spirit is the source and suchness of the entire sequence. (You have to be very careful with terminology here—you can almost reverse the sequence of wording, depending upon your definition of "implicate." If by implicate you mean enfolded as in "enveloped," then prana envelopes or implicates matter, or contains it. This might seem trivial but I have seen many writers use Bohm's concept in what are really diametrically opposed senses. I am using implicate to mean the larger ground out of which the explicate emerges.) Anyway, in my opinion, because Bohm originally didn't distinguish systematically between matter, prana and mind, he started looking horizontally for hidden dimensions of implicateness, failing to see that those three realms are already vertical dimensions of implicateness with regard to each other. But I think he's looking carefully at his scheme, but we'll have to wait and see.

RV: One last question. Anybody who knows you knows that you'd much rather work on your own writing than critique the works of others. Besides such published books as *Atman Project* and *Up From Eden*, you are now almost finished with two other books that further outline the comprehensive paradigm you have discussed briefly with us in this interview. What jarred you away from your own work?

WILBER: Well, the notion was rapidly spreading that all you have to do to be a mystic is learn a new mental world view. If you actually think you can include the absolute Tao in a new paradigm—and get anything other than a mass of contradictions and paradoxes—then you foster the idea that by merely learning the new paradigm, whatever it may be, you are actually transcending—really transcending. I have actually heard that claim made. That is a disaster. So naturally you're moved to put your two cents in and then shut-up, which is what I hope to do after this interview. But the fact that spiritual transformation takes years of meditative or contemplative practice, that it takes moral and physical purification, that it takes, or is helped by, direct contact with a living adept in divine realization, that it takes a direct opening of the eye of contemplation and has nothing to do with merely learning another mental paradigm—all of that was being left out. You know, we went through all this with Alan Watts. God knows nobody did more for mystical studies, especially Zen, than Alan, and I don't know a single person of my generation interested in transcendence who wasn't touched deeply by the man. Nobody could write like Watts, nobody. But it was just that—words. It was only at the end of his life that he rather surreptitiously began to admit that the core of Zen is, in fact, zazen. But by then, most of the people who began with Alan were now with Suzuki Roshi or Sazaki or Soen or Katigari or Baker—that is, they were actually practicing, actually working on spiritual trans-formation. That is not square Zen, as Alan finally admitted. Thus, the only good function of a book on Zen should be to persuade the reader to engage in zazen and to encourage those already practicing to continue and deepen their efforts. In the same way, the only major purpose of a book on mysticism should be to persuade the reader to engage in mystical practice. It is precisely like a cook book. You give recipes and invite the reader to go out and perform the recipe, actually do it, and then taste the results. You are not sup-posed merely to learn the recipes, memorize the recipes and then claim you're a cook. But that is exactly what many—not all—of the proponents of the new paradigm have in mind. Like Watts himself would say, it's like eating the menu instead of the meal. The new paradgim is just a new menu, but nobody's talking about the meal anymore, and that bothers me.

RV: You said "not all."

WILBER: There are many new-age thinkers perfectly aware of what I'm talking about. Marilyn Ferguson always emphasizes the need for actual attention deployment for transformation. David Bohm is fa-natical about the need for radical transformation or mutation in awareness, as is Renée Weber and Bill Harman and Fritjof Capra and many others. I just wanted my voice added because sometimes these themes simply don't get emphasized enough, so anxious are we to forge a new mental picture of that which is really transmental. And the only way you actually know the trans-mental is to actually transform. You cook the meal and eat it, you don't emboss the menu. So that's what we're trying to say.

CONTRIBUTORS

DAVID BOHM is Professor of Theoretical Physics at Birkbeck College, University of London. He holds a Ph.D. in physics from Berkeley, where he has taught, and has also held positions at Princeton, the University of Sao Paolo and at Haifa. Dr. Bohm is the author of *Causality and Chance in Modern Physics, Quantum Theory, The Special Theory of Relativity* and *Wholeness and the Implicate Order*.

FRITJOF CAPRA received his doctorate at the University of Vienna and has taught at the University of Paris, the University of California at Santa Cruz and the Imperial College in London. He is currently doing research in theoretical high energy physics at the Lawrence Berkeley Laboratory and is lecturing at the University of California at Berkeley. Dr. Capra is the author of *The Tao of Physics* and *The Turning Point*.

MARILYN FERGUSON is the editor of the *Brain/Mind Bulletin*, an advisor to *ReVision Journal* and the author of *The Brain Revolution* and *The Aquarian Conspiracy*.

KARL PRIBRAM is a professor of neuroscience at Stanford University. He is the author of *Languages of the Brain*.

RENÉE WEBER is Professor of Philosophy at Rutgers, where she teaches Oriental philosphy. She holds a Ph.D. from Columbia University. Dr. Weber has written numerous articles and is a consulting editor for *ReVision Journal*.

KEN WILBER is the editor-in-chief of *ReVision Journal* and a consulting editor for the *Journal of Transpersonal Psychology* and Shambhala Publications. He holds a graduate degree in biochemistry, and is the author of *The Spectrum of Consciousness, No Boundary, The Atman Project, Up from Eden, A Sociable God* and *Eye to Eye*.

ReVision Journal: A Journal of Consciousness and Change is a biannual publication. The subscription is $15 per year, and can be ordered from:

ReVision Journal
P.O. Box 316
Cambridge, Massachusetts 02138

INDEX

Note: Additional bibliographical references follow most chapters.